United States Department of Justice

Death of Michael Brown – The Fatal Shot Which Lit Up the Nationwide Riots & Protests

Madison & Adams Press 2019

Reading suggestions (available from Madison & Adams Press as Print & eBook)

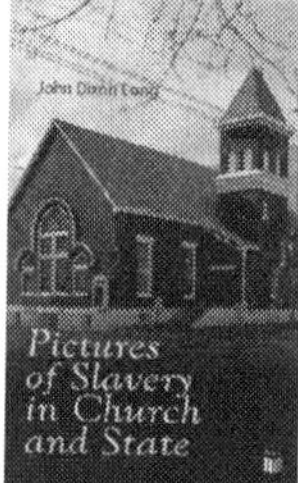

John Dixon Long
Pictures of Slavery in Church and State

Henry Bibb
Narrative of the Life and Adventures of an American Slave, Henry Bibb

Charles Ball
Fifty Years in Chains-Life of an American Slave

Elizabeth Keckley
Behind the Scenes: Thirty Years a Slave and Four Years in the White House

Booker T. Washington
Up From Slavery: The Incredible Life Story of Booker T. Washington

Frederick Douglass
Narrative of the Life of Frederick Douglass, an American Slave

Harriet Jacobs
Incidents in the Life of a Slave Girl

Sarah H. Bradford
Scenes in the Life of Harriet Tubman

William Craft, Ellen Craft
Running a Thousand Miles for Freedom: The Escape of William and Ellen Craft From Slavery

Austin Steward
Twenty-Two Years a Slave and Forty Years a Freeman

United States Department of Justice

Death of Michael Brown - The Fatal Shot Which Lit Up the Nationwide Riots & Protests

Complete Official Investigations of the Policing Practices and the Shooting - Constitutional Violations, Unlawful Police and Court Practices, Racial Discrimination, Physical & Forensic Evidence, Witness Accounts and Legal Analysis of the Ferguson Case

Madison & Adams Press, 2019. No claim to original U.S. Government Works
Contact: info@madisonadamspress.com

ISBN 978-80-273-3374-5

This is a publication of Madison & Adams Press. Our production consists of thoroughly prepared educational & informative editions: Advice & How-To Books, Encyclopedias, Law Anthologies, Declassified Documents, Legal & Criminal Files, Historical Books, Scientific & Medical Publications, Technical Handbooks and Manuals. All our publications are meticulously edited and formatted to the highest digital standard. The main goal of Madison & Adams Press is to make all informative books and records accessible to everyone in a high quality digital and print form.

Contents

Investigation into the Shooting of Michael Brown

I. Introduction

At approximately noon on Saturday, August 9, 2014, Officer Darren Wilson of the Ferguson Police Department ("FPD") shot and killed Michael Brown, an unarmed 18-year-old. The Criminal Section of the Department of Justice Civil Rights Division, the United States Attorney's Office for the Eastern District of Missouri, and the Federal Bureau of Investigation ("FBI") (collectively, "The Department") subsequently opened a criminal investigation into whether the shooting violated federal law. The Department has determined that the evidence does not support charging a violation of federal law. This memorandum details the Department's investigation, findings, and conclusions. Part I provides an introduction and overview. Part II summarizes the federal investigation and the evidence uncovered during the course of the investigation, and discusses the applicable federal criminal civil rights law and standards of federal prosecution. Part III provides a more in-depth summary of the evidence. Finally, Part IV provides a detailed legal analysis of the evidence and explains why the evidence does not support an indictment of Darren Wilson.

The Department conducted an extensive investigation into the shooting of Michael Brown. Federal authorities reviewed physical, ballistic, forensic, and crime scene evidence; medical reports and autopsy reports, including an independent autopsy performed by the United States Department of Defense Armed Forces Medical Examiner Service ("AFMES"); Wilson's personnel records; audio and video recordings; and internet postings. FBI agents, St. Louis County Police Department ("SLCPD") detectives, and federal prosecutors and prosecutors from the St. Louis County Prosecutor's Office ("county prosecutors") worked cooperatively to both independently and jointly interview more than 100 purported eyewitnesses and other individuals claiming to have relevant information. SLCPD detectives conducted an initial canvass of the area on the day of the shooting. FBI agents then independently canvassed more than 300 residences to locate and interview additional witnesses. Federal and local authorities collected cellular phone data, searched social media sites, and tracked down dozens of leads from community members and dedicated law enforcement email addresses and tip lines in an effort to investigate every possible source of information.

The principles of federal prosecution, set forth in the United States Attorneys' Manual ("USAM"), require federal prosecutors to meet two standards in order to seek an indictment. First, we must be convinced that the potential defendant committed a federal crime. *See* USAM § 9-27.220 (a federal prosecution should be commenced only when an attorney for the government "believes that the person's conduct constitutes a federal offense"). Second, we must also conclude that we would be likely to prevail at trial, where we must prove the charges beyond a reasonable doubt. *See* USAM § 9-27.220 (a federal prosecution should be commenced only when "the admissible evidence will probably be sufficient to sustain a conviction"); Fed R. Crim P. 29(a)(prosecution must present evidence sufficient to sustain a conviction). Taken 4 together, these standards require the Department to be convinced both that a federal crime occurred and that it can be proven beyond a reasonable doubt at trial.[1]

In order to make the proper assessment under these standards, federal prosecutors evaluated physical, forensic, and potential testimonial evidence in the form of witness accounts. As detailed below, the physical and forensic evidence provided federal prosecutors with a benchmark against which to measure the credibility of each witness account, including that of Darren Wilson. We compared individual witness accounts to the physical and forensic evidence, to other credible witness accounts, and to each witness's own prior statements made throughout the investigations, including the proceedings before the St. Louis County grand jury ("county grand jury"). We worked with federal and local law enforcement officers to interview witnesses, to include re-interviewing certain witnesses in an effort to evaluate inconsistencies in their accounts and to obtain more detailed information. In so doing, we assessed the witnesses' demeanor, tone, bias, and ability to accurately perceive or recall the events of August 9, 2014. We credited and determined that a jury would appropriately credit those witnesses whose accounts were consistent with the physical evidence and consistent with other credible witness accounts. In the case of witnesses who made multiple statements, we compared those statements to determine whether they were materially consistent with each other and considered the timing and circumstances under which the witnesses gave the statements. We did not credit and determined that a jury appropriately would not credit those witness accounts that were contrary to the physical and forensic evidence, significantly inconsistent with other credible witness accounts, or significantly inconsistent with that witness's own prior statements.

Based on this investigation, the Department has concluded that Darren Wilson's actions do not constitute prosecutable violations under the applicable federal criminal civil rights statute, 18 U.S.C. § 242, which prohibits uses of deadly force that are "objectively unreasonable," as defined by the United States Supreme Court. The evidence, when viewed as a whole, does not support the conclusion that Wilson's uses of deadly force were "objectively unreasonable" under the Supreme Court's definition. Accordingly, under the governing federal law and relevant standards set forth in the USAM, it is not appropriate to present this matter to a federal grand jury for indictment, and it should therefore be closed without prosecution.

II. Summary of the Evidence, Investigation, and Applicable Law

A. Summary of the Evidence

Within two minutes of Wilson's initial encounter with Brown on August 9, 2014, FPD officers responded to the scene of the shooting, and subsequently turned the matter over to the SLCPD for investigation. SLCPD detectives immediately began securing and processing the scene and conducting initial witness interviews. The FBI opened a federal criminal civil rights investigation on August 11, 2014. Thereafter, federal and county authorities conducted cooperative, yet independent investigations into the shooting of Michael Brown.

The encounter between Wilson and Brown took place over an approximately two-minute period of time at about noon on August 9, 2014. Wilson was on duty and driving his department-issued Chevy Tahoe SUV westbound on Canfield Drive in Ferguson, Missouri when he saw Brown and his friend, Witness 101,[2] walking eastbound in the middle of the street. Brown and Witness 101 had just come from Ferguson Market and Liquor ("Ferguson Market"), a nearby convenience store, where, at approximately 11:53 a.m., Brown stole several packages of cigarillos. As captured on the store's surveillance video, when the store clerk tried to stop Brown, Brown used his physical size to stand over him and forcefully shove him away. As a result, an FPD dispatch call went out over the police radio for a "stealing in progress." The dispatch recordings and Wilson's radio transmissions establish that Wilson was aware of the theft and had a description of the suspects as he encountered Brown and Witness 101.

As Wilson drove toward Brown and Witness 101, he told the two men to walk on the sidewalk. According to Wilson's statement to prosecutors and investigators, he suspected that Brown and Witness 101 were involved in the incident at Ferguson Market based on the descriptions he heard on the radio and the cigarillos in Brown's hands. Wilson then called for backup, stating, "Put me on Canfield with two and send me another car." Wilson backed up his SUV and parked at an angle, blocking most of both lanes of traffic, and stopping Brown and Witness 101 from walking any further. Wilson attempted to open the driver's door of the SUV to exit his vehicle, but as he swung it open, the door came into contact with Brown's body and either rebounded closed or Brown pushed it closed.

Wilson and other witnesses stated that Brown then reached into the SUV through the open driver's window and punched and grabbed Wilson. This is corroborated by bruising on Wilson's jaw and scratches on his neck, the presence of Brown's DNA on Wilson's collar, shirt, and pants, and Wilson's DNA on Brown's palm. While there are other individuals who stated that Wilson reached out of the SUV and grabbed Brown by the neck, prosecutors could not credit their accounts because they were inconsistent with physical and forensic evidence, as detailed throughout this report.

Wilson told prosecutors and investigators that he responded to Brown reaching into the SUV and punching him by withdrawing his gun because he could not access less lethal weapons while seated inside the SUV. Brown then grabbed the weapon and struggled with Wilson to gain control of it. Wilson fired, striking Brown in the hand. Autopsy results and bullet trajectory, skin from Brown's palm on the outside of the SUV door as well as Brown's DNA on the inside of the driver's door corroborate Wilson's account that during the struggle, Brown used his right hand to grab and attempt to control Wilson's gun. According to three autopsies, Brown sustained a close range gunshot wound to the fleshy portion of his right hand at the base of his right thumb. Soot from the muzzle of the gun found embedded in the tissue of this wound coupled with indicia of thermal change from the heat of the muzzle indicate that Brown's hand was within inches of the muzzle of Wilson's gun when it was fired. The location of the recovered bullet in the side panel of the driver's door, just above Wilson's lap, also corroborates Wilson's account of the struggle over the gun and when the gun was fired, as do witness accounts that Wilson fired at least one shot from inside the SUV.

Although no eyewitnesses directly corroborate Wilson's account of Brown's attempt to gain control of the gun, there is no credible evidence to disprove Wilson's account of what occurred inside the SUV. Some witnesses claim that Brown's arms were never inside the SUV. However, as discussed later in this report, those witness accounts could not be relied upon in a prosecution because credible witness accounts and physical and forensic evidence, *i.e.* Brown's DNA inside the SUV and on Wilson's shirt collar and the bullet trajectory and close-range gunshot wound to Brown's hand, establish that Brown's arms and/or torso were inside the SUV.

After the initial shooting inside the SUV, the evidence establishes that Brown ran eastbound on Canfield Drive and Wilson chased after him. The autopsy results confirm that Wilson did not shoot Brown in the back as he was running away because there were no entrance wounds to Brown's back. The autopsy results alone do not indicate the direction Brown was facing when he received two wounds to his right arm, given the mobility of the arm. However, as detailed later in this report, there are no witness accounts that could be relied upon in a prosecution to prove that Wilson shot at Brown as he was running away. Witnesses who say so cannot be relied upon in a prosecution because they have given accounts that are inconsistent with the physical and forensic evidence or are significantly inconsistent with their own prior statements made throughout the investigation.

Brown ran at least 180 feet away from the SUV, as verified by the location of bloodstains on the roadway, which DNA analysis confirms was Brown's blood. Brown then turned around and came back toward Wilson, falling to his death approximately 21.6 feet west of the blood in the roadway. Those witness accounts stating that Brown never moved back toward Wilson could not be relied upon in a prosecution because their accounts cannot be reconciled with the DNA bloodstain evidence and other credible witness accounts.

As detailed throughout this report, several witnesses stated that Brown appeared to pose a physical threat to Wilson as he moved toward Wilson. According to these witnesses, who are corroborated by blood evidence in the roadway, as Brown continued to move toward Wilson, Wilson fired at Brown in what appeared to be self-defense and stopped firing once Brown fell to the ground. Wilson stated that he feared Brown would again assault him because of Brown's conduct at the SUV and because as Brown moved toward him, Wilson saw Brown reach his right hand under his t-shirt into what appeared to be his waistband. There is no evidence upon which prosecutors can rely to disprove Wilson's stated subjective belief that he feared for his safety.

Ballistics analysis indicates that Wilson fired a total of 12 shots, two from the SUV and ten on the roadway. Witness accounts and an audio recording indicate that when Wilson and Brown were on the roadway, Wilson fired three gunshot volleys, pausing in between each one. According to the autopsy results, Wilson shot and hit Brown as few as six or as many as eight times, including the gunshot to Brown's hand. Brown fell to the ground dead as a result of a gunshot to the apex of his head. With the exception of the first shot to Brown's hand, all of the shots that struck Brown were fired from a distance of more than two feet. As documented by crime scene photographs, Brown fell to the ground with his left, uninjured hand balled up by his waistband, and his right, injured hand palm up by his side. Witness accounts and cellular phone video prove that Wilson did not touch Brown's body after he fired the final shot and Brown fell to the ground.

Although there are several individuals who have stated that Brown held his hands up in an unambiguous sign of surrender prior to Wilson shooting him dead, their accounts do not support a prosecution of Wilson. As detailed throughout this report, some of those accounts are inaccurate because they are inconsistent with the physical and forensic evidence; some of those accounts are materially inconsistent with that witness's own prior statements with no explanation, credible for otherwise, as to why those accounts changed over time. Certain other witnesses who originally stated Brown had his hands up in surrender recanted their original accounts, admitting that they did not witness the shooting or parts of it, despite what they initially reported either to federal or local law enforcement or to the media. Prosecutors did not rely on those accounts when making a prosecutive decision.

While credible witnesses gave varying accounts of exactly what Brown was doing with his hands as he moved toward Wilson – *i.e.*, balling them, holding them out, or pulling up his pants up – and varying accounts of how he was moving – *i.e.* , "charging," moving in "slow motion," or "running" – they all establish that Brown was moving toward Wilson when Wilson shot him. Although some witnesses state that Brown held his hands up at shoulder level with his palms facing outward for a brief moment, these same witnesses describe Brown then dropping his hands and "charging" at Wilson.

B. Initial Law Enforcement Investigation

Wilson shot Brown at about 12:02 p.m. on August 9, 2014. Within minutes, FPD officers responded to the scene, as they were already en route from Wilson's initial radio call for assistance. Also within minutes, residents began pouring onto the street. At 12:08 p.m., FPD officers requested assistance from nearby SLCPD precincts. By 12:14 p.m., some members of the growing crowd became increasingly hostile in response to chants of "[We] need to kill these motherfuckers," referring to the police officers on scene. At around the same time, about 12:15 p.m., Witness 147, an FPD sergeant, informed the FPD Chief that there had been a fatal officer-involved shooting. At about 12:23 p.m., after speaking with one of his captains, the FPD Chief contacted the SLCPD Chief and turned over the homicide investigation to the SLCPD. Within twenty minutes of Brown's death, paramedics covered Brown's body with several white sheets.

The SLCPD Division of Criminal Investigation, Bureau of Crimes Against Persons ("CAP") was notified at 12:43 p.m. to report to the crime scene to begin a homicide investigation. When they received notification, SLCPD CAP detectives were investigating an armed, masked hostage situation in the hospice wing at St. Anthony's Medical Center in the south part of St. Louis County, nearly 37 minutes from Canfield Drive. They arrived at Canfield Drive at approximately 1:30 p.m. During that time frame, between about 12:45 p.m. and 1:17 p.m., SLCPD reported gunfire in the area, putting both civilians and officers in danger. As a result, canine officers and additional patrol officers responded to assist with crowd control. SLCPD expanded the perimeter of the crime scene to move the crowd away from Brown's body in an effort to preserve the crime scene for processing.

Upon their arrival, SLCPD detectives from the Bureau of Criminal Identification Crime Scene Unit erected orange privacy screens around Brown's body, and CAP detectives alerted the St. Louis County Medical Examiner ("SCLME") to respond to the scene. To further protect the integrity of the crime scene, and in accordance with common police practice, SLCPD personnel did not permit family members and concerned neighbors into the crime scene (with one brief exception). Also in accordance with common police practice, crime scene detectives processed the crime scene with Brown's body present. According to SLCPD CAP detectives, they have one opportunity to thoroughly investigate a crime scene before it is forever changed upon the removal of the decedent's body. Processing a homicide scene with the decedent's body present allows detectives, for example, to accurately measure distances, precisely document body position, and note injury and other markings relative to other aspects of the crime scene that photographs may not capture.

In this case, crime scene detectives had to stop processing the scene as a result of two more reports of what sounded like automatic weapons gunfire in the area at 1:55 p.m. and 2:11 p.m., as well as some individuals in the crowd encroaching on the crime scene and chanting, "Kill the Police," as documented by cell phone video. At each of those times, having exhausted their existing resources, SLCPD personnel called emergency codes for additional patrol officers from throughout St. Louis County in increments of twenty-five. Livery drivers sent to transport Brown's body upon completion of processing arrived at 2:20 p.m. Their customary practice is to wait on scene until the body is ready for transport. However, an SLCPD sergeant briefly stopped them from getting out of their vehicle until the gunfire abated and it was safe for them to do so. The SLCME medicolegal investigator arrived at 2:30 p.m. and began conducting his investigation when it was reasonably safe to do so. Detectives were at the crime scene for approximately five and a half hours, and throughout that time, SLCPD personnel continued to seek additional assistance, calling in the Highway Safety Unit at 2:38 p.m. and the Tactical Operations Unit at 2:44 p.m. Witnesses and detectives described the scene as volatile, causing concern for both their personal safety and the integrity of the crime scene. Crime scene detectives and the SLCME medicolegal investigator completed the processing of

Brown's body at approximately 4:00 p.m, at which time Brown's body was transported to the Office of the SLCME.

C. Legal Summary

1. The Law Governing Uses of Deadly Force by a Law Enforcement Officer

The federal criminal statute that enforces Constitutional limits on uses of force by law enforcement officers is 18 U.S.C. § 242, which provides in relevant part, as follows:

> Whoever, under color of any law, . . . willfully subjects any person . . . to the deprivation of any rights, privileges, or immunities secured or protected by the Constitution or laws of the United States [shall be guilty of a crime].

To prove a violation of Section 242, the government must prove the following elements beyond a reasonable doubt: (1) that the defendant was acting under color of law, (2) that he deprived a victim of a right protected by the Constitution or laws of the United States, (3) that he acted willfully, and (4) that the deprivation resulted in bodily injury and/or death. There is no dispute that Wilson, who was on duty and working as a patrol officer for the FPD, acted under color of law when he shot Brown, or that the shots resulted in Brown's death. The determination of whether criminal prosecution is appropriate rests on whether there is sufficient evidence to establish that any of the shots fired by Wilson were unreasonable, as defined under federal law, given the facts known to Wilson at the time, and if so, whether Wilson fired the shots with the requisite "willful" criminal intent.

i. *The Shootings Were Not Objectively Unreasonable Uses of Force Under 18 U.S.C. § 242*

In this case, the Constitutional right at issue is the Fourth Amendment's prohibition against unreasonable seizures, which encompasses the right of an arrestee to be free from "objectively unreasonable" force. *Graham v. Connor*, 490 U.S. 386, 396-97 (1989). "The 'reasonableness' of a particular use of force must be judged from the perspective of a reasonable officer on the scene, rather than with the 20/20 vision of hindsight." *Id.* at 396. "Careful attention" must be paid "to the facts and circumstances of each particular case, including the severity of the crime at issue, whether the suspect poses an immediate threat to the safety of the officers or others, and whether he is actively resisting arrest or attempting to evade arrest by flight." *Id.* Allowance must be made for the fact that law enforcement officials are often forced to make split-second judgments in circumstances that are tense, uncertain, and rapidly evolving. *Id.* at 396-97.

The use of deadly force is justified when the officer has "probable cause to believe that the suspect pose[s] a threat of serious physical harm, either to the officer or to others." *Tennessee v. Garner*, 471 U.S. 1, 11 (1985); *see Nelson v. County of Wright*, 162 F.3d 986, 990 (8th Cir. 1998); *O'Bert v. Vargo*, 331 F.3d 29, 36 (2d Cir. 2003) (same as *Garner*); *Deluna v. City of Rockford*, 447 F.3d 1008, 1010 (7th Cir. 2006), *citing Scott v. Edinburg*, 346 F.3d 752, 756 (7th Cir. 2003) (deadly force can be reasonably employed where an officer believes that the suspect's actions place him, or others in the immediate vicinity, in imminent danger of death or serious bodily injury).

As detailed throughout this report, the evidence does not establish that the shots fired by Wilson were objectively unreasonable under federal law. The physical evidence establishes that Wilson shot Brown once in the hand, at close range, while Wilson sat in his police SUV, struggling with Brown for control of Wilson's gun. Wilson then shot Brown several more times from a distance of at least two feet after Brown ran away from Wilson and then turned and faced him. There are no witness accounts that federal prosecutors, and likewise a jury, would credit to support the conclusion that Wilson fired at Brown from behind. With the exception of the two wounds to Brown's right arm, which indicate neither bullet trajectory nor the direction in which Brown was moving when he was struck, the medical examiners' reports are in agreement that the entry wounds from the latter gunshots were to the front of Brown's body, establishing that Brown was facing Wilson when these shots were fired. This includes the fatal shot to the top of Brown's head. The physical evidence also establishes that Brown moved forward toward Wilson after he turned around to face him. The physical evidence is corroborated by multiple eyewitnesses.

Applying the well-established controlling legal authority, including binding precedent from the United States Supreme Court and Eighth Circuit Court of Appeals, the evidence does not establish that it was unreasonable for Wilson to perceive Brown as a threat while Brown was punching and grabbing him in the SUV and attempting to take his gun. Thereafter, when Brown started to flee, Wilson was aware that Brown had attempted to take his gun and suspected that Brown might have been part of a theft a few minutes before. Under the law, it was not unreasonable for Wilson to perceive that Brown posed a threat of serious physical harm, either to him or to others. When Brown turned around and moved toward Wilson, the applicable law and evidence do not support finding that Wilson was unreasonable in his fear that Brown would once again attempt to harm him and gain control of his gun. There are no credible witness accounts that state that Brown was clearly attempting to surrender when Wilson shot him. As detailed throughout this report, those witnesses who say so have given accounts that could not be relied upon in a prosecution because they are irreconcilable with the physical evidence, inconsistent with the credible accounts of other eyewitnesses, inconsistent with the witness's own prior statements, or in some instances, because the witnesses have acknowledged that their initial accounts were untrue.

ii. Wilson Did Not Willfully Violate Brown's Constitutional Right to Be Free from Unreasonable Force

Federal law requires that the government must also prove that the officer acted willfully, that is, "for the specific purpose of violating the law." *Screws v. United States*, 325 U.S. 91, 101-107 (1945) (discussing willfulness element of 18 U.S.C. § 242). The Supreme Court has held that an act is done willfully if it was "committed" either "in open defiance or in reckless disregard of a constitutional requirement which has been made specific or definite." *Screws*, 325 U.S. at 105. The government need not show that the defendant knew a federal statute or law protected the right with which he intended to interfere . *Id.* at 106-07 ("[t]he fact that the defendants may not have been thinking in constitutional terms is not material where their aim was not to enforce local law but to deprive a citizen of a right and that right was protected"); *United States v. Walsh*, 194 F.3d 37, 52-53 (2d Cir. 1999) (holding that jury did not have to find defendant knew of the particular Constitutional provision at issue but that it had to find intent to invade interest protected by Constitution). However, we must prove that the defendant intended to engage in the conduct that violated the Constitution and that he did so knowing that it was a wrongful act. *Id.*

"[A]ll the attendant circumstances" should be considered in determining whether an act was done willfully. *Screws*, 325 U.S. at 107. Evidence regarding the egregiousness of the conduct, its character and duration, the weapons employed and the provocation, if any, is therefore relevant to this inquiry. *Id.* Willfulness may be inferred from blatantly wrongful conduct. *See id.* at 106; *see also United States v. Reese*, 2 F.3d 870, 881 (9th Cir. 1993) ("Intentionally wrongful conduct, because it contravenes a right definitely established in law, evidences a reckless disregard for that right; such reckless disregard, in turn, is the legal equivalent of willfulness."); *United States v. Dise*, 763 F.2d 586, 592 (3d Cir. 1985) (holding that when defendant "invades personal liberty of another, knowing that invasion is violation of state law, [defendant] has demonstrated bad faith and reckless disregard for [federal] constitutional rights"). Mistake, fear, misperception, or even poor judgment does not constitute willful conduct prosecutable under the statute. *See United States v. McClean*, 528 F.2d 1250, 1255 (2d Cir. 1976) (inadvertence or mistake negates willfulness for purposes of 18 U.S.C. § 242).

As detailed below, Wilson has stated his intent in shooting Brown was in response to a perceived deadly threat. The only possible basis for prosecuting Wilson under 18 U.S.C. § 242 would therefore be if the government could prove that his account is not true – *i.e.*, that Brown never punched and grabbed Wilson at the SUV, never attempted to gain control of Wilson's gun, and thereafter clearly surrendered in a way that no reasonable officer could have failed to perceive. There is no credible evidence to refute Wilson's stated subjective belief that he was acting in self-defense. As discussed throughout this report, Wilson's account is corroborated by physical evidence and his perception of a threat posed by Brown is corroborated by other credible eyewitness accounts. Even if Wilson was mistaken in his interpretation of Brown's conduct, the fact that others interpreted that conduct the same way as Wilson precludes a determination that he acted for the purpose of violating the law.

III. Summary of the Evidence

As detailed below, Darren Wilson has stated that he shot Michael Brown in response to a perceived deadly threat. This section begins with Wilson's account because the evidence that follows, in the form of forensic and physical evidence and witness accounts, must disprove his account beyond a reasonable doubt in order for the government to prosecute Wilson.

A. Darren Wilson's Account

Darren Wilson made five voluntary statements following the shooting. Wilson's first statement was to Witness 147, his supervising sergeant at the FPD, who responded to Canfield Drive within minutes and immediately spoke to Wilson.[3] Wilson's second statement was made to an SLCPD detective about 90 minutes later, after Wilson returned to the FPD. This interview continued at a local hospital while Wilson was receiving medical treatment. Third, SLCPD detectives conducted a more thorough interview the following morning, on August 10, 2014. Fourth, federal prosecutors and FBI agents interviewed Wilson on August 22, 2014. Wilson's attorney was present for both interviews with the SLCPD detectives. Two attorneys were present for his interview with federal agents and prosecutors. Wilson's fifth statement occurred when he appeared before the county grand jury for approximately 90 minutes on September 16, 2014.

According to Wilson, he was traveling westbound on Canfield Drive, having just finished another call, when he saw Brown and Witness 101 walking single file in the middle of the street on the yellow line. Wilson had never before met either Brown or Witness 101. Wilson approached Witness 101 first and told him to use the sidewalk because there had been cars trying to pass them. When pressed by federal prosecutors, Wilson denied using profane language, explaining that he was on his way to meet his fiancée for lunch, and did not want to antagonize the two subjects. Witness 101 responded to Wilson that he was almost to his destination, and Wilson replied, "What's wrong with the sidewalk?" Wilson stated that Brown unexpectedly responded, "Fuck what you have to say." As Wilson drove past Brown, he saw cigarillos in Brown's hand, which alerted him to a radio dispatch of a "stealing in progress" that he heard a few minutes prior while finishing his last call. Wilson then checked his rearview mirror, and realized that Witness 101 matched the description of the other subject on the radio dispatch.

Wilson requested assistance over the radio, stating that he had two subjects on Canfield Drive. Wilson explained that he intended to stop Brown and Witness 101 and wait for backup before he did any further investigation into the theft. Wilson reversed his vehicle and parked in a manner to block Brown and Witness 101 from walking any further. Upon doing so, he attempted to open his driver's door, and said, "Hey, come here." Before Wilson got his leg out, Brown responded, "What the fuck are you gonna do?"[4] Brown then slammed the door shut and Wilson told him to "get back." Wilson attempted to open the door again. Wilson told the county grand jury that he then told Brown, "Get the fuck back," but Brown did not comply and, using his body, pushed the door closed on Wilson.

Brown placed his hands on the window frame of the driver's door, and again Wilson told Brown to "get back." To Wilson's surprise, Brown then leaned into the driver's window, so that his arms and upper torso were inside the SUV. Brown started assaulting Wilson, "swinging wildly." Brown, still with cigarillos in his hand, turned around and handed the items to Witness 101 using his left hand, telling Witness 101 "take these." Wilson used the opportunity to grab Brown's right arm, but Brown used his left hand to twice punch Wilson's jaw. As Brown assaulted Wilson, Wilson leaned back, blocking the blows with his forearms. Brown hit Wilson on the side of his face and grabbed his shirt, hands, and arms. Wilson feared that Brown's blows could potentially render him unconscious, leaving him vulnerable to additional harm.

Wilson explained that he resorted to his training and the "use of force triangle" to determine how to properly defend himself. Wilson explained that he did not carry a taser, and therefore, his options were mace, his flashlight, his retractable asp baton, and his firearm. Wilson's mace was on his left hip and Wilson explained that he knew that the space within the SUV was too small to use it without incapacitating himself in the process. Wilson's asp baton was located on the back of his duty belt. Wilson determined that not only would he have to lean forward to reach it, giving more of an advantage to Brown, but there was not enough space in the SUV to expand the baton. Wilson's flashlight was in his duty bag on the passenger seat, out of his reach. Wilson explained that his gun, located on his right hip, was his only readily accessible option.

Consequently, while the assault was in progress and Brown was leaning in through the window with his arms, torso, and head inside the SUV, Wilson withdrew his gun and pointed it at Brown. Wilson warned Brown to stop or he was going to shoot him. Brown stated, "You are too much of a pussy to shoot,"[5] and put his right hand[6] over Wilson's right hand, gaining control of the gun. Brown then maneuvered the gun so that it was pointed down at Wilson's left hip. Wilson explained that Brown's size and strength, coupled with his standing position outside the SUV relative to Wilson's seated position inside the SUV, rendered Wilson completely vulnerable. Wilson stated that he feared Brown was going to shoot him because Brown had control of the gun. Wilson managed to use his left elbow to brace against the seat, gaining enough leverage to push the gun forward until it lined up with the driver's door, just under the handle. Wilson explained that he twice pulled the trigger but the gun did not fire, most likely because Brown's hand was preventing the gun from functioning properly. Wilson pulled the trigger a third time and the gun fired into the door. Immediately, glass shattered because the window had been down, and Wilson noticed blood on his own hand. Wilson initially thought he had been cut by the glass.

Brown appeared to be momentarily startled because he briefly backed up. Wilson saw Brown put his hand down to his right hip, and initially assumed the bullet went through the door and struck Brown there. Wilson then described Brown becoming enraged, and that Brown "looked like a demon." Brown then leaned into the driver's window so that his head and arms were inside the SUV and he assaulted Wilson again. Wilson explained that while blocking his face with his left hand, he tried to fire his gun with his right hand, but the gun jammed. Wilson lifted the gun, without looking, and used both hands to manually clear the gun while also trying to shield himself. He then successfully fired another shot, holding the gun in his right hand. According to Wilson, he could not see where he shot, but did not think that he struck Brown because he saw "smoke" outside the window, seemingly from the ground, indicating to him a point of impact that was farther away.

Brown then took off running. Wilson radioed for additional assistance, calling out that shots were fired. Wilson then chased after Brown on foot. Federal prosecutors questioned Wilson as to why he did not drive away or wait for backup, but instead chose to pursue Brown despite the attack he just described. Wilson explained that he ran after Brown because Brown posed a danger to others, having just assaulted a police officer and likely stolen from Ferguson Market. Given Brown's violent and otherwise erratic behavior, Wilson was concerned that Brown was a danger to anyone who crossed his path as he ran.

Wilson denied firing any shots while Brown was running from him. Rather he kept his gun out, but down in a "low ready" position. Wilson explained that he chased after Brown, repeatedly yelling at him to stop and get on the ground. Brown kept running, but when he was about 20 to 30 feet from Wilson, abruptly stopped, and turned around toward Wilson, appearing "psychotic," "hostile," and "crazy," as though he was "looking through" Wilson. While making a "grunting noise" and with what Wilson described as the "most intense aggressive face" that he had ever seen on a person, Brown then made a hop-like movement, similar to what a person does when he starts running. Brown then started running at Wilson, closing the distance between them to about 15 feet. Wilson explained that he again feared for his life, and backed up as Brown came toward him, repeatedly ordering Brown to stop and get on the ground. Brown failed to comply and kept coming at Wilson. Wilson explained that he knew if Brown reached him, he "would be done." During Brown's initial strides, Brown put his right hand in what appeared to be his waistband, albeit covered by his shirt. Wilson thought Brown might be reaching for a weapon. Wilson fired multiple shots. Brown paused. Wilson explained that he then paused, again yelled for Brown to get on the ground, and again Brown charged at him, hand in waistband. Wilson backed up and fired again. The same thing happened a third time where Brown very briefly paused, and Wilson paused and yelled for Brown to get on the ground. Brown continued to "charge." Wilson described having tunnel vision on Brown's right arm, all the while backing up as Brown approached, not understanding why Brown had yet to stop.

Wilson fired the last volley of shots when Brown was about eight to ten feet from him. When Wilson fired the last shot, he saw the bullet go into Brown's head, and Brown "went down right there." Wilson initially estimated that on the roadway, he fired five shots and then two shots, none of which had any effect on Brown. Then Brown leaned forward as though he was getting ready to "tackle" Wilson, and Wilson fired the last shot.

Federal prosecutors questioned Wilson about his actions after the shooting. Wilson explained that he never touched Brown's body. Using the microphone on his shoulder, Wilson radioed, "Send me every car we got and a supervisor." Within seconds, additional officers and his sergeant arrived on scene. In response to specific questions by federal prosecutors, Wilson explained that he had left his keys in the ignition of his vehicle and the engine running during the pursuit, so he went back to his SUV to secure it. In so doing, he was careful only to touch the door and the keys. Wilson then walked over to his sergeant, Witness 147, and told him what happened.[7] Both Wilson and Witness 147 explained that Witness 147 told Wilson to wait in his SUV, but Wilson refused, explaining that if he waited there, it would be known to the neighborhood that he was the shooter. Wilson explained that the atmosphere was quickly becoming hostile, and he either needed to be put to work with his fellow officers or he needed to leave. Per Witness 147's orders, Wilson drove Witness 147's vehicle to the FPD. It was during the drive that Wilson realized he was not bleeding, but had what he thought was Brown's blood on both hands.

As soon as Wilson got to the police department, he scrubbed both hands. When federal prosecutors challenged why he did so in light of the potential evidentiary value, Wilson explained that he realized after the fact that he should not have done so, but at the time he was reacting to a potential biohazard while still under the stress of the moment. Wilson then rendered his gun safe and packaged it with the one remaining round in an evidence envelope. When federal prosecutors further questioned why he packaged his own gun, Wilson explained that he wanted to ensure its preservation for analysis because it would prove what happened. At first, he hoped Brown's fingerprints or epithelial DNA from sweat on his hand might be present from when Brown grabbed the gun. But then Wilson actually saw blood on the gun, and assumed that since he was not bleeding, the blood likely belonged to Brown, and therefore, Brown's DNA would be present.

During Wilson's interview with federal authorities, prosecutors and agents focused on whether he was consistent with his previous statements, the motivation for his actions, and his training and experience relative to when the use of deadly force is appropriate. Federal prosecutors challenged Wilson with specificity about why he stopped Brown and whether he was aware that Brown and Witness 101 were suspects in the Ferguson Market robbery. Similarly, prosecutors challenged Wilson about his decision to use deadly force inside the SUV, to chase after Brown, and to again use deadly force on Brown in the roadway. Wilson responded to those challenges in a credible manner, offering reasonable explanations to the questions posed.

At the time of his interview, federal prosecutors and agents were aware of the autopsy, DNA, and ballistics results, as detailed below. Wilson's account was consistent with those results, and consistent with the accounts of other independent eyewitnesses, whose accounts were also consistent with the physical evidence. Wilson's statements were consistent with each other in all material ways, and would not be subject to effective impeachment for inconsistencies or deviation from the physical evidence.[8] Therefore, in analyzing all of the evidence, federal prosecutors found Wilson's account to be credible.

B. Physical and Forensic Evidence

1. Crime Scene

As noted above, SLCPD detectives from the Bureau of Criminal Identification, Crime Scene Unit processed the scene of the shootings. During processing, they photographed and took video of the crime scene, including Brown's body and Wilson's SUV. They measured distances from Brown's body, Wilson's SUV, and various pieces of evidence. As described in detail below, they recovered twelve spent shell casings.[9] One was located on the ground between the driver's door and back passenger door of the SUV and another was located near the sidewalk, diagonally across from the driver's door. Seven casings and one spent projectile were located in the general vicinity of Brown's body. Those casings were located on the ground next to the left side of his body (on the south side of Canfield Drive), with four closer to his body, and three in the grassy area of the sidewalk. The projectile was located on the right side of Brown's body (on the north side of Canfield Drive). Three additional casings were further east, or further away from where Brown came to rest. Crime scene detectives also recovered a spent projectile fragment from the wall of an apartment building located east of Brown's body, in the direction toward which Wilson had been shooting.[10] As described below, crime scene detectives noted apparent blood[11] in the roadway approximately 17 feet and 22 feet east of where Brown's body was found and east of the casings that were recovered, consistent with Brown moving toward Wilson before his death. There was no other blood found in the roadway, other than the pool of blood surrounding Brown's body.

Crime scene detectives recovered Brown's St. Louis Cardinals baseball cap by the driver's door of the SUV. Two bracelets, one black and yellow, and the other beaded, were found on either side of the SUV.[12] Brown's Nike flip flops were located in the roadway, the left one near the front of the driver's side of the vehicle, approximately 126 feet west of where Brown's head came to rest, and the right one in the center of the roadway, 82.5 feet west of where Brown's head came to rest and just south of the center line. This is consistent with witness descriptions that Brown, wearing his socks, described as bright yellow with a marijuana leaf pattern, ran diagonally away from the SUV, crossing over the center line.

Prior to transport of Brown's body, the SLCME medicolegal investigator documented the position of Brown's body on the ground. Brown was on his stomach with his right cheek on the ground, his buttocks partially in the air. His uninjured left arm was back and partially bent under his body with his left hand at his waistband, balled up in a fist. His injured right arm was back behind him, almost at his right side, with his injured right hand at hip level, palm up. Brown's shorts were midway down his buttocks, as though they had partially fallen down.

The forensic analysis of the seized evidence is detailed below:

2. Autopsy Findings

There were three autopsies conducted on Michael Brown's body. SLCME conducted the first autopsy. A private forensic pathologist conducted the second autopsy at the request of Brown's family. AFMES conducted the third autopsy at the Department's request.

The SLCME, AFMES, and the private forensic pathologist were consistent in their findings unless otherwise noted. Brown was shot at least six and at most eight times. As described below, two entrance wounds may have been re-entry wounds, accounting for why the number of shots that struck Brown is not definite.

Of the eight gunshot wounds, two wounds, a penetrating gunshot wound to the apex of Brown's head, and a graze or tangential wound to the base of Brown's right thumb, have the most significant evidentiary value when determining the prosecutive merit of this matter. The former is significant because the gunshot to the head would have almost immediately incapacitated and immobilized Brown; the latter is significant because it is consistent with Brown's hand being in close range or having near-contact with the muzzle of Wilson's gun and corroborates Wilson's account that Brown struggled with him to gain control of the gun in the SUV.

The skin tags, or flaps of skin created by the graze of the bullet associated with the right thumb wound, indicate bullet trajectory. They were oriented toward the tip of the right thumb, indicating the path of the bullet went from the tip of the thumb toward the base. Microscopic analysis of the wound indicates that Brown's hand was near the muzzle of the gun when Wilson pulled the trigger. Both AFMES and SLCME pathologists observed numerous deposits of dark particulate foreign debris, consistent with gunpowder soot from the muzzle of the gun embedded in and around the wound. The private forensic pathologist called it gunshot residue, opining that Brown's right hand was less than a foot from the gun. The SLCME pathologist opined that the muzzle of the gun was likely six to nine inches from Brown's hand when it fired. AFMES pathologists opined that the particulate matter was, in fact, soot and was found at the exact point of entry of the wound. The soot, along with the thermal change in the skin resulting from heat discharge of the firearm, indicates that the base of Brown's right hand was within inches of the muzzle of Wilson's gun when it fired. AFMES pathologists further opined that, given the tangential nature of the wound, the fact that the soot was concentrated on one side of the wound, and the bullet trajectory as detailed below, the wound to the thumb is consistent with Brown's hand being on the barrel of the gun itself, though not the muzzle, at the time the shot was fired.

The presence of soot also proves that the wound to the thumb was the result of the gunshot at the SUV.[13] As detailed below, several witnesses described Brown at or in Wilson's SUV when the first shot was fired, and a bullet was recovered from within the driver's door of the SUV. There is no evidence that Wilson was within inches of Brown's thumb other than in the SUV at the outset of the incident. Additionally, according to the SLCME pathologist and the private forensic pathologist, a piece of Brown's skin recovered from the exterior of the driver's door of the SUV is consistent with skin from the part of Brown's thumb that was wounded. It is therefore a virtual certainty that the first shot fired was the one that caused the tangential thumb wound.

The order of the remaining shots cannot be determined, though the shot to Brown's head would have killed him where he stood, preventing him from making any additional purposeful movement toward Wilson after the final shots were fired.[14] The fatal bullet entered the skull, the brain, and the base of the skull, and came to rest in the soft tissues of the right face. The trajectory of the bullet was downward, forward, and to the right. Brown could not have been standing straight when Wilson fired this bullet because Wilson is slightly shorter than Brown. Brown was likely bent at the waist or falling forward when he received this wound. It is also possible, although not consistent with credible eyewitness accounts, that Brown had fallen to his knees with his head forward when Wilson fired this shot. However, the lack of stippling and soot indicates that Wilson was at least two to three feet from Brown when he fired.

The remaining gunshots, like the thumb wound, were all on Brown's right side and none of them would have necessarily immediately immobilized Brown. The lack of soot and stippling indicates that the shots were fired from a distance of at least two to three feet. However, as described below, because of environmental conditions and because Brown's shirt was blood soaked, it was not suitable for gunshot residue analysis to determine muzzle-to-target distance. Therefore, we cannot reliably say whether gunshot residue on Brown's shirt might have provided evidence of muzzle-to-target distance. Regardless, gunshot residue is inherently delicate and easily transferrable.[15]

In addition to the thumb wound and the fatal shot to the head, Brown sustained a gunshot wound to his central forehead, with a corresponding exit wound of the right jaw. The bullet tracked through the right eye and right orbital bone, causing fractures of the facial bones. Brown sustained another gunshot wound to the upper right chest, near the neck. The bullet tracked though the right clavicle and upper lobe of the right lung, and came to rest in the right chest. Brown sustained another entrance wound to his lateral right chest. The bullet tracked through and fractured the eighth right rib, puncturing the lower lobe of the right lung. The bullet was recovered from the soft tissue of the right back. The AFMES pathologists and the private forensic pathologist opined that the right chest wound could have been a re-entry wound from an arm wound as described below, and the clavicle wound could have been a re-entry wound from the bullet that entered Brown's forehead and exited his jaw. The SLCME pathologist also allowed for the possibility of re-entry wounds, but did not opine with specificity due to the variability of such wounds.

Brown also sustained a gunshot wound to the front of the upper right arm, near the armpit, with a corresponding gunshot exit wound of the back of the upper right arm. The remaining gunshot wounds were also to the right arm. These bullet trajectories are described according to the standard anatomic diagram, that is, standing, arms at sides, palms facing forward. That said, Brown sustained a gunshot wound to the dorsal (back) right forearm, below the elbow. The bullet tracked through the bone in the forearm, fracturing it, and exiting through the ventral (front) right forearm. Finally, Brown sustained a tangential or graze gunshot wound to the right bicep, above the elbow.

Given the mobility of the arm, it is impossible to determine the position of the body relative to the shooter at the time the arm wounds were inflicted. Therefore, the autopsy results do not indicate whether Brown was facing Wilson or had his back to him. They do not indicate whether Brown sustained those two arm wounds while his hands were up, down, or by his waistband. The private forensic pathologist opined that he would expect a re-entry wound across Brown's stomach if Brown's hand was at his waistband at the time Wilson fired. However, as mentioned, there is no way to know the exact position of Brown's arm relative to his waistband at the time the bullets struck. Therefore, these gunshot wounds neither corroborate nor discredit Wilson's account or the account of any other witness. However, the concentration of bullet wounds on Brown's right side is consistent with Wilson's description that he focused on Brown's right arm while shooting.

The autopsy established that Brown did not sustain gunshot wounds to his back.[16] There was no evidence to corroborate that Wilson choked, strangled, or tightly grasped Brown on or around his neck, as described by Witness 101 in the summary of his account below. There were no bruises, abrasions, hemorrhaging of soft tissues, or any other injuries to the neck, nor was there evidence of petechial hemorrhaging of Brown's remaining left eye. The private forensic pathologist opined that although the lack of injury does not signify the absence of strangulation, it would be "surprising," given Brown's size, if Wilson attempted to strangle Brown. The private forensic pathologist explained that the act of strangling is often committed by the stronger person, as it is rarely effective if attempted by the person of smaller size or weaker strength.[17]

Brown sustained a one inch superficial incised wound to the right middle of the front of his left arm. SCLME differed with AFMES, characterizing this wound as an abrasion, but AFMES opined that this was more like a cut, consistent with being caused by broken window glass. Brown also sustained abrasions to the right side of the head and face, including abrasions near the right forehead, the lateral right face, and the upper right cheek, consistent with Brown falling and impacting the ground with his face. The private forensic pathologist opined that the severity of these abrasions could have been caused by involuntary seizures as Brown died. He also opined, as did the SLCME pathologist, that these abrasions were consistent with Brown impacting the ground upon death and sliding on the roadway due to the momentum from quickly moving forward.

According to the AFMES and SCLME pathologists, Brown also had small knuckle abrasions, but the pathologists could not link them to any specific source. The SLCME pathologist opined they may have been inflicted post mortem, while the AFMES pathologist opined that they were too small to determine whether they were caused pre or post-mortem.[18] The private forensic pathologist did not note any knuckle abrasions or injury to Brown's hands, explaining that he would expect Brown to have knuckle injury if Wilson sustained broken bones, but not necessarily bruising. AFMES pathologists likewise concurred that lack of injury to Brown's hands is not inconsistent with bruising to Wilson's face.

3. DNA Analysis

The SLCPD Crime Laboratory conducted DNA analysis on swabs taken from Wilson, Brown, Wilson's gun, and the crime scene. Brown's DNA was found at four significant locations: on Wilson's gun; on the roadway further away from where he died; on the SUV driver's door and inside the driver's cabin area of the SUV; and on Wilson's clothes. A DNA mixture from which Wilson's DNA could not be excluded was found on Brown's left palm.

Analysis of DNA on Wilson's gun revealed a major mixture profile that is 2.1 octillion times more likely a mixture of DNA from Wilson and DNA from Brown than from Wilson and anyone else. This is conclusive evidence that Brown's DNA was on Wilson's gun.[19]

Brown is the source of the DNA found in two bloodstains on Canfield Drive, approximately 17 and 22 feet east of where Brown fell to his death, proving that Brown moved forward toward Wilson prior to the fatal shot to his head.

Brown's DNA was found both on the inside and outside of the driver's side of the SUV.

Brown is the source of DNA in blood found on the exterior of the passenger door of the driver's side of the SUV. Likewise, a piece of Brown's skin was recovered from the exterior of the driver's door of the SUV, consistent with Brown sustaining injury while at that door. Brown is also the source of the major contributor of a DNA mixture found on the interior driver's door handle of the SUV. A DNA mixture obtained from the top of the exterior of the driver's door revealed a major mixture profile that is 6.9 million times more likely a mixture of DNA from Wilson and DNA from Brown than from Wilson and anyone else.

Brown's DNA was found on Wilson's uniform shirt collar and pants. With respect to the left side of Wilson's shirt and collar, it is 2.1 trillion times more likely that the recovered DNA mixture is DNA from Wilson and DNA from Brown than from Wilson and anyone else. Similarly, with respect to a DNA mixture obtained from the left side of Wilson's pants, it is 34 sextillion times more likely that the mixture is DNA from Wilson and DNA from Brown than from Wilson and anyone else. Brown is also the source of the major male profile found in a DNA mixture found in a bloodstain on the upper left thigh of Wilson's pants.

DNA analysis of Brown's left palm revealed a DNA mixture with Brown as the major contributor, and Wilson being 98 times more likely the minor contributor than anyone else.

DNA analysis of Brown's clothes, right hand, fingernails, and clothes excluded Wilson as a possible contributor.

4. Dispatch Recordings

According to FPD records, at about 11:53 a.m., a dispatcher called out a "stealing in progress" at the address of Ferguson Market while Wilson was in the midst of a sick infant call. During his interview with federal officials, Wilson told prosecutors and agents that he heard the call on his portable radio, but did not hear the specifics about the location of the "stealing in progress." He also stated that he heard that one of the suspects was wearing a "black shirt," that they had stolen cigarillos, and were going toward the Quick-Trip. The actual description given was that of a "black male in a white t-shirt," "running toward the Quick-Trip," and that "he took a whole box of Swisher cigars." Two officers, Witness 145 and Witness 146, the same two FPD officers who first responded to Canfield Drive after the shooting, responded to the Ferguson Market. At approximately 11:56 a.m., Witness 145, via radio, added, "He's with another male. He's got a red Cardinals hat, white t-shirt, yellow socks, and khaki shorts."

Wilson left the sick call at approximately 11:58 a.m., after EMS arrived to transport the mother and sick child to the hospital. Twenty-seven seconds later, Wilson radioed to Witness 145 and Witness 146, "Do you guys need me?," corroborating that Wilson was aware of the theft at Ferguson Market prior to his encounter with Brown. Witness 145 responded that the suspect "disappeared into the woodwork." Wilson, having not heard him, asked the dispatcher to "relay." The dispatcher then clarified, "He thinks that they...disappeared." Wilson then said "clear," indicating that he understood.

Wilson drove his police SUV west on Canfield Drive, where he encountered Brown and Witness 101 walking east in the middle of the street. Wilson's last recorded radio transmission occurred at approximately noon when he called out, "Put me on Canfield with two and send me another car," consistent with Wilson's account that he radioed for backup once he interacted with Brown and Witness 101.

Several radio transmissions followed from dispatch and from Officer 145 seeking a response from Wilson to no avail. About one minute and forty seconds following Wilson's last transmission, Witness 145 called out to send the supervising sergeant to Canfield Drive and Copper Creek Court, the location of the shooting incident. There were no recorded radio transmissions from Wilson from the time Wilson called for assistance to the time that Witness 145 called for a supervisor.

As noted above, Wilson stated that he also radioed for backup after the initial shots when Brown ran from the SUV, and then again after he shot Brown to death. According to Wilson, as he left the shooting scene, he realized that his radio must have switched from channel 1, which he had been using, to channel 3 during the initial struggle. Channel 3 is a dedicated channel for the North County Fire Department. It only receives transmissions, and therefore, officers cannot use that channel to transmit messages to dispatch. While this is not definitive evidence that Wilson attempted to call for assistance both after the initial shots in the SUV and after he killed Brown, it offers a plausible explanation for the lack of radio transmissions. Moreover, as detailed below, there are several witnesses who state that Wilson paused in the SUV after Brown took off running, arguably giving him enough time to attempt to radio dispatch. Likewise, several witnesses saw Wilson appear to use his shoulder microphone after Brown fell to the ground, presumably to radio dispatch.

5. Ballistics

Witness 143, a firearms and toolmarks examiner with the SLCPD, conducted the ballistics analysis for the St. Louis County Police Laboratory. Witness 144, an FBI firearms and toolmarks examiner, conducted gunshot residue analysis and reconstructed the shooting incident.

i. *Wilson's Firearm and Projectiles Fired*

There were a total of five projectiles, and a fragment from another projectile, recovered from the crime scene and Brown's autopsy. There were a total of 12 shell casings recovered from the crime scene. Wilson's gun can hold up to 13 rounds, 12 in the magazine and one in the chamber. Witness 143 test-fired Wilson's Sig Sauer S&W .40 caliber semi-automatic pistol, noting apparent blood on the gun. He compared the test bullets and casings to those seized as evidence from Brown's body and the crime scene. Witness 143 confirmed that all 12 shell casings were fired from Wilson's gun, consistent with the one round remaining in the gun after the shooting. Witness 143 also confirmed that four of the recovered projectiles, as well as the recovered fragment, were fired from Wilson's gun. The remaining projectile, recovered from the inside of the driver's door of Wilson's SUV, was too damaged to conclusively find that it came from Wilson's gun.

ii. *Projectile Recovered from SUV*

Witness 144 conducted a shooting incident reconstruction of the interior driver's door panel of Wilson's SUV to determine the trajectory of the bullet that was recovered there. The trajectory of the bullet was at a downward angle from left to right, striking the armrest near the interior door handle, entering the door from inside the SUV, and coming to rest inside the door. This is consistent with Wilson's description of the initial gunshot.

Witness 144 conducted gunshot residue analysis on the inside of the driver's door. Particulate and vaporous lead residues found on the interior driver's door panel near the interior window weather stripping and on the interior side frame of the driver's door were, like the recovery of the bullet itself, consistent with the discharge of a firearm. These residues were unsuitable for muzzle-to-target distance determinations. However, vaporous lead residues rarely are deposited at a distance greater than 24 inches, consistent with Wilson discharging his firearm while seated in the driver's seat, less than two feet from the driver's door.

iii. *Gunshot Residue on Brown's Shirt*

Witness 144 conducted gunshot residue analysis on Brown's shirt. For the most part, gunshot residue analysis can only determine whether defects in an item, *i.e.*, the holes in his shirt, are the result of gunshots. Analysis cannot determine the directional travel of bullets.

Witness 144 examined seven holes in the shirt. Gunshot residues in the form of nitrite and bullet wipe lead residues were found near some of the holes. This does not necessarily suggest that the remaining holes were not created by bullets. According to Witness 144, lack of gunshot residue could be due to the possibility of intervening conditions, like large amounts of blood, environmental conditions, or the way the shirt was folded and packaged.

Likewise, the presence of nitrite residues tells very little. Nitrite residues were found near three holes in Brown's right sleeve, and one hole in the right chest of this shirt. Test-firing of the gun showed that nitrite residues appear at a muzzle-to-target distance of eight feet or less, consistent with Wilson's description and several other witness descriptions that Wilson and Brown were about eight feet apart during the final shots. However, the residues were not in a measurable pattern. This means that they may not even be associated with the specific holes in the shirt that they are near, but rather may be just indiscriminate residue from any of the shots, including the close range shots at the SUV, or transferred from one shot to another during the handling and packaging of the clothes.

6. Fingerprints

Wilson's gun was not tested for the presence of Brown's fingerprints. After SLCPD crime scene detectives recovered Wilson's gun, they submitted the gun for DNA analysis rather than for fingerprints analysis. The detectives told federal prosecutors that they knew that typically testing for one would preclude testing for the other, and there was a high likelihood of DNA given the presence of apparent blood on the gun. They also knew that even according to Wilson, Brown never had sole possession of the gun, and if Brown ever had control of the gun at all, it was only when Brown's hand was over Wilson's hand during a struggle for the gun, lessening the likelihood of fingerprints. Furthermore, based on their training and experience, there was a greater likelihood of finding a DNA profile on the gun than lifting fingerprints with enough fine ridge detail to make it suitable for comparison.[20] Because the gun was swabbed in its entirety, it could not later undergo latent fingerprint analysis.[21]

SLCPD crime scene detectives lifted five latent fingerprints from the outside of the driver's door of the SUV. Two were unsuitable for comparison; one was determined to be Wilson's fingerprint; and the remaining two prints, although suitable for comparison, belonged to neither Brown nor Wilson. The leather interior of the SUV was unsuitable for recovering latent prints. Fingerprint examiners also tested Wilson's duty belt for fingerprints, but none recovered was suitable for comparison.

7. Audio Recording of Shots Fired

Witness 136 was in his apartment using a video chat application on his mobile phone when the shooting occurred. According to Witness 136, he heard "maybe three" gunshots followed by a five to six second pause. After those first gunshots, Witness 136 recorded the remainder of his chat and turned it over to the FBI. The recording is about 12 seconds long and captured a total of 10 gunshots. The gunshots begin after the first four seconds. The recording then captured six gunshots in two seconds. There was a three second pause, followed by a seventh gunshot. There was a quick pause of less than one second before the final three-shot volley within two seconds. The recording was not time-stamped. As detailed below, this recording is consistent with several credible witness accounts as well as Wilson's account, that he fired several volleys of shots, briefly pausing between each one.

8. Wilson's Medical Records

Paramedics examined Wilson when he returned to the FPD after the shooting, and recommended that he go to the hospital for follow-up treatment. Wilson sought medical treatment at Christian Northwest Hospital within two hours of the shooting. Witness 117, a nurse practitioner, examined Wilson. For the purpose of making a medical diagnosis, Witness 117 questioned Wilson about what happened. Wilson stated that he was twice punched in the jaw. Witness 117 noted acute or fresh pink scratch marks on the back of Wilson's neck as well as swelling to his jaw. Wilson sustained a contusion of the mandibular joint or jaw area, but did not break his jaw or any other bones. According to Witness 117, Wilson's injuries were consistent with his description of what transpired.

Wilson submitted to a drug and alcohol screen. His blood alcohol content was 0.00% and he tested negative for cocaine, marijuana metabolites, amphetamines, opiates, and phencyclidine, the chemical commonly known as PCP.

9. Brown's Toxicology

A toxicologist with the St. Louis University (SLU) Toxicology Laboratory and the Chief of the Division of Forensic Toxicology at AFMES each conducted blood and urine screens on samples collected from Brown's body. Brown tested positive for the presence of cannabinoids, the hallucinogenic substances associated with marijuana use. The SLU Toxicology Laboratory found 12 nanograms per milliliter of Delta-9-THC, the active ingredient in marijuana, where AFMES found 11 nanograms per milliliter of Delta-9-THC in Brown's blood.

According to both laboratories, these levels of Delta-9-THC are consistent with Brown having ingested THC within a few hours before his death. This concentration of THC would have rendered Brown impaired at the time of his death. As a general matter, this level of impairment can alter one's perception of time and space, but the extent to which this was true in Brown's case cannot be determined. THC affects individuals differently depending on unknown variables such as whether Brown was a chronic user and the concentration of the THC ingested.

10. Ferguson Market Surveillance Video

At approximately 11:53 a.m. on August 9, 2014, about ten minutes prior to the shooting, Brown and Witness 101 went to Ferguson Market, a nearby convenience store. Surveillance video shows Brown stealing several packages of cigarillos and then forcefully shoving the store clerk who tried to stop him from leaving the store without paying. Evidence of this theft and assault likely would be admissible by the defense in a prosecution of Wilson because it is relevant to show Brown's state of mind at or near the time of the shooting, and arguably corroborates Wilson's self-defense claim.

Surveillance cameras captured the incident without audio. SLCPD detectives, FBI agents, and federal prosecutors jointly interviewed the store employees who were present at the time. The employees, a father (the clerk who was assaulted) and his adult daughter, are of Indian origin. The father does not speak English well, and therefore, was not as able as his daughter to recount with specificity what Brown said during the incident.

The video depicts Brown and Witness 101 entering the store and proceeding to the front counter. Brown stood at the register, as Witness 101 waited behind him. Brown asked the clerk behind the counter for cigarillos. The clerk put a package of cigarillos on the counter. Brown then "snatched" the package of cigarillos from the counter. Using his left hand, Brown reached behind him and gave them to Witness 101.[22] Brown then reached over the counter, as Witness 101 described and the video shows, and took additional packages of cigarillos. In so doing, Brown dropped some of the cigarillos and had an exchange with the clerk during which he refused to pay. Witness 101 then placed the cigarillos that Brown had given him back on the register counter, as Brown picked up his stolen goods from the floor.

Brown and Witness 101 proceeded to the exit and the clerk, who is about 5'6" and 150 lbs, attempted to stop them. The clerk first tried to hold the store door closed to prevent Brown's exit. However, Brown shoved the clerk aside, and as Witness 101 walked out the door, Brown menacingly re-approached the clerk. According to the store employees, Brown, looking "crazy" and using profane language, said something like, "What are you gonna do about it?" Brown then exited the store and the clerk's daughter called 911.

C. Witness Accounts

As the first responding investigators, SLCPD detectives interviewed witnesses on Canfield Drive within the first few hours of the shooting. One week later, on August 16, 2014, in an effort to identify additional witnesses who may have been reluctant to speak with local law enforcement, the FBI conducted a neighborhood canvass of more than 300 residences. Federal and county authorities largely conducted additional interviews jointly, unless a witness expressed discomfort with the presence of either federal agents or SLCPD detectives. To evaluate the merits of a potential federal prosecution, federal prosecutors and FBI agents conducted follow-up interviews. Many witnesses also testified before the county grand jury. Unless otherwise noted, witnesses did not know, or know of, Brown or Wilson prior to the shooting.

For ease of review, this report divides the summaries of witness accounts into three sections based on the nature and credibility of their accounts to a jury. First, the report summarizes the accounts of those witnesses whose statements have been materially consistent, are consistent with the physical evidence, and that are mutually corroborative. For these reasons, prosecutors determined these witness accounts were reliable and would be credible to jurors.

This section is further broken down into subsections for those witness accounts that support Wilson's claim of self-defense and those that support a criminal prosecution of Wilson. Of course, to support a prosecution of Wilson under 18 U.S.C. § 242, the weight of the evidence from those witness accounts that support a prosecution must be prove the violation beyond a reasonable doubt to twelve reasonable jurors. A prosecution will fail if the credible evidence creates "reasonable doubt" of Wilson's guilt by supporting Wilson's statements that he acted reasonably and in self-defense. The second section of summaries contains those accounts that neither inculpate Wilson nor fully corroborate Wilson's account. These witnesses, regardless of whether prosecutors determined their accounts to be credible, would not strengthen the government's case in a prosecution of Wilson. The third section of summaries contains those witness accounts that are inconsistent with the physical and forensic evidence, materially inconsistent with that witness's own prior statements, or those witnesses who have recanted large portions of their accounts, admitting that they did not in fact witness the shooting as they initially claimed. Therefore, for this last category of witnesses, federal prosecutors either could not rely on their accounts to support a prosecution of Darren Wilson or did not consider their accounts in making a prosecutive decision.

1. Witnesses Materially Consistent with Prior Statements, Physical Evidence, and Other Witnesses and Therefore, Give Credible Accounts

i. *Witnesses Materially Consistent with Prior Statements, Physical Evidence, and Other Witnesses Who Corroborate That Wilson Acted in Self-Defense*

a. Witness 102

Witness 102 is a 27-year-old bi-racial male. Witness 102 gave three statements. First, SLCPD detectives interviewed him; second, FBI agents interviewed him; third, Witness 102 testified before the county grand jury.

Witness 102 was doing house repairs on a residence on Canfield Drive when the shooting occurred. Witness 102 first noticed Brown and Witness 101 walking down Canfield Drive about 20 minutes prior to the shooting when he went to his truck to retrieve a broom. Brown's size initially drew Witness 102's attention. When Witness 102 later came back outside to get another tool, he noticed Wilson's SUV parked in the middle of the street at an angle, with the driver's side closer to the center of the street. Witness 102's vantage point was street level, about 450 feet from the SUV with a view of the driver's side of the SUV.

According to Witness 102, he saw Brown standing on the driver's side of the SUV, bent over with his body through the driver's window from the waist up. Witness 102 explained that Brown was "wrestling" through the window, but he was unable to see what Wilson was doing. After a few seconds, Witness 102 heard a gunshot. Immediately, Brown took off running in the opposite direction from where Witness 102 was standing. Witness 102 heard something metallic hit the ground. Witness 102 thought that he had just witnessed the murder of a police officer because a few seconds passed before Wilson emerged from the SUV. Wilson then chased Brown with his gun drawn, but not pointed at Brown, until Brown abruptly turned around at a nearby driveway. Witness 102 explained that it made no sense to him why Brown turned around. Brown did not get on the ground or put his hands up in surrender. In fact, Witness 102 told investigators that he knew "for sure that [Brown's] hands were not above his head." Rather, Brown made some type of movement similar to pulling his pants up or a shoulder shrug, and then "charged" at Wilson. It was only then that Wilson fired five or six shots at Brown. Brown paused and appeared to flinch, and Wilson stopped firing. However, Brown charged at Wilson again, and again Wilson fired about three or four rounds until Brown finally collapsed on the ground. Witness 102 was in disbelief that Wilson seemingly kept missing because Brown kept advancing forward. Witness 102 described Brown as a "threat," moving at a "full charge." Witness 102 stated that Wilson only fired shots when Brown was coming toward Wilson. It appeared to Witness 102 that Wilson's life was in jeopardy. Witness 102 was unable to hear whether Brown or Wilson said anything.

Witness 102 did not see Brown's friend, Witness 101, at any time during the incident until Witness 101 "came out of nowhere," shouting, "'They just killed him!'" Witness 101 seemed to be shouting toward a blue Monte Carlo[23] that had stopped behind Wilson's SUV. Witness 101 then ran off. Witness 102 explained that once he saw officers putting up police tape, he went down to the scene and began telling another onlooker what he had witnessed. Witness 102 later learned via a "friend" on Facebook that his voice was inadvertently captured on another bystander's cell phone recording. Federal prosecutors reviewed this recording and Witness 102 identified his voice on the recording when he testified before the county grand jury. In it, Witness 102 can be heard correcting someone else who was recounting what he heard from others, that Wilson "stood over [Brown] and shot while on the ground." In response, Witness 102 stated that Wilson shot Brown because Brown came back toward Wilson. Witness 102 "kept thinking" that Wilson's shots were "missing" Brown because Brown kept moving.

Witness 102 did not stay on Canfield Drive long after the shooting, but rather started to leave the area after about five minutes because he felt uncomfortable. According to Witness 102, crowds of people had begun to gather, wrongly claiming the police shot Brown for no reason and that he had his hands up in surrender. Two black women approached Witness 102, mobile phones set to record, asking him to recount what he had witnessed. Witness 102 responded that they would not like what he had to say. The women responded with racial slurs, calling him names like "white motherfucker."

Witness 102 called 911 the following day to report what he saw. He then went to the FPD on Monday, August 11, 2014, where he was referred to the SLCPD. Witness 102 explained that he came forward because he "felt bad about the situation," and he wanted to "bring closure to [Brown's] family," so they would not think that the officer "got away with murdering their son." He further explained that "most people think that police are bad for 'em up until the time they're in need of the police," and he felt that witnesses would not come forward to tell the truth in this case because of community pressure.

As described above, all of Witness 102's statements were materially consistent with each other, with physical and forensic evidence, and with other credible witness accounts. Witness 102 does not have a criminal history. Therefore, if called as a defense witness in a prosecution of Darren Wilson, this witness's account would not be vulnerable to meaningful cross-examination and would not be subject to impeachment due to bias or inconsistencies in his prior statements. Accordingly, after a thorough review of all the evidence, federal prosecutors determined his account to be credible and likewise determined that a jury appropriately would credit his potential testimony.

b. Witness 103

Witness 103 is a 58-year-old black male who gave two statements. First, Witness 103 was reluctant to meet with SLCPD detectives, FBI agents, and federal prosecutors because he has no particular allegiance to law enforcement. Witness 103 is a convicted felon who served time in federal prison, and has a son who was shot and injured by law enforcement during the commission of a robbery. Witness 103 expressed concerns because there were signs in the neighborhood of Canfield Drive stating, "snitches get stitches." Therefore, he agreed to be interviewed only on the condition of confidentiality. Witness 103 later testified before the county grand jury.

According to Witness 103, he was driving his blue pickup truck in the opposite direction of Wilson's SUV, and ended up virtually next to the driver's side of the SUV when it stopped. Relative to Witness 102, Witness 103 had a similar, but much closer view of the driver's side of the SUV. If the parked SUV is viewed as dividing Canfield Drive in half, both Witness 102 and Witness 103 were on the same side, with a view of Brown's back as he ran from Wilson, and a view of Brown's front as he ran toward Wilson.

When Witness 103 stopped his truck on Canfield Drive, although he did not see what led up to it, he saw Brown punching Wilson at least three times in the facial area, through the open driver's window of the SUV. Witness 103 described Wilson and Brown as having hold of each other's shirts, but Brown was "getting in a couple of blows." Wilson was leaning back toward the passenger seat with his forearm up, in an effort to block the blows. Then Witness 103 heard a gunshot and Brown took off running. Wilson exited the SUV, appeared to be using his shoulder microphone to call into his radio, and chased Brown with his gun held low.

Witness 103 explained that Brown came to a stop near a car, put his hand down on the car, and turned around to face Wilson. Brown's hands were then down at his sides. Witness 103 did not see Brown's hands up. Wanting to leave, Witness 103 began to turn his car around in the opposite direction that Brown had been running when he heard additional shots. Witness 103 turned to his right, and saw Brown "moving fast" toward Wilson. Witness 103 then drove away.

Witness 103 had a passenger in his truck. Although Witness 103 tried to facilitate contact between federal and state authorities and the passenger, the passenger refused to identify himself or provide any information.

When Witness 103 was initially subpoenaed to testify before the county grand jury, he expressed even more reluctance than he did during his investigative interview, this time alleging memory loss. However, he ultimately testified consistently with his original account, with the physical and forensic evidence, and with other credible witness accounts. Therefore, if called as a defense witness in a federal prosecution of Darren Wilson, Witness 103 would be subject to limited impeachment for his two felony convictions, including a theft conviction, but his apparent antipathy toward law enforcement would bolster testimony that corroborates Wilson. Accordingly, after a thorough review of all the evidence, federal prosecutors determined his account to be credible, and likewise determined that a jury appropriately would credit his potential testimony.

c. Witness 104

Witness 104 is a 26-year-old bi-racial female. Witness 104 gave three statements. SLCPD detectives interviewed her, federal prosecutors and agents interviewed her, and she testified before the county grand jury.

Witness 104 was in a minivan that had been traveling in the opposite direction of Wilson, and came to a halt in front of Wilson's SUV, and somewhat behind, yet adjacent to Witness 103's blue pickup truck. Witness 104 was on the same side of the SUV as Witness 102 and Witness 103. She was seated in the middle row behind the driver's seat of the minivan, leaning over toward the center, with a direct view of Brown running away from Wilson, a frontal view of Brown coming back toward Wilson, and the shooting thereafter. Witness 104 is the adult daughter of the two witnesses in the driver and passenger front seats, Witness 105 and Witness

106, respectively. She is the sister of Witness 107, who was seated in the middle row passenger seat to her right.

According to Witness 104, she was leaning over, talking to her sister, Witness 107, when she heard two gunshots. She looked out the front window and saw Brown at the driver's window of Wilson's SUV. Witness 104 knew that Brown's arms were inside the SUV, but she could not see what Brown and Wilson were doing because Brown's body was blocking her view. Witness 104 saw Brown run from the SUV, followed by Wilson, who "hopped" out of the SUV and ran after him while yelling "stop, stop, stop." Wilson did not fire his gun as Brown ran from him. Brown then turned around and "for a second" began to raise his hands as though he may have considered surrendering, but then quickly "balled up in fists" in a running position and "charged" at Wilson. Witness 104 described it as a "tackle run," explaining that Brown "wasn't going to stop." Wilson fired his gun only as Brown charged at him, backing up as Brown came toward him. Witness 104 explained that there were three separate volleys of shots. Each time, Brown ran toward Wilson, Wilson fired, Brown paused, Wilson stopped firing, and then Brown charged again. The pattern continued until Brown fell to the ground, "smashing" his face upon impact. Wilson did not fire while Brown momentarily had his hands up. Witness 104 explained that it took some time for Wilson to fire, adding that she "would have fired sooner." Wilson did not go near Brown's body after Brown fell to his death.

Witness 104 explained that she first saw Brown's friend, Witness 101, when he took off running as soon as the first two shots were fired. She never saw him again.

All three of Witness 104's statements were consistent with each other, consistent with the physical and forensic evidence, and consistent with other credible witness accounts. Witness 104 does not have a criminal history. Therefore, if called as a defense witness in a prosecution of Darren Wilson, this witness's account would not be vulnerable to meaningful cross-examination and would not be subject to impeachment due to bias or inconsistencies in prior statements. Accordingly, after a thorough review of all the evidence, federal prosecutors determined her account to be credible, and likewise determined that a jury appropriately would credit her potential testimony.

d. Witness 105

Witness 105 is a 50-year-old black female. She gave two statements. SLCPD detectives interviewed her, and federal prosecutors explained the nature of the two parallel criminal investigations to Witness 105 prior to her testimony before the county grand jury. Witness 105 was driving a minivan in which Witness 104, her daughter, was seated behind the driver's seat in the middle row. Her husband, Witness 106, was next to her in the front passenger seat, and her other daughter, Witness 107, was seated behind her husband and next to Witness 104. Witness 105 had been traveling east on Canfield Drive, when she stopped in front of Wilson's vehicle with a view of the driver's side of his vehicle. Her view was also of the back of Brown as he first ran away, and then the front of Brown as he turned around and came back toward Wilson.

According to Witness 105, Wilson was driving a car, not an SUV, and a gunshot drew her attention to the vehicle. She noticed Brown's hands on Wilson's "car." Brown then ran eastbound and Wilson chased after him, gun in hand but held low. Witness 105 explained that Brown put his hands up "for a brief moment," and then turned around and made a shuffling movement. Wilson told Brown to "get down," but Brown did not comply. Instead, Brown put his hands down "in a running position." Witness 105 could not tell whether Brown was "charging" at Wilson or whether his plan was to run past Wilson, but either way, Brown was running toward Wilson. According to Witness 105, Wilson only shot at Brown when Brown was moving toward him. She could not see Brown's hands as he was running, but saw him reaching down as he began to fall to the ground. Witness 105 saw Wilson shoot Brown in the face before he began to stumble. Once Brown was on the ground, it appeared to Witness 105 that Wilson was calling out on the radio using his shoulder microphone.

When Witness 105 contacted SLCPD detectives, she was reluctant to identify herself and ultimately met with them in a library parking lot. She explained that she was coming forward because in speaking with her neighbors, she realized that what they believed had happened was inconsistent with what actually happened. She further explained that that she had not been paying attention to media accounts, and had been unaware of the inaccuracies being reported.

Both of Witness 105's statements were consistent with each other, materially consistent with the physical and forensic evidence, and consistent with other credible witness accounts in all material ways. Witness 105 has no criminal history. If called as a defense witness in a prosecution of Darren Wilson, this witness's account would be subject to limited impeachment on her ability to accurately perceive what occurred, *e.g.* , that she perceived Wilson driving a car, rather than an SUV. However, that line of cross-examination does not undermine the overall consistency of her account with other credible witness accounts and with the physical evidence. Accordingly, after a thorough review of all the evidence, federal prosecutors determined her account to be largely credible and likewise determined that a jury appropriately would credit her potential testimony.

e. Witness 108

Witness 108 is a 74-year-old black male who claimed to have witnessed the shooting, stated that it was justified, but repeatedly refused to give formal statements to law enforcement for fear of reprisal should the Canfield Drive neighborhood find out that his account corroborated Wilson. He was served with a county grand jury subpoena and refused to appear.

During the initial canvass of the crime scene on August 9, 2014, in the hours after the shooting, SLCPD detectives approached Witness 108, who was sitting in his car on Canfield Drive. They asked if he witnessed what happened. Witness 108 refused to identify himself or give details, but told detectives that the police officer was "in the right" and "did what he had to do," and the statements made by people in the apartment complex were inaccurate. Both state and federal investigators later attempted to locate and interview Witness 108, who repeatedly expressed fear in coming forward. During the investigators' attempts to find Witness 108, another individual reported that two days after the shooting, Witness 108 confided in her that he "would have fucking shot that boy, too." In saying so, Witness 108 mimicked an aggressive stance with his hands out in front of him, as though he was about to charge. SLCPD detectives finally tracked down Witness 108 at a local repair shop, where he reluctantly explained that Wilson told Brown to "stop" or "get down" at least ten times, but instead Brown "charged" at Wilson. Witness 108 told detectives that there were other witnesses on Canfield Drive who witnessed the same thing. An SLCPD detective and federal prosecutor again tracked down Witness 108 in hopes of obtaining a more formal statement. However, Witness 108 refused to provide additional details to either county or federal authorities, citing community sentiment to support a "hands up" surrender narrative as his reason to remain silent. He explained that he would rather go to jail than testify before the county grand jury.

Witness 108 has no criminal history. Witness 108's accounts, although quite general, are clearly exculpatory as to Wilson and consistent with other credible evidence. His reluctance to testify in opposition to community sentiment lends further credence to his account.

f. Witness 109

Witness 109 is a 53 year-old black male. Like Witness 108, Witness 109 claimed to have witnessed the shooting, stated that it was justified, and repeatedly refused to give formal statements to law enforcement for fear of reprisal should the Canfield Drive neighborhood find out that his account corroborated Wilson. He was served with a county grand jury subpoena and refused to appear. Likewise, Witness 109 repeatedly refused to formally meet with SLCPD detectives, FBI agents, or federal and county prosecutors.

Law enforcement identified Witness 109 through a phone call that he made to the SLCPD information line at 5:19 p.m. on the day of the shooting. During that six-minute recorded call, the operator transferred Witness 109 to an SLCPD detective, and Witness 109 provided the following information, repeatedly refusing to meet with detectives in person. Witness 109 stated that he did not want his phone number traced, and would deny everything if it was traced. Witness 109 stated that he did not know Brown or his friend, Witness 101. However, he was calling because Witness 101, whom he described as the "guy with the dreads," lied on national television. Witness 109 described Brown and Witness 101 walking on the center line of the street when the officer asked them to get out of street. Brown responded something to the effect of, "Fuck the police." According to Witness 109, Wilson got out of his vehicle and Brown, the "young guy that died," hit him in the face. Witness 109 explained that Wilson reached for what appeared to be a taser but dropped it, and then grabbed a gun. Witness 109 explained that Brown reached for Wilson's gun. Although Witness 109's description was somewhat disjointed, he also stated that at first Brown ran away from Wilson, but then kept coming toward Wilson. Wilson told Brown to stop and lie down, but Brown failed to comply. Witness 109 said that Wilson fired in self-defense, explaining that Wilson did not shoot to kill at first, but "he unloaded on him when [Brown] wouldn't stop." Witness 109 said that "a lot of people saw that it was justified," ending the call by stating, "I know police get a bad rap, but they're here to protect us."

Federal and county prosecutors and investigators tried to no avail to interview Witness 109. True to his word on that initial phone call, he would not discuss what he saw. He did, however, acknowledge that he placed a call to the SLCPD information line.

Witness 109 does have a criminal history that would be admissible in federal court. Witness 109 has a misdemeanor theft conviction from 1985 and a felony arrest, both of which likely would be inadmissible in federal court for impeachment purposes. Witness 109's account is exculpatory as to Wilson and although Witness 109 may be subject to limited impeachment, the majority of his description is consistent with the physical and forensic evidence, and consistent with other credible witness accounts. Community sentiment and therefore his reluctance to testify on behalf of Wilson would likely bolster his account.

g. Witness 113

Witness 113 is a 31-year-old black female. She was interviewed one time by FBI agents during their canvass on August 16, 2014, and gave an account that generally corroborated Wilson, but only after she was confronted with untruthful statements she initially made in an effort to avoid neighborhood backlash. When local authorities tried to serve Witness 113 with a subpoena to testify before the county grand jury, she blockaded her door with a couch to avoid service.

Witness 113 was on her brother's balcony, located opposite and to the left of the aforementioned minivan, when she first saw Brown walking in the street. Contrary to other witness accounts, Witness 113 saw what she believed to be three black males walking in the street, and two police vehicles present, calling into question whether she actually witnessed the beginning of the incident. She explained that one of the police officers told Brown and his friends to go on the sidewalk, and then subsequently called Brown over to his vehicle, where a struggle occurred.

Witness 113 then gave an account that was contrary to physical evidence, internally inconsistent, and admittedly untrue. She first explained that Brown ran east, away from Wilson, as Wilson shot at him. However, she then explained that she watched as Brown ran west past Wilson, who shot Brown right next to the SUV. Witness 113 stated that Wilson fired shots into Brown's back as he lay flat on his stomach on the ground. When the FBI told Witness 113 that the autopsy results and other evidence were inconsistent with her account, she admitted that she lied. She explained to the FBI that, "You've gotta live the life to know it," and stated that she feared offering an account contrary to the narrative reported by the media that Brown held his hands up in surrender.

Witness 113 then admitted that she saw Brown running toward Wilson, prompting Wilson to yell, "Freeze." Brown failed to stop and Wilson began shooting Brown. Witness 113 told the FBI that it appeared to her that Wilson's life was in danger. She explained there was a pause in the shots before the firing resumed, but Witness 113 had ducked down for cover and did not see anything after the first volley of shots.

Witness 113 was with her brother and boyfriend when the shooting occurred. Witness 113 refused to provide their contact information, and they both repeatedly evaded law enforcement's attempts to meet with them.

Witness 113 has no criminal history that would be admissible in federal court. Witness 113 has past arrests but no convictions, which likely would be inadmissible in federal court. In a federal prosecution, if served and called to testify on behalf of Wilson, federal prosecutors could subject Witness 113 to cross-examination due to her admittedly untruthful statements during the first part of her interview with the FBI. However, her reasons for being untruthful, coupled with the fact that she immediately changed course when her statements were challenged, give her account reliability. Accordingly, prosecutors did not discount her narrative in its entirety, but rather in examining all of the evidence, considered this witness's account in making a prosecutive decision.

h. Witness 134

Witness 134 is a 36-year-old white female. She was interviewed one time by federal authorities. At the time of her interview with federal agents and prosecutors, she was Wilson's fiancée and was Wilson's field training officer in 2011. Prosecutors considered her potential bias when interviewing Witness 134, but sought out and evaluated her account for several reasons. First, as noted below in the legal analysis, to make a determination as to whether a potential civil rights defendant has the requisite criminal intent, prosecutors must consider a subject officer's training as part of an evaluation of his overall understanding of when the use of deadly force is permissible. Second, Witness 134 spoke to Wilson minutes after the shooting, while he was arguably still under the stress of the situation and immediately after he perceived it. It is possible that in a prosecution of Wilson, defense counsel would be permitted to introduce Wilson's initial statements to Witness 134 through the "present sense impression" or "excited utterance" hearsay exceptions. Fed. R. Evid. 803(1); 803(2).

Witness 134 explained that when she was Wilson's field training officer for the FPD, he did not require a lot of training because he had prior experience as a law enforcement officer. Wilson knew and understood that he was permitted to use physical force when he or someone else was met with a physical threat. As Wilson's training officer, she never had concerns as to whether he understood when he was permitted to use force.

Witness 134 was on light duty on August 9, 2014, working at the police department building because she was pregnant. She was working the same shift as Wilson and was waiting to join him for lunch. Witness 134 stated that when Wilson arrived at the FPD at about 12:15 p.m., he did not seem like himself. His face was red and puffy, consistent with injury. Knowing something was wrong, she asked Wilson what happened. Wilson responded, "I just killed someone." Wilson also told her that he had washed blood from his hands.

Witness 134 also explained that other than facial injuries, she did not notice additional injuries or blood on Wilson, but she did notice blood on the hammer of his gun, still holstered in his belt. Wilson asked her to retrieve latex gloves for him, which Wilson then used to clear and package his gun. Witness 134 did not actually see Wilson do this because her back was to him, although she could hear what he was doing. She also saw the envelope, presumably containing the gun, sealed with evidence tape, but did not know who eventually took it to an evidence locker.

Prior to packaging his gun, Wilson gave Witness 134 a narrative consistent with the accounts he later gave throughout the course of the investigation. Federal agents and prosecutors asked Witness 134 to be specific about what Wilson told her at the police department in the immediate aftermath as opposed to subsequent conversations that they have had since the shooting. Witness 134 was certain that Wilson told her the following: He told Brown and his friend to get out of the street, but did not say anything "ignorant" that would anger them. As Wilson was passing Brown and his friend, he saw cigarillos in Brown's hand and noticed Witness 101's black shirt and realized that they matched the description of the suspects involved in the "stealing in progress." As Brown was attacking Wilson, Wilson explained that in his mind, he went through the weapons available to him on his gun belt. He knew that he had no choice but to use his gun.

Wilson explained to Witness 134 that he was able to shoot inside the SUV, but did not know where the bullet went and whether it hit Brown. Brown ran off and Wilson chased him, explaining to Witness 134 that "all of a sudden," Brown stopped, turned around, and started "charging" him. Witness 134 explained that although she could not remember the exact words Wilson said he used, he said something like, "Get on the ground," trying to get Brown to stop. However, Wilson told her that Brown did not stop and continued to charge at Wilson. Wilson fired at Brown and continued to do so until Brown was on the ground because Brown "just wouldn't stop."

Witness 134 explained that Wilson was shaken, but confident that he did the right thing in the moment, although he became worried in the few minutes that followed the shooting because the neighborhood was quickly becoming hostile.

Witness 134 explained that in all of their conversations, Wilson had been adamant that Brown's hands were not up, but rather, Brown's right hand was in his waistband with his left hand in a fist, as though he was running. Witness 134 said that she was relieved to see the results of the private autopsy in the media because it showed a series of shots in Brown's right arm, consistent with Wilson's explanation that he had tunnel vision during the shooting.

After learning of Witness 101's account alleging that Wilson grabbed Brown's throat by reaching out the driver's window and then subsequently shooting him while he was surrendering, Wilson told Witness 134 that Witness 101 was not present for the shooting because he saw Witness 101 run off as soon as Brown handed him the cigarillos during the assault at the SUV window. Wilson and Witness 134 agreed that the notion that a police officer would attempt to pull an individual into his vehicle, especially someone as big as Brown, is contrary to training. Wilson described Brown as Hulk Hogan-like, such that he could have easily overpowered Wilson.

Witness 134 has no criminal history. If called as a defense witness in a prosecution of Darren Wilson, Witness 134 would be subject to cross- examination due to obvious bias. However, her account of what Wilson told her is consistent with Wilson's previous statements, with other credible witness accounts, and with the forensic and physical evidence. Accordingly, having met Witness 134 and considered her manner and demeanor, federal prosecutors found her account credible. Nonetheless, because of Witness 134's relationship with Wilson and because most of her information came directly from Wilson, prosecutors did not heavily rely on her account when making a prosecutive decision.

ii. Witnesses Consistent with Prior Statements, Physical Evidence, and Other Witnesses Who Inculpate Wilson

There are no witnesses who fall under this category.

2. Witnesses Who Neither Inculpate Nor Fully Corroborate Wilson

i. Witness 107

Witness 107 is a 30-year-old black female. Witness 107 was seated in the passenger seat in the middle row of a minivan that was stopped opposite Wilson's SUV at the time of the shooting. Witness 107 was seated next to her sister Witness 104 and behind her father, Witness 106. Witness 105, her mother, was seated in the driver's seat. However, when Witness 107 initially described what happened, she mistakenly thought she was in the front passenger seat and forgot that her father was present. She also mistakenly thought that they had been driving in the same direction as Wilson.

Witness 107 gave three statements. First, an SLCPD detective and an FBI agent jointly interviewed her. Federal prosecutors and agents conducted a follow-up interview to address inconsistencies with the physical evidence in her original account. Witness 107 also testified before the county grand jury.

According to Witness 107, she was looking at her mobile phone when she heard two gunshots. She looked up and out the front windshield, and saw Brown run away from Wilson. Witness 107 mistakenly thought that Wilson was standing toward the front of the passenger side of the police vehicle, and could not remember whether the vehicle was an SUV or a car. Wilson then chased after Brown and drew his gun, shooting three times. Contrary to the autopsy results, Witness 107 stated that Wilson shot Brown in the leg and hip as Brown was running away. Brown then turned around and briefly put his hands with up, palms forward, near his shoulders, as though he was "giving up." But then Brown put his hands down, one of them holding his chest, as he came back toward Wilson, though Witness 107 was unsure whether Brown was stumbling or running. Wilson fired the last shots from 10 to 15 feet away from Brown, and kept shooting as Brown was falling to the ground.

Witness 107 explained that immediately following the shooting, her mother drove to a nearby parking lot. She and her family members discussed what they witnessed, and they all seemed to have witnessed different things. Her sister, Witness 104, for example, was adamant that Brown "charged" at Wilson, whereas Witness 107 expressed uncertainty. The family also could not reach a consensus as to the number of shots fired.

When Witness 107 met with federal prosecutors and agents, she was visibly shaken by what she witnessed, articulating the difficulty of watching someone die. However, given the differences among what she and her family saw, and realizing that she was factually incorrect about the direction of the police vehicle, the location where Wilson stood, and where the bullets struck Brown, she was not certain about what she believed she witnessed.

Witness 107 has one prior misdemeanor arrest that likely would not be admissible in federal court. As detailed above, Witness 107 was admittedly mistaken or unsure about some of what she perceived, rendering her account vulnerable to effective cross-examination. Regardless of credibility, her account does not inculpate Darren Wilson and does not support a federal prosecution.

ii. Witness 106

Witness 106 is a 45-year-old white male. As mentioned, he was seated in the front passenger seat of a minivan, driven by his wife, Witness 105. Witness 106's daughters, Witness 104 and Witness 107, were seated in the middle row of the minivan, behind the driver and front seat passenger, respectively. According to Witness 106, although his wife saw Wilson emerge from what she remembered was a police car, he first saw Wilson and Brown when they were in the street. It initially looked to Witness 106 like Brown had a gun and there was a firefight happening, although he has since realized that not to be the case. Regardless, Witness 106's overall impression was that he witnessed a police officer "taking down a gunman in a residential neighborhood before anyone else got hurt." It was for that reason that Witness 106 agreed to speak with SLCPD detectives. He otherwise does not "have any love" for law enforcement, having served 18 years in prison. Witness 106 also testified before the county grand jury.

Witness 106 explained that he first saw Brown as he ran from Wilson. Wilson fired one shot which seemed to hit Brown in the leg because Brown appeared to stagger. Brown's arms then "briefly flung" out and he turned around to face Wilson. Witness 106 then explained that even though the neighborhood had been talking about Brown having his "hands up," Brown "did not have his hands up." Brown's arms were down at his sides, such that Witness 106 could not even see Brown's hands. Witness 106's vantage point was over Wilson's shoulder. Witness 106 saw Brown walk toward Wilson and thought that Brown was about to shoot Wilson, as Wilson shot Brown until he fell to his death. Wilson was about six to 10 feet from Brown when he fired the final shots at Brown.

Witness 106's account is inconsistent with the physical and forensic evidence and other credible witness accounts. He has a conviction for sexual abuse that would likely be admissible in federal court as impeachment evidence, although his bias tends to bolster his account. Regardless of its credibility, Witness 106's account does not inculpate Darren Wilson and therefore does not support a federal prosecution.

iii. Witness 110

Witness 110 is a 51-year-old black male who is married to Witness 111. Witness 110 spoke to SLCPD detectives on two occasions. As noted below, the second interview occurred because Witness 111 was too upset to complete the first interview. Witness 110 also testified before the county grand jury.

Witness 110 and Witness 111 first came into contact with SLCPD detectives because they were attending a social function the evening of August 9, 2014. The couple told a friend, an attorney, what they had witnessed, and the friend called the SLCPD on their behalf. SLCPD detectives responded to the venue of the social function to interview Witness 110 and Witness 111, but they were reluctant to speak to law enforcement, fearing retaliation from people in the community. They agreed to speak only on the condition of confidentiality. However, during that initial contact with SLCPD detectives, Witness 111 began crying and could not talk about what she witnessed. Witness 110 was too shaken to give a full account, but he did explain that earlier that day, he and his wife were at the Canfield Green Apartments complex visiting Witness 110's elderly mother and brother, Witness 112. He then gave a brief account which he detailed a few days later when he met again with SLCPD detectives.

According to Witness 110, he and Witness 111 were driving on Canfield Drive when they noticed Brown and his friend, Witness 101, walking in the center of the street and had to veer around them to avoid hitting them. Witness 111 commented to Witness 110, "Why don't they just get on the sidewalk?" As they were pulling into the driveway of the building they were visiting, they noticed Wilson driving in the opposite direction. During his initial interview with SLCPD detectives, Witness 110 explained that while in the driveway, he noticed Brown standing beside the driver's door of the SUV, with the upper portion of his body inside the driver's area of the SUV. Witness 110 did not mention this during his second interview with SLCPD detectives or when he testified in front of the county grand jury.

Witness 110 then explained that he and Witness 111 went up to the second floor apartment balcony, located opposite and off to the right of the minivan with Witness 104, Witness 105, Witness 106, and Witness 107. Their vantage point was of the passenger side of the SUV, followed by the right profile of Brown as he ran away from Wilson, and then the left profile of Brown as he turned around and moved toward Wilson.

Witness 110 stated that he witnessed an exchange between Wilson, Brown, and Witness 101, but did not hear what was said. Wilson reversed his vehicle, using it to block Brown and Witness 101. Brown and Wilson engaged in a back and forth "scuffle," although Witness could not see exactly what happened because the SUV blocked his view of Brown. They then heard a shot and Witness 101 "disappeared." Brown remained at the SUV and the scuffle continued until there was a second gunshot and Brown took off running. When Brown reached a nearby driveway, he stopped and looked down at his hand, which Witness 111 noted had blood on it. Witness 110 believed that Brown looked at his left hand. Brown put his hands out at his sides, palms up, as though asking, "What the heck?" Brown then moved toward Wilson with his hands in that same position, and Wilson shot Brown. Brown then paused, the shooting stopped, and then Brown advanced again. Witness 110 stated that Wilson shot Brown only when Brown was moving toward him, and did not shoot at Brown as he ran away. Witness 110 initially told SLCPD detectives that Brown moved "quickly," although he testified in the county grand jury that he could not describe how Brown was moving toward Wilson, though he was not "charging" or "running." At no time were Brown's hands up in surrender or otherwise.

Witness 110 has no criminal history. As noted, Witness 110's second interview was consistent with his grand jury testimony, though partially inconsistent with what he initially told SLCPD detectives. Nonetheless, Witness 110's account was consistent with the physical and forensic evidence. Regardless of the credibility of his account, it does not inculpate Wilson, and therefore does not support a federal prosecution.

iv. Witness 111

Witness 111 is a 48-year-old black female who is married to Witness 110. As mentioned, she was too upset to speak with SLCPD detectives on the evening of August 9, 2014, but did speak to law enforcement on August 18, 2014, when she was jointly interviewed by SLCPD detectives, FBI agents, and federal prosecutors. Federal authorities also met with Witness 110 at that time. Witness 111 subsequently testified before the county grand jury.

Witness 111's account is consistent with the account of Witness 110, with two exceptions. First, when she witnessed Brown turn around after fleeing from Wilson, Witness 111 explained that Brown looked down at his right hand, which was bleeding. This is contrary to Witness 110, who said that Brown looked down at his left hand and did not mention seeing blood. Second, Witness 111 described Brown as moving back toward Wilson in "slow motion," where Witness 110 at one time described Brown walking "quickly," but later could not characterize his pace. According to Witness 111, at no time were Brown's hands up in surrender or otherwise.

Witness 111 has no criminal history. Witness 111's statements were consistent with each other, and with the physical and forensic evidence, and therefore, Witness 111 would not be vulnerable to cross-examination on those grounds. However, Witness 111 was especially distraught during her investigatory interview, stating that she, too, has a teenage son and commenting that she wished Wilson had used a form of less lethal force. Her bias could subject her to effective cross-examination, and led federal prosecutors to question whether her bias was affecting her ability to accurately recall events. Regardless, Witness 111's account does not inculpate Wilson, and therefore does not support a federal prosecution.

v. Witness 115

Witness 115 is a 32-year-old black male. Witness 115 gave three investigatory statements and was interviewed by the media on several occasions. First, SLCPD detectives interviewed Witness 115 within hours of Brown's death. Second, federal agents and prosecutors conducted a follow-up interview, during which they challenged Witness 115 on what he actually witnessed as opposed to what he assumed had taken place. Witness 115 also testified before the county grand jury.

According to Witness 115, he was in his second floor apartment at the time of the shooting, on the same side of the SUV as the minivan occupied by Witness 104, Witness 105, Witness 106, and Witness 107, but with a view of Brown's right profile as he was coming back toward Wilson. Just before noon, Witness 115 was in his bedroom when he heard what he thought was an altercation. He described hearing "strong voices" or loud grunts, but could not make out specific words or sounds. Witness 115 went to his window and looked through horizontal blinds by pushing them apart. He saw Brown at the driver's door of the SUV and "arms were being exchanged." Federal prosecutors and agents asked Witness 115 to demonstrate Brown's actions, and he did so by making a fist and a punching motion. Witness 115 demonstrated that Wilson had his arm bent across his chest in a defensive position, but he was reluctant to state that Brown "punched" Wilson. However, after federal prosecutors played Witness 115's own cell phone video back to him, he acknowledged that on the video, recorded right after Brown died, he narrated, "Dude was all up in his car; dude was punching on him," and that "dude" was Brown. Witness 115 explained that his initial impression was that Brown was punching Wilson because Brown was on the outside, standing on the street, and appeared to have the upper hand.

Witness 115 explained that he suddenly saw both Brown and his friend, Witness 101, who had been standing toward the front part of the SUV, start running. Witness 115 did not know why they started to run and he did not hear a gunshot, though he acknowledged that the suddenness with which they ran was consistent with a shot being fired. Brown ran down the middle of the street and Witness 101 started to crouch down by a white Monte Carlo. According to Witness 115, Wilson then got out of his SUV, gun drawn, and immediately fired shots as he began to quickly walk in Brown's direction. With each shot, Witness 101 ducked down a little more, creeping around the Monte Carlo until he went from the driver's side to the passenger side, and out of Witness 115's view. Witness 115 explained that while he was watching Witness 101, he was not watching Brown, who had disappeared from his range of view once he ran from Wilson.

Witness 115 stated that there was a pause in the shooting and he used this opportunity to go out on his balcony to get a better look. As he did, he realized that he left his mobile phone on his dresser. He went back to his bedroom, retrieved his phone, and returned to his balcony. At the same time, he called to his wife, Witness 124, who joined him with their three children. By the time Witness 115 saw Brown again, Brown was walking back toward Wilson with his arms folded across his stomach. Witness 115 said he "assumed" that Wilson had shot Brown in the stomach, although he did not see this happen. This assumption is inconsistent with the autopsy findings.

Witness 115 stated that he did not see Brown with his hands up and Brown did not appear to be surrendering. Rather, Brown looked as though he was slowly going down to the ground as he walked toward Wilson. Wilson then fired another volley of shots and Brown fell to the ground with one arm under him and the other at his side. Consistent with Wilson's account, Witness 115 explained that once Brown was on the ground, Wilson kept his gun drawn and appeared to be talking in his radio on his shoulder. According to Witness 115, at no time did Wilson touch Brown's body.

Witness 115 described the crowds that began to form immediately after the shooting, as people began to gather and talk about what happened. Witness 115 explained that although he initially spoke to SLCPD detectives only four hours after the incident, by then, he had already discussed the incident with Witness 124 and with a passerby on the street. He explained that this passerby can be heard on Witness 115's cell phone video, attempting to correct Witness 115, as Witness 115 narrated that Brown had been punching Wilson.

Witness 115 expressed that he felt comfortable with federal prosecutors and agents who were questioning him about assumptions and inconsistencies. However, Witness 115 was concerned that because of the constant talk in the neighborhood and his multiple media appearances without the presence of a lawyer, he may have unwittingly made inconsistent statements in the past.

Witness 115 has one prior misdemeanor conviction, which likely would be inadmissible in federal court as impeachment evidence. Witness 115 is vulnerable to effective cross-examination because he did not witness significant parts of the shooting and based parts of his account on assumption. Regardless of credibility, Witness 115's account does not inculpate Darren Wilson and therefore does not support a federal prosecution.

vi. Witness 141

Witness 141 is a 19-year-old black male who moved out of Missouri after the shooting. Witness 141 gave three statements. First, FBI agents based in Texas interviewed him. Federal prosecutors and agents conducted a follow-up interview. Finally, Witness 141 testified before the county grand jury.

According to Witness 141, he was sitting on his balcony when he saw Brown and Witness 101 walking down the middle of Canfield Drive. Witness 141 knew Brown through a friend, but did not have regular interaction with him. Unrelated to the shooting incident, Witness

141 went into his apartment to retrieve his mobile phone. While inside, he heard gunshots, prompting him to go back out to the balcony. Witness 141 saw Wilson pointing his gun at Brown, who had his hand across his front torso or waist. Brown never had his hands up in surrender or otherwise. Brown appeared to be stumbling or walking toward Wilson, who fired about five to seven shots at Brown from a distance of about eight feet. Brown collapsed to the ground. Witness 141 did not see Witness 101 anywhere. Witness 141 used his mobile phone to record a video in the aftermath of Brown's death.

Witness 141 testified before the county grand jury that he thought that after Wilson fired the first shot, the additional shots were "excessive," an opinion that would be inadmissible in federal court, and a misstatement of the applicable federal law. Witness 141 based that opinion on the fact that he did not perceive Brown to be a physical threat. However, he acknowledged that he did not see what led up to the initial shots, and did not see Brown run from Wilson, turn around to face Wilson, or any of Brown's actions during that time. Rather, he only saw Wilson shoot Brown as Brown moved toward him.

Witness 141 has no criminal history. Witness 141's statements were consistent with each other, but he did not witness large parts of the incident. Regardless of whether his account is credible, it does not inculpate Darren Wilson and therefore does not support a federal prosecution.

vii. Witness 114

Witness 114 is a 75-year-old black female. She gave two statements. First, she was interviewed by the FBI, and she later testified before the county grand jury.

Witness 114 saw the initial interaction between Brown and Wilson from her second floor window. Witness 114's view was of the passenger side of Wilson's SUV. Witness 114 saw Brown and Witness 101 walking in the middle of Canfield Drive, when Wilson stopped his SUV and leaned his head out of the driver's window as though saying something to Brown. Brown then made some sort of hand gesture, indicating to Witness 114 that he was responding to Wilson. Wilson continued driving, but then jerked back his SUV and parked it at an angle, with the back of the SUV closer to the center of the street. According to Witness 114, Brown remained there, while Witness 101 kept walking. She did not see Witness 101 again.

Next, Witness 114 saw Wilson hold onto Brown, though she was unsure how the physical contact began. Witness 114 stated that Wilson and Brown were "tussling," explaining that she could see Brown's hands inside the SUV by looking through the passenger side window. However, she did not see any other part of his body go into the SUV because Brown was standing straight up. From her perspective, it looked like Brown was trying to pull away. Yet Witness 114 acknowledged that had Wilson un-holstered his gun in the manner he described, it was also possible, given Brown's position, that Brown reached for Wilson's gun.

Witness 114 watched Brown run from the SUV, followed by Wilson with his gun drawn, until they both disappeared from her line of sight. She heard two gunshots followed by six more gunshots, but did not see Wilson fire any shots. Witness 114 changed her clothes and went down to street level to see Brown's body in the street.

Witness 114 has no criminal history. Witness 114's statements were consistent with each other, however, she did not see the majority of the shooting. Accordingly, her account does not inculpate Wilson and therefore does not support a federal prosecution.

viii. Witness 129

Witness 129 is a 22-year-old black male. He gave two statements. First, FBI agents interviewed him as part of their canvass on August 16, 2014. Second, Witness 129 testified before the county grand jury.

Witness 129 was outside his apartment when he saw Brown and his friend, Witness 101, walking in the middle of Canfield Drive. Wilson pulled up next to them in his SUV. Brown and Witness 101 kept walking and Wilson backed up to cut them off. Brown and Wilson then engaged in a "scuffle." Witness 129's view was of the passenger side of the SUV. Therefore, although he could tell that Wilson remained in the driver's seat of the SUV while Brown was standing outside of the SUV, Witness 129 could not describe exactly what Brown and Wilson were doing or how the upper half of Brown's body was positioned relative to the SUV. Witness 129 then heard a gunshot, but Brown remained at the SUV and the scuffle continued for another 20 to 30 seconds. A second shot then went off and Brown ran eastbound down Canfield Drive. Witness 129 explained that Witness 101 ducked behind a white car, ran around it, and went in the other direction. Wilson got out of the SUV and fired one or two shots, though Witness 129 did not see whether the shots struck Brown, nor did he see what Brown was doing, because a nearby building blocked his view.

Witness 129 has no criminal history. Witness 129's statements were materially consistent with each other and consistent with other credible evidence. However, Witness 129's account does not inculpate Wilson, and therefore does not support a federal prosecution.

ix. Witness 116

Witness 116 is a 16-year-old black male. He gave three statements. First, he met with SLCPD detectives within hours of the shooting in the presence of his father and father's girl-friend. He subsequently met with federal agents and prosecutors. Finally, he testified before the county grand jury.

Witness 116 explained that he was in his apartment watching television when he heard screams, prompting him to go to the window and look out of the vertical blinds. Witness 116 saw Brown with his hands inside the driver's side of the SUV. He then saw Wilson take out what appeared to be a taser. Wilson shot the taser one time, but missed, which is why Witness 116 surmised that Wilson took out his gun. Brown's friend, Witness 101, took off running somewhere into the apartment complexes.

Wilson shot once or twice, and Brown, with arms at his sides, ran out of view. Witness 116 looked away because he assumed that Brown had been apprehended. He then heard five or six more shots and looked back out the window to see Brown dead on the ground. Witness 116 did not see what happened leading up to Brown standing by the SUV.

Witness 116's statements were consistent, but he also mistakenly believed that Wilson used a taser. Regardless of the reliability of his account, Witness 116 did not witness significant parts of the shooting. Like several of the witnesses in this section of the report, that which he did see does not inculpate Darren Wilson and therefore does not support a federal prosecution.

3. Witnesses Whose Accounts Do Not Support a Prosecution Due to Materially Inconsistent Prior Statements or Inconsistencies With the Physical and Forensic Evidence

i. Witness 101

Witness 101 is a 22-year-old black male who was walking in the middle of Canfield Drive with Brown when they encountered Wilson. Witness 101 made multiple statements to the media immediately following the incident that spawned the popular narrative that Wilson shot Brown execution-style as he held up his hands in surrender. These media interviews occurred prior to Witness 101 giving his two statements. First, FBI and SLCPD jointly interviewed Witness 101 on August 13, 2014, in the presence of Witness 101's mother, Witness 101's two attorneys, and an individual who explained that he was in charge of Witness 101's personal security. Witness 101 subsequently testified before the county grand jury.

According to Witness 101, he and Brown had been friends for about two to three months as of the day of the shooting. Witness 101 viewed himself as a role model or mentor to Brown. Witness 101 came into contact with Brown on August 9, 2014, at about 7:00 a.m. At some point between then and just prior to noon, he and Brown decided to go to Ferguson Market to get cigarillos. Witness 101 could not recall in detail what the pair was doing in those five intervening hours, other than to explain that they were playing video games and talking. However, Witness 101 explained that just prior to going to Ferguson Market, Brown engaged in a 25-minute conversation about marijuana with one of two contractors who were working in the apartment complex.

Witness 101 explained that when they went to Ferguson Market, Brown stole cigarillos from behind the counter as though he was entitled to them, and then subsequently shoved the store clerk, who was substantially smaller in stature than Brown, who was 6'5" and 289 lbs. Witness 101 initially minimized these events when speaking with law enforcement, but then acknowledged to the county grand jury that Brown was surprisingly aggressive. Brown's behavior caught Witness 101 off guard because it was uncharacteristic of Brown and contrary to Brown's usual behavior. Witness 101 expected to encounter the police when they left Ferguson Market because he heard the clerk say he was going to call the police. Witness 101 described Brown's behavior as "bold" when Brown openly carried the stolen cigarillos as they walked down Canfield Drive. Witness 101 and Brown were walking eastbound, single-file, on Canfield Drive in the center of the street on the yellow line when they encountered Wilson driving in the opposite direction in his marked FPD SUV. Witness 101 explained that they had not been obstructing traffic, although several cars had to avoid Brown and Witness 101 as they drove by. Wilson told them to "get the fuck on the sidewalk," and Witness 101 responded that they were "not but one minute from their destination." Brown and Witness 101 did not move onto the sidewalk, but continued to walk in the middle of the street. As Wilson drove past them, he reversed his SUV and parked it at an angle, blocking both lanes in the road and almost hitting them, asking, "What did you just say?" According to Witness 101, Wilson attempted to open the driver's side in an "aggressive" and "forceful" manner. The door opened less than an inch because of Brown and Witness 101's proximity to the door. The door quickly bounced off of Brown and Witness 101 and shut on Wilson. According to Witness 101, this angered Brown. Witness 101 also stated that he understood how Wilson could have perceived that Brown shut the door on him.

According to Witness 101, Wilson then reached out the window and up with his left hand, grabbing Brown by the throat. The private forensic pathologist termed such an action "surprising," based on the autopsy results and his experience as a forensic pathologist. Wilson and Brown engaged in a "tug of war," during which Wilson unsuccessfully tried to pull Brown toward the SUV as Brown attempted to pull away, while still holding the cigarillos. Witness 101 told county and federal investigators that Brown told Wilson, "Get the fuck off me. We're not doin' anything wrong. Leave us the fuck alone." However, Witness 101 explained that even though Wilson had his grip on Brown, Brown had the upper hand both because of his stature and his physical position relative to the car. As Witness 101 told investigators, Wilson would have to be "superhuman" to "overpower" Brown. Witness 101 told the county grand jury that Brown was getting "the best of the officer" because Wilson was only using his left hand. During this tug of war, Wilson's grip gradually slipped from Brown's throat to his shirt, down to his shoulder and arm. Although Witness 101 told the county grand jury that Wilson gripped Brown's right arm, Witness 101 told investigators that Wilson mostly was gripping Brown's shirt by pulling it down over Brown's forearm. According to Witness 101, at no point did Brown ever strike, punch, or grab any part of Wilson. He could offer no explanation as to how Wilson sustained injury, other than to speculate that it was the result of their "tug of war."

As the "tug of war" continued, Brown was then able to turn to his right toward Witness 101 and hand off the cigarillos with both hands. Brown then put his left hand on the door frame under the rearview mirror, while Wilson, using his left hand, maintained hold of Brown's right arm or sleeve. According to Witness 101, Wilson used his right hand to grab hold of Brown's left arm, although it is unclear from Witness 101's accounts whether he actually saw that happen or assumed it happened. Wilson, also using his right hand, then took out his gun and said, "I'm going to shoot." Witness 101 saw Wilson holding the gun and aiming it out the window when Wilson again started to say, "I'm going to shoot."

Witness 101 explained that Wilson fired, hitting Brown in the torso. Witness 101 described blood on the right side of Brown's torso. At the time of the shot, Brown was standing straight, his midsection up against the door, with his left hand down at his side and Wilson gripping Brown's right arm. Contrary to the autopsy results, particularly with regard to the thumb wound and the round recovered from the inside of the driver's door, Witness 101 was adamant that Wilson neither fired a shot within the SUV, nor did Brown have his hand(s) near the gun when the first shot was fired. Witness 101 explained that Wilson fired the shot and "the bullet traveled outside the car and struck [Brown] in the chest." Witness 101 was equally adamant that Brown's hands and arms never entered the SUV, telling investigators that the only hand that would have been "free" would have been Brown's left hand, and that hand neither entered the vehicle nor "reached for" Wilson's gun. However, when he testified before the county grand jury, Witness 101 made room for the possibility that Brown's arm entered the SUV when he was not looking.

According to Witness 101, after the first shot, Brown and Witness 101 simultaneously ran eastbound, away from the SUV. Witness 101 explained that he got ahead of Brown, such 45 that his back was to both Brown and Wilson. Fearing for his life, Witness 101 crouched down among the cars that had now stopped in the middle of the street because of the parked SUV. Witness 101 attempted to get into a nearby car, a gray Sunfire, but the occupants would not allow him inside. Brown ran past Witness 101, telling him, "Keep running, bro." After a pause, Witness 101 explained that he heard Wilson emerge from the SUV. Witness 101 stood up and watched "in plain sight" as Wilson passed him and chased after Brown.

According to Witness 101, Wilson then fired a second shot which appeared to strike Brown in the back. Brown's arms were not raised at that time. During his investigative interview, Witness 101 stated that the bullet "definitely struck [Brown] in the back." During his county grand jury testimony, Witness 101 stated that the bullet likely "grazed" Brown's arm, acknowledging that since he had made his original statements, he had watched media reports of the privately-commissioned autopsy of Brown. Witness 101 said that he assumed that had Brown not been struck, he would have kept on running. Instead, Brown stopped. Brown put his hands up above his head, in the air, and turned around to face Wilson. In so doing, one arm was lower than the other, though Witness 101 could not say whether it was the left or right arm. According to Witness 101, Brown then stated, "I don't have a gun" or "I'm unarmed." Brown started to say it again, but Wilson, while walking toward Brown, fired one volley of at least four shots and Brown fell to his death. Wilson never said a word; he never commanded Brown to stop or freeze. Witness 101 was steadfast that Brown fell to the ground right where he initially stopped and turned around. At most, Brown took a half-step forward, but he did not move toward Wilson. Witness 101 was also steadfast that Brown never put his hand(s) near his waist. As described earlier, the physical evidence establishes that Brown moved forward about 20 feet toward Wilson, and the SLCME medicolegal investigator found Brown with his left hand at his waistband.

Witness 101 also told the county grand jury that he "stood and watched face-to-face as every shot was fired as [Brown]'s body [fell] to the ground," but was unaware that Wilson shot Brown in the face and head until he saw media reports of the privately-commissioned autopsy. Until then, he thought the only shots were to Brown's "upper region" and chest.

Witness 101 ran from the scene, saying, "He just killed my friend." Witness 101 went home and changed his shirt, so he later would not be recognized by the police. By the time he went back to the scene of the shooting, the streets were crowded with people, but, contrary to the dispatch recordings and cellular phone video, there were no police officers on scene. When police officers did arrive, he did not want to speak with them. Instead, Witness 101 went to Brown's grandmother's home and told her and other family members what happened. With the encouragement of Brown's family, Witness 101 went back out onto the street and gave an interview to the media.

During his testimony before the county grand jury, Witness 101 acknowledged that he had discussed the incident with another witness, Witness 118. Witness 101 explained that he was friendly with Witness 118, and noticed her standing on her balcony when he and Brown first encountered Wilson on Canfield Drive. He explained that he was surprised that so many other witnesses came forward because Witness 118 was the only person he saw outside, and she was the only person who saw the incident from the "first shot to the last shot." However, as detailed below, Witness 118 was not out on her balcony for the majority of the incident, and it is unknown at what point she actually witnessed the shootings, if at all.

Witness 101 has a misdemeanor conviction for a crime of dishonesty likely admissible in federal court as impeachment evidence. As described above, material parts of Witness 101's account are inconsistent with the physical and forensic evidence, internally inconsistent from one part of his account to the next, and inconsistent with other credible witness accounts that are corroborated by physical evidence. It is also unclear whether Witness 101 had the ability to accurately perceive the shootings. Witness 101 likely crouched down next to a white Monte Carlo as Wilson chased Brown. The Monte Carlo was facing west with a view of the passenger side of the SUV. Brown ran in the opposite direction that the Monte Carlo was facing. Witness accounts vary as to whether Witness 101 was ducking for cover on the passenger side of the Monte Carlo with his back to the shooting, or whether he fled the scene prior to the final shots being fired. Both Witness 101's inconsistencies and his ability to perceive what happened, or lack thereof, make his account vulnerable to effective cross-examination and extensive impeachment. Accordingly, after a thorough review of all of the evidence, federal prosecutors determined material portions of Witness 101's account lack credibility and therefore determined that his account does not support a prosecution of Darren Wilson.

ii. Witness 123

Witness 123 is a 29-year-old black male who gave two statements. First, he was jointly interviewed by FBI agents and SLCPD detectives. Second, he testified before the county grand jury.

Witness 123 was in the front passenger seat of a white Monte Carlo that was traveling west on Canfield Drive behind Wilson before Wilson stopped his SUV. Witness 133, a black female, was driving the Monte Carlo. Witness 123 first observed Brown and his friend, Witness 101, walking in the street in the opposite direction of the SUV. It seemed to Witness 123 that Brown and Witness 101 failed to comply with a directive from Wilson because the SUV quickly swerved back, and stopped while Brown and Witness 101 were still standing on the yellow line in the middle of the street.

The SUV was then positioned such that Witness 123 and Witness 133 had a view of its passenger side. Therefore, although Witness 123 described a tussle involving Brown at the driver's window, he could not be more specific. During the tussle, Witness 101 looked startled and ran off. Witness 123 then heard a gunshot and told Witness 133 to back up. He heard a second gunshot just as Brown was running past the driver's window of the Monte Carlo. Witness 123 ducked after the second shot and, therefore, could not see if Brown was injured. Between four and six seconds later, he looked out the front windshield to see Wilson emerge from the SUV with his gun held low. At about the same time, Witness 101 approached the Monte Carlo's passenger side door, which Witness 123 had already opened to allow him more room to duck. Witness 101 asked if he could get into their car, but Witness 123 would not permit him to do so, instead instructing him to duck down. Witness 123 then turned his attention to Witness 133, who was shaking. While Witness 123 attempted to calm Witness 133, Witness 101 disappeared and they never saw him again.

Witness 123 explained to the FBI and the SLCPD that he turned around and watched through the back window as Brown turned around with hands half-way up, shoulder height, and crunched up as though he was about to go to the ground. Witness 123 did not know what prompted Brown to turn around. He then heard a volley of about five shots in addition to the two initial shots, and Brown fell forward to his death, palms face forward and arms tucked under him. Witness 123 told the county grand jury that he saw Brown turn around and hold his hands up. Wilson shot Brown three times and Brown fell to the ground dead. Contrary to the physical evidence, Witness 123 explained that Brown died where he turned around and did not move toward Wilson. After the final shots, Wilson appeared to be looking at his (Wilson's) arms.

Witness 133 quickly drove around the SUV and away from the scene after the shooting. Witness 123 and Witness 133 subsequently discussed what they had seen with each other while watching media reports.

Witness 123 has no criminal history. Witness 123's accounts to investigators and to the county grand jury were inconsistent with the physical and forensic evidence, making him vulnerable to effective cross-examination. His focus was split among the driver of the vehicle, Witness 101, and the shooting itself. For those reasons, prosecutors questioned his ability to accurately perceive the incident and could not rely upon his account to support prosecution of Darren Wilson.

iii. Witness 133

Witness 133 is a 33-year-old black female who gave three statements. SLCPD detectives first interviewed Witness 133 within hours of the shooting. She subsequently met with federal agents and prosecutors who questioned her more in-depth. She then testified before the county grand jury.

As previously noted, Witness 133 was driving a white Monte Carlo west on Canfield Drive when she was forced to stop behind Wilson's SUV. Witness 123 was seated in Witness 133's front passenger seat. Witness 133 initially saw Brown and Witness 101 walking down the center line of the street in the opposite direction in which she was traveling. Wilson stopped his SUV alongside Brown and Witness 101, and it appeared to Witness 133 that "something had to have been said between the two parties." However, Witness 133 could not hear anything. Once the SUV stopped, her vantage point was of its passenger side. She was able to see that there was some sort of "tussle" on the driver's side of the SUV between Wilson, who was seated in the SUV, and Brown, whose feet she could see moving underneath the SUV. The SUV was shaking. Witness 101, who was standing closer to the front of the SUV, was trying to see what was happening.

Witness 133 then heard a gunshot from within the SUV. Witness 133 stated that the "suspect who got shot, backed up, and seemed amazed." Both Brown and Witness 101 then ran eastbound past her vehicle down Canfield Drive. The gunshot "terrified" Witness 133, and when she saw Wilson get out of the SUV, she immediately ducked down for cover. It was then that Witness 101 appeared at her passenger side door, asking if he could get in the car, saying "Can you get me away from here? It's crazy." Witness 133 refused to allow Witness 101 into her car, instead telling him to duck. Witness 123, Witness 133, and Witness 101 all ducked for cover together. During her interview with federal authorities, Witness 133 added that she likely "blacked out" while all of this was happening.

Shortly thereafter, Witness 133 looked in her rearview mirror, and saw Brown's face, indicating to her that Brown had turned to face Wilson. She described hearing two or three shots and then Brown fell to the ground. At some point, Witness 101 disappeared, but having been focused on Brown, she did not know where he went or when he left. Wanting to leave quickly, Witness 133 drove on the grass and around the SUV to get out of the area.

During both her interview with SLCPD and her follow-up interview with federal agents and prosecutors, Witness 133 was repeatedly asked if there was anything else that she saw or anything she thought investigators would need to know. In both instances, Witness 133 denied knowing any more information, telling federal authorities that she had given "everything [she's] got." However, she expressed sorrow as the mother of a teenaged son.

Despite her repeated assurances that she saw nothing else, Witness 133 testified before the county grand jury that when she looked in the rearview mirror, Brown had his hands up before he fell to his death. When questioned by the county prosecutor about providing this new information, Witness 133 acknowledged that the transcripts from her prior statements were correct, and that she told SLCPD detectives, FBI agents and federal prosecutors everything she could think of that was important. Witness 133 never offered an explanation as to why she did not previously disclose that Brown's hands were up. Witness 133 also acknowledged that she has been watching the news and "hands up" had become the "mantra" of the protesters.

Witness 133 has no criminal history. Witness 133's repeated omission of a material detail that goes directly to whether Wilson used unreasonable force, coupled with the fact that she told federal authorities that she "blacked out" before later testifying that she saw Brown's hands up, would subject her to effective cross-examination if called as a prosecution witness. It calls into question whether she actually saw Brown's hands at all, had "blacked out," or had been distracted by Witness 101. Accordingly, federal prosecutors determined material portions of her account to be unreliable, and therefore it does not support a prosecution of Darren Wilson.

iv. Witness 119

Witness 119 is a 15-year-old black male. He initially told SLCPD detectives that he witnessed the shooting. However, he later recanted, telling federal agents and prosecutors that he lied to SLCPD detectives because he just wanted to be involved in the investigation. Witness 119 reiterated the same thing to county prosecutors and did not testify before the county grand jury.

Witness 119 initially spoke to SLCPD detectives within hours of the shooting, while standing on Canfield Drive. In part because of the chaos around him during the interview, and in larger part because he was lying, much of Witness 119's initial account did not make sense.

Witness 119 seemed to claim that Wilson shot Brown in the side from out of the window of the SUV, possibly while he was still driving. Wilson then chased after Brown, and ultimately shot him to death in the head while Brown had his hands in the air.

Federal agents and prosecutors sought to follow up with Witness 119 to clarify his account. Witness 119 readily admitted that he never saw the shooting, but was sitting near a flowerbed playing video games on his phone when he heard gunshots. Witness 119 could not see the SUV from his vantage point. He and his brother waited until the gunshots stopped before going to the scene because they did not want to get hit by a stray bullet. By the time they arrived on scene, Brown was dead. Witness 119 claimed that he told the police that he was a witness because he was traumatized and because he "wanted to be a part of it."

Because Witness 119 admitted that he gave a false account, federal prosecutors did not consider his account in the prosecutive decision.

v. Witness 125

Witness 125 is a 23-year-old black female. She initially told law enforcement that she witnessed the shooting, but later recanted, claiming that she wanted to be involved from the outset and therefore lied to investigators.

SLCPD detectives briefly interviewed Witness 125 during their initial canvass after the shooting. Witness 125 claimed that she was asleep for the first two gunshots. Her boyfriend, Witness 131, told her to get up and go to the window. Witness 125 then gave an internally inconsistent account, first saying that Brown's arms were by his waist, followed by his hands going up. When asked for clarification, she said the same thing in reverse, explaining that it all occurred while Brown was kneeling.

In an effort to reconcile this inconsistency and help inform the prosecutive decision, federal prosecutors sought to meet with Witness 125. Witness 125 refused to meet with federal prosecutors but did meet with FBI agents. She reiterated that she was asleep during the first few shots, but then went to her window where she witnessed Brown standing with his hands up in surrender. Although she could not see who was shooting Brown due to a tree blocking her line of sight, Witness 125 explained that she witnessed two volleys of shots, one which caused Brown to grab his torso with his left hand and a second volley causing his head to snap back before he fell to the ground. Witness 125 did not see Brown move from his position. Despite saying otherwise in her recorded statement to the SLCPD, she denied telling FBI agents that she originally told SLCPD detectives that Brown was kneeling prior to his death.

When Witness 125 appeared at the St. Louis County Prosecutor's Office to testify before the county grand jury, she was accompanied by an attorney. Prior to her testimony, Witness 125 told the county prosecutors that she lied to the FBI and to SLCPD detectives. Witness 125 was then given immunity from federal prosecution for making material false statements to federal agents so long as she testified truthfully in the grand jury. She testified that she did not, in fact, witness any part of the incident, but claimed she did so because she wanted to be "part of something." She claimed that a friend in the community told her to tell the SLCPD and the FBI what her boyfriend saw, but to claim it as her own.

Witness 125 has no criminal history. Because Witness 125 admitted that she gave false accounts, federal prosecutors did not consider her accounts in the prosecutive decision.

vi. Witness 131

Witness 131 is a 22-year-old black male. As previously mentioned, Witness 131 is the fiancé of Witness 125, who first told SLCPD detectives and then FBI agents that she saw Wilson shoot Brown while he had his hands in the air, and then admitted to county prosecutors that she lied to law enforcement and did not, in fact, see anything. Witness 131 gave two statements, first to FBI agents and then he testified before the county grand jury.

Witness 131 told the FBI that he was in his apartment when he heard three gunshots, prompting him to call Witness 125 to come look out their living room window. However, he changed his account when he testified before the county grand jury, claiming that he only called to his fiancée once the shooting had stopped.

Witness 131 stated that he initially did not see Wilson, but saw only Brown, who was taking a few steps forward. Witness 131 testified before the county grand jury that his view was somewhat obstructed, but he also saw Witness 101 run across the yard. Witness 131 then heard about five more shots, and watched as Brown grabbed his torso with his left hand, while holding his right hand in the air, in front him at a 45 degree angle. Witness 131 then heard another volley of shots and Brown's arms dropped. Brown fell to his knees and collapsed face down in the street. Witness 131 explained to the FBI that once Brown stopped moving forward, the shooting stopped. It was then that Witness 131 noticed a police officer approach Brown just as other officers arrived on scene.

Despite Witness 131 telling the FBI that Brown was shot only when he moved forward, he testified to the contrary in front of the county grand jury. There, he testified that Brown stood still as he was shot to death and denied that Brown moved forward at all. When county prosecutors confronted Witness 131 with his inconsistency, he denied that he said anything different to the FBI.

Witness 131 has no criminal history. Witness 131's accounts are inconsistent with each other, and his most recent version is inconsistent with the physical and forensic evidence. He also claimed that his fiancée was present for something she admitted she did not witness. Accordingly, based on a thorough review of all of the evidence, federal prosecutors determined his account not to be credible, and it therefore does not support a prosecution of Darren Wilson.

vii. Witness 112

Witness 112 is a 62-year-old black male who was with his brother, Witness 110, and sister-in-law, Witness 111, when he witnessed the shooting. As described above, they witnessed the shooting from the second floor balcony located opposite and off to the right of the minivan occupied by Witness 104, Witness 105, Witness 106, and Witness 107. Their view was of the passenger side of the SUV, followed by the right profile of Brown as he ran away from Wilson, and then the left profile of Brown as he turned around and moved toward Wilson.

Witness 112 gave three investigative statements, and he also spoke to the print media. He spoke first with SLCPD detectives. He then met with federal prosecutors and agents, and subsequently testified before the county grand jury.

Witness 112 agreed to meet with SLCPD detectives only because he spoke to his pastor, and realized that what he witnessed was "weighing on [him]." Witness 112 explained that Witness 101 could not have seen what he is claiming to have seen in his media interviews. According to Witness 112, he was sitting by his bedroom window when he saw Brown and Witness 101 walking in the center of the street. Witness 112 knew Brown from the neighborhood and always found him to be respectful.

Witness 112 saw Wilson's SUV pass Brown and Witness 101, and then back up. Witness 112 then went out to his balcony to get a better view. Once there, he saw a "tussling" at the SUV, and acknowledged that he did not know whether Wilson grabbed Brown or vice versa. However, Witness 112 was adamant that, contrary to what he kept hearing from people in his neighborhood, at least one of Brown's arms was inside the SUV. Wilson fired a shot from within the SUV, likely in an effort to get Brown off of him because Brown was so big. After that initial shot, Brown looked startled and took off running. Witness 101 took off running as well, and did not reappear until much later, once Brown's body was covered.

Witness 112 explained that it appeared that Brown stopped running because either the pain or shock hit him. Brown turned around, and looked down, as though checking himself for injury. In so doing, Witness 112 explained that Brown raised his arms partly, palms up, clarifying that he "didn't have his hands all the way up." Brown then moved his arms out at a 35 to 45 degree angle, as if to say, "What?" It was then that Wilson trained his gun on Brown, and as Brown moved forward, Wilson repeatedly yelled, "Stop!" When Brown failed to stop, Wilson fired shots. Brown's arms went limp at his sides, but he kept moving toward Wilson, though Witness 112 characterized it as "not in a menacing way." Witness 112 explained that at no time did Brown say a word. Instead, Witness 112 yelled out from his balcony for Brown to stop, but Brown kept slowly advancing, bent forward, and Wilson kept shooting.

When Witness 112 subsequently met with federal agents and prosecutors, he gave a similar account, except that he steadfastly claimed that when Brown turned around in the roadway, he held his arms up in surrender, at ninety degree angles with his palms facing out. When asked about his previous description, Witness 112 became agitated and angry, and refused to listen to a recording of his previous statement. He was unable to explain the difference in his accounts, and why his statement had changed. Witness 112 similarly described that Brown held his hands up in surrender when he testified before the county grand jury.

Subsequent to his meeting with federal authorities and his appearance before the county grand jury, Witness 112 gave an "anonymous" interview to the local print media. Although Witness 112 never identified himself, based on the account given that was almost verbatim to his initial SLCPD interview and the proximity in time to his county grand jury testimony, federal and county prosecutors and investigators recognized that it was Witness 112. In that media interview, Witness 112 reverted to his initial version that he told SLCPD detectives, explaining that Brown did not have his hands up in surrender, but rather partly raised his arms, palms up, checking for injury. This stood in stark contrast to what he told the FBI and federal prosecutors, and to his testimony in the county grand jury.

Witness 112 has a felony conviction for stealing from 18 years ago that likely would be inadmissible in federal court as impeachment evidence. Witness 112 made it clear in all of his statements that he believes that Wilson should not have shot and killed Brown, stating that it was "overkill," without offering more of an explanation. Witness 112's accounts are inconsistent as to whether Brown held his hands up in surrender, and his most recent account is that Brown's hands were not up in surrender. Because federal prosecutors cannot discern the truth among Witness 112's versions, and his most recent account does not inculpate Wilson, federal prosecutors cannot rely upon it to support a prosecution of Darren Wilson.

viii. Witness 135

Witness 135 is a 20-year-old black female. She was walking on Canfield Drive at the time of the initial interaction between Brown and Wilson. She gave three statements. The FBI first interviewed Witness 135 during their canvass on August 16, 2014, and she subsequently met with federal prosecutors. She then testified before the county grand jury.

According to Witness 135, as she was standing on the south side of the street, she saw Wilson's SUV back up and bump up against Brown and his friend. Brown then "charged over" to the driver's side of the SUV and put his arms inside the driver's window. She was unable to see what transpired inside the vehicle because the width of Brown's back obstructed her view. She did, however, explain that Brown's arms were moving aggressively and his head, shoulders, and top half of his body were in the window.

Witness 135 stated that this interaction lasted about 15 seconds during which time she saw a gun fall to the ground and then heard a gunshot. She moved to a nearby tree where she initially waited, and then continued her walk home. Brown ran anywhere from five to 10 steps, and then turned around to face Wilson who had emerged from the SUV seconds after Brown took off running. Witness 135 explained that she was both walking away and scanning the street as this was happening, so she did not see the entire incident. She recalled that as Brown turned around, he put his hands up with his arms, "scrunched up," pulled tight against his body, palms out at about shoulder height. According to Witness 135, Brown was hunched forward, though he took a few steps backward, and was shot about five times before he fell to his death. According to Witness 135, there was only this one additional volley of shots after the initial shot, Brown never moved forward, and Wilson never shot Brown as he was running away.

Witness 135 readily acknowledged to federal prosecutors that she has poor vision, and was not wearing her contact lenses on the date of the shooting. She was able to see shapes and figures, but could not see details or facial expressions from where she stood once Brown ran from the SUV. Because the physical evidence proves that Brown moved forward before he fell to his death, federal prosecutors and agents asked Witness 135 if it was possible that Brown moved forward, but she did not see it. Witness 135 responded that it was possible, not only because of her vision problems but because she was not watching Brown the entire time. Instead, she was scanning the block, and was worried for her own safety due to the ringing of gunshots.

Witness 135 explained to federal prosecutors that Brown's friend ran off as soon as the first shot was fired and she never saw him again. However, she described a similarly built black male with dreadlocks who was later running around the Canfield apartments, saying something to the effect of, "The police shot my friend and his hands were up." Witness 135 explained that quickly became the narrative on the street, and to her frustration, people used it both as an excuse to riot and to create a "block party" atmosphere.

During her county grand jury testimony, Witness 135 characterized Wilson's actions as "murder," an opinion that would be inadmissible in federal court. When county prosecutors pressed her for an explanation, she stated that she sees it that way because Wilson should have used a taser, night stick, or similar weapon. Witness 135 also stated that when she saw the gun drop by the SUV, she assumed it belonged to Brown, acknowledging that it was not unreasonable for Wilson to think that Brown had a weapon. Witness 135 also testified about her own negative experience with the FPD, when an officer arrested her and "basically beat [her] up." That officer was not Darren Wilson, nor did she ever have prior interactions with Wilson.

Witness 135 has no criminal history. As detailed above, Witness 135's initial account was inconsistent with the forensic and physical evidence and inconsistent with other credible witness accounts. She admittedly was unsure of what she saw, both because she was distracted and because she has poor vision. Because of her admitted inconsistencies along with her questionable ability to have accurately perceived what happened, federal prosecutors determined material parts of this witness's account to lack reliability and therefore, her account does not support a prosecution of Darren Wilson

ix. Witness 124

Witness 124 is a 31-year-old black female. As previously noted, Witness 124 is the wife of Witness 115. In addition to testifying before the county grand jury, Witness 124 gave two interviews to law enforcement, first to SLCPD detectives and then to FBI agents during their canvass one week after the shooting.

In her initial interview to SLCPD detectives, Witness 124 explained that she was on the phone and eating when her husband, Witness 115, called to her, "Baby, Look out the window. They're shooting." She went to the window and saw Brown running from Wilson, who was walking and steadily shooting at Brown from behind. Brown then disappeared from her sight, making her think that Brown got away. However, Brown then reappeared and came back toward Wilson. Witness 124 then joined Witness 115 on the balcony with their three children. Once on the balcony, Witness 124 saw Wilson shoot Brown in the chest area, firing two shots, followed by three shots until Brown tipped over and fell to the pavement. She further told the SLCPD detective that Brown had nothing in his hands, and Wilson did not go near Brown's body. At no point did Witness 124 describe Brown's arm across his torso as her husband described. At no point did she describe Brown's hands up in surrender.

However, during her interview with the FBI, Witness 124 described that she first saw Wilson's SUV when Wilson tried to run over Brown and Witness 101. This directly contradicts her prior statement that Witness 115 called to her to look out the window after the first shots were fired. During her FBI interview, Witness 124 also added that she saw Brown turn around and put his hands up. This also directly contradicts her initial statement in which she claimed that Brown disappeared from sight and that she did not see him until he reappeared in her line of sight. Witness 124 also added that, contrary to virtually every other witness account, Wilson walked toward Brown and shot him to death.

Witness 124 has no criminal history. In an effort to reconcile the apparent inconsistencies in Witness 124's accounts and determine what she actually witnessed as opposed to what she may have heard from others, federal prosecutors sought to meet with her. However, Witness 124 failed to appear for a scheduled meeting and refused to reschedule at any time or place of her convenience. Therefore, federal prosecutors did not have the opportunity to assess her credibility and determine which parts of her account, if any, were accurate. Because the substance of her two investigative accounts stood in stark contrast to each other, without further explanation, federal prosecutors determined her accounts not to be credible and therefore did not consider them in its prosecutive decision.

x. Witness 127

Witness 127 is a 27-year-old black female who gave three investigative statements, including testifying before the county grand jury. SLCPD detectives initially interviewed Witness 127 within two hours of the shooting. She subsequently appeared in the media several times. Federal agents and prosecutors interviewed Witness 127, in the presence of her lawyer, because parts of her account were inconsistent with the physical evidence.

According to Witness 127, she was driving east on Canfield Drive, traveling in the opposite direction of Wilson's SUV. and heard tires screeching as she rounded a curve. When she pulled up to where the SUV was stopped, Witness 127 saw Brown "rassling" at the driver's window. Brown's head was bent at the window, with his palms on the outside of the door. Witness

127 said that it looked like Brown was either pushing off of the door or pulling away and that someone was pulling him into the car, in a "tug of war" manner. However, she did not see anyone or anything pulling Brown. At the same time this was happening, Witness 127 was looking at her mobile phone, trying to no avail to record what was transpiring "because it didn't look right." Witness 127 then heard a gunshot, but did not see blood or injury. She said that Brown broke free, indicating that it looked like Brown's right shirtsleeve was being pulled, though she could not see anything pulling it.

Upon hearing that gunshot, Witness 127 drove around the SUV and turned left into a nearby parking lot. She parked her car and got out. By that time, she saw Brown running and heard shots being fired. Witness 127 did not actually see Wilson exit the SUV, but she saw him chase after Brown. Witness 127 described volleys of gunshots without specificity. She explained that once she was out of her car, she began walking on the sidewalk as the shooting continued. She saw Brown's body make a jerking movement such that his hands started going up involuntarily. In one quick motion, Brown turned around with his hands up at right angles at his shoulders. Wilson then shot him, and Brown fell to his death where he stood. Witness 127 did not see injury to either of Brown's hands when his hands were up. Witness 127 was adamant that, contrary to DNA evidence with regard to the blood east of Brown's body, Brown never moved toward Wilson. She insisted that he fell to his death right where he turned around. She was equally adamant that Brown's hands remained outside the SUV during the initial interaction between Wilson and Brown, despite forensic and physical evidence to the contrary. When questioned by federal prosecutors and then by county prosecutors during her county grand jury testimony, she disallowed any possibility that perhaps her perception was compromised because she was using her phone, driving, and parking, among other reasons. Additionally, Witness 127 appeared in the media with her friend, Witness 118, allowing for the possibility that their accounts became conflated .

Witness 127 has no criminal history. Although Witness 127's statements are materially consistent with each other, significant portions are contrary to the forensic and physical evidence and inconsistent with credible witness accounts. Witness 127 was unable to give reasonable explanations as to why the physical evidence might be inconsistent with what she remembers, and therefore prosecutors were left to conclude that she inaccurately perceived material portions of the shootings either because of the stress of incidents or because she was distracted. Accordingly, after a thorough review of the evidence, federal prosecutors determined material portions of this witness's account not reliable and therefore cannot be used to support prosecution of Darren Wilson.

xi. Witness 118

Witness 118 is a 19-year-old black female who lives in the Canfield Green neighborhood and knew Brown through a mutual friend, Witness 120. Witness 118 also knew Witness 101, with whom she became friendly when she moved into the neighborhood. Prior to the shootings, Witness 118 and Witness 101 socialized almost weekly. Witness 118 denied speaking with Witness 101 since the shootings, contrary to what Witness 101 said during his testimony before the county grand jury. However, Witness 118 acknowledged speaking to Witness 120 about the shooting. As detailed later in this memorandum, Witness 120 was admittedly untruthful about what he claimed to have witnessed.

Witness 118 gave three investigative statements, and testified before the county grand jury. A SLCPD detective initially interviewed Witness 118 approximately two hours after the shooting. She subsequently appeared in the media several times. During those media interviews, Witness 118 added details that she did not report to local law enforcement, claiming in the news that she saw the "whole scenario play out." In an effort to evaluate the inconsistencies between her statements to law enforcement and her statements to the media as well as inconsistencies with physical evidence, federal agents and prosecutors interviewed Witness 118 in the presence of her lawyer.

During her initial SLCPD interview, Witness 118 stated that just before the shooting, she was in her apartment when she heard the screech of tires and thought someone might be hurt. She then heard three gunshots and went to look out her bedroom window. Witness 118 denied to the SLCPD detective that she witnessed any "tussle" at the side of the SUV. In fact, her view was of the passenger side of the SUV, which would have limited her ability to see a struggle at the driver's side even if she had looked out the window in time.

Witness 118 told the SLCPD detective that she then saw Wilson get out of the SUV and run in a hurry. She did not see anyone else at that time. She left her bedroom window to go to her patio door when she heard no less than four more shots. Those shots occurred about 30 seconds after the first three shots. Witness 118 thought someone was trying to shoot Wilson. She did not see Brown until she got to her patio door, when she peeked through the blinds to see him running. While looking through her glass door, she was distracted for about 10 to 30 seconds by Witness 101 ducking behind a black Monte Carlo and trying to hide. Witness 101 was creeping westward, toward the front of the Monte Carlo, with his back to Wilson and Brown as they ran east on Canfield Drive.

Witness 118 told the SLCPD detective that she then looked back toward Brown as he turned around, put his hands in the air, and got shot two times. Brown fell to the ground face down, with his arms at 90 degree angles on either side of his head, contrary to what the crime scene photos depict and the SLCME medicolegal investigator noted, *i.e.,* Brown's left hand was at his waistband and his right hand was down at his side.

At the conclusion of the interview with the SLCPD, Witness 118 assured the detective that what she reported was her best recollection of the incident and that she was not leaving anything out. Nonetheless, Witness 118's accounts to the media and to federal prosecutors and agents were different from her initial statement to the SLCPD, even though her grand jury testimony was ultimately more consistent with her initial SLCPD account.

Witness 118 claimed to the media that she "saw" screeching tires as the SUV swerved at Brown and Witness 101. She further claimed that she watched Brown as he was reaching, pulling, and "hassling" through the window of the SUV, in what appeared to be "arm wrestling."

Witness 118 told the media that Wilson was pulling Brown into the SUV while Brown was trying to flee. She claimed to have seen the first gunshots hit Brown as he pulled away and fled. She also claimed that she saw a bullet strike a nearby building, but acknowledged that she inferred this because she saw SLCPD detectives attempting to remove one from a building wall.

Witness 118 added to her media narrative that Wilson shot Brown in the back from three feet away and that Brown never moved back towards Wilson. Physical evidence is inconsistent with both of those added details. Also, contrary to her initial account, Witness 118 told federal agents and prosecutors that Brown's arms were at his sides and his hands were around his hips when he came to rest on the ground.

When federal prosecutors and agents challenged the inconsistencies in her accounts, Witness 118 conceded that she likely assumed facts that she did not witness herself based on talking with other residents in the Canfield Green complex and watching the news, but was not specific about which facts. Witness 118 also added that she did not have a lawyer when she was first interviewed by the SLCPD, though there was nothing to indicate that interview was custodial or coercive and Witness 118 expressed no apprehension or hesitation when speaking with the SLCPD.

Witness 118 has no criminal history. Witness 118's accounts are riddled with internal inconsistencies, inconsistencies with the physical and forensic evidence, and inconsistencies with credible witness accounts. Her attention was admittedly diverted away from the shooting when she watched Witness 101 ducking for cover and she acknowledged that her account was also based on assumption and media coverage. Accordingly, after a thorough review of the evidence, federal prosecutors determined the various versions of this witness's account to lack credibility and therefore it does not support a prosecution of Darren Wilson.

xii. Witness 122

Witness 122 is a 46-year-old white male. He was laying drain pipe on Canfield Drive with Witness 130 on the morning of the shooting. Witness 122 gave six statements, including testimony before the county grand jury. SLCPD detectives and an FBI agent twice jointly interviewed him, and SLCPD detectives once independently interviewed him. Witness 122 and Witness 130 authored one-page written statements on advice of a former boss. Witness 122 and Witness 130 claimed that they did not discuss what they witnessed, though Witness 130 admitted that they read each other's statements after they were written. Witness 122 gave a media interview on the condition of anonymity. As noted throughout this memorandum, federal prosecutors interviewed many potential witnesses in an effort to assess credibility and reconcile internal inconsistencies and inconsistencies with physical evidence, as is necessary to make a fair prosecutive decision. Witness 122 agreed to meet with federal prosecutors only after assurances that he would not be held against his will at the FBI office, claiming that he had heard of instances where individuals go to the FBI office and do not emerge for days.

According to Witness 122, Witness 122 and Witness 130 (collectively, "the contractors") twice encountered Brown during the morning of the shootings, first when Brown was alone and then when Brown was with Witness 101. Witness 122 and Brown did most of the talking, and the topics included God and smoking marijuana. About 20 minutes after their last conversation with Brown, the contractors heard a loud bang. Witness 122 saw Brown running, staggering, or falling forward. Contrary to the autopsy results, Witness 122 described Brown being shot in the back and "knew he had gotten hit." In fact, both contractors claimed to have witnessed bullets go through Brown and exit his back, as evidenced by his shirt "popping back" and "stuff coming through." However, in his interview with federal prosecutors, Witness 122 explained that he thought that Brown was shot in the back and stumbled until he saw media reports about the autopsy commissioned by Brown's family. After learning about that autopsy, he realized that Brown was not shot in the back and admittedly changed his account.

Witness 122 also claimed that Brown put his right hand to the ground to regain his balance when he was hit and as he turned around. According to both contractors, Brown then turned around with his hands up and repeatedly screamed "Okay!" as many as eight times, an exclamation heard by no other witness. When Witness 122 demonstrated the position of Brown's hands for federal prosecutors and agents, he wavered from a position of surrender to one indicative of a person trying to maintain balance.

Contrary to the autopsy results establishing that the shot to the top of Brown's head would have incapacitated Brown almost immediately, both contractors insisted that Brown continued to move toward Wilson as far as 20, 25, or even 30 feet after the final shots. Witness 122 described Brown as walking "dead on his feet, and then he just fell forward." Later, both contractors admitted that they did not actually see Brown fall to the ground, because their view was obstructed by the corner of a building.

Witness 122 insisted that there were three officers present during the shootings, demonstrating the inaccuracy of his perception. Witness 122 described three uniformed police officers engaged with Brown in a "triangle formation" at the time of the shootings. Witness 122 described a heavyset, older officer, and two "skinny, little people," one of whom was possibly a female and the other with dark hair and a moustache, who was a head shorter than the heavyset officer. Witness 122 described the shooter as the heavyset officer. Witness 122 explained that the heavset officer shot until he ran out of bullets, and then the shorter officer with the moustache trained his gun on Brown, but did not shoot. These statements cannot be reconciled with the fact that Wilson was the only officer present when Brown was shot and that Wilson has a slim build.

Witness 122 also explained that he did not see Witness 101 at all during the shooting itself, and did not understand how Witness 101 could claim to see everything if he was hiding behind a car. Witness 122 also said that contrary to what was reported in the media, Brown did not say, "Don't shoot."

The contractors, apparently unwittingly, were captured on a widely circulated video taken several minutes after the shooting while responding officers were securing the scene with crime scene tape. That video depicts another individual yelling, "He wasn't no threat at all," as Witness 122 put his hands up and stated, "He had his fucking hands in the air." As detailed below, two other witnesses, Witness 128 and Witness 137, each took credit for making the statement, "He wasn't no threat at all."[24] Both of those witnesses have since acknowledged to federal agents and prosecutors that they did not, in fact, know whether Brown was a threat.

According to the Brown family, Witness 122 called them after the shooting and told them that he had seen Wilson shoot Brown execution-style as Brown was on his knees holding his hands in the air. However, Witness 122 denied making any statements about the nature of the shooting to the Brown family. As mentioned, despite his earlier statements, Witness 122 recanted the claim that he actually saw Brown fall dead to the ground.

Witness 122 has no criminal history. As detailed above, material portions of Witness 122's accounts are irreconcilable with the physical and forensic evidence. These accounts are also inconsistent with each other and inconsistent with credible witness accounts. Accordingly, after a thorough review of all of the evidence, federal prosecutors determined this witness's accounts not to be credible and therefore do not support a prosecution of Darren Wilson.

xiii. Witness 130

Witness 130 is a 26–year-old white male. As previously noted, he was laying drain pipe on Canfield Drive with Witness 122, on the morning of the shooting. Witness 130 gave five statements, including testimony before the county grand jury. SLCPD detectives and an FBI agent twice jointly interviewed him, and SLCPD detectives once independently interviewed him. Like Witness 122, Witness 130 authored a one-page written statement on advice of a former boss. Witness 122 and Witness 130 claimed that they did not discuss what they witnessed, though Witness 130 admitted that they read each other's statements after they were written. Like Witness 122, Witness 130 gave a media interview on the condition of anonymity.

As noted, Witness 122 and Witness 130 twice encountered Brown during the morning of the shootings, first when Brown was alone and then when Brown was with Witness 101. Witness 122 and Brown did most of the talking, and Witness 130 admitted that at times, Brown seemed paranoid and aggressive, clenching his fists and causing Witness 130 some concern. Witness 130 thought Brown "was not in his right mind," based upon how paranoid he seemed.

About 20 minutes after their last conversation with Brown, Witness 130 heard a loud bang. Witness 130 stepped around the corner of an apartment building that was obstructing his view, and saw Brown "fast walk[ing]" east on Canfield Drive. According to both contractors, Brown then turned around with his hands up and repeatedly screamed "Okay!" as many as eight times, an exclamation heard by no other witness According to Witness 130, after Brown turned around, he continued to stumble or otherwise approach Wilson, although he did not know whether Brown was speeding up to come after Wilson, or whether his momentum was carrying him forward. Wilson then fired at least seven shots, but as Witness 130 told the grand jury, Wilson only fired when Brown moved forward. Witness 130 described Wilson "unloading his clip" into Brown, although Witness 130 acknowledged that Brown put his arms down after the third shot.

Witness 130 explained that Wilson backed up as Brown approached him. Contrary to the autopsy results establishing that the shot to the top of Brown's head would have incapacitated Brown almost immediately, like Witness 122, Witness 130 insisted that Brown continued to move toward Wilson as far as 20, 25, or even 30 feet after the final shots. Contrary to his initial account, Witness 130 admitted that he did not actually see Brown fall to the ground because his view was obstructed by the corner of a building.

Witness 130 has no criminal history. Federal prosecutors attempted to meet with Witness 130 to evaluate inconsistencies in his various statements. Witness 130 refused to meet with federal prosecutors, making reliance on his account problematic because his statements are inconsistent with each other, inconsistent with the physical and forensic evidence, and inconsistent with credible witness accounts. Therefore, federal prosecutors could not rely on Witness 130's account to support a prosecution of Darren Wilson.

xiv. Witness 142

Witness 142 is a 48-year-old black male. Witness 142 briefly spoke to SLCPD detectives within hours of the shooting incident and denied that he witnessed the shooting. However, the SLCPD and the FBI then followed up with Witness 142 after SLCPD detectives learned that Witness 142 called in to an Atlanta-based podcast on August 11, 2014, where he described the shootings. Witness 142 then testified before the county grand jury.

During the podcast, Witness 142 explained that he was sitting on his front patio when he heard the first gunshot. He then moved closer to get a better look at what he termed a "scuffle," and saw "the brother (referring to Brown) leaning over into the window." Witness 142 further described Brown's "upper body in the windshield." The podcast announcer then asked if what "the officer is saying is true," relative to what happened at the SUV. Witness 142 responded, "yes." Witness 142 explained that Brown then took off running and Wilson chased after him. Witness 142 thought that Wilson shot at Brown while Brown was running away. Brown then turned around and came back toward Wilson. Wilson "unloaded on him" and Brown fell to the ground.

The podcast announcer then asked if Brown's hands were up. Witness 142 responded, "Well, I don't know. I didn't see that." He went on to explain that "the crowd" was saying that Brown's hands were up, and that he was ducking to avoid getting hit by gunfire. The announcer later asked, "If you had to say from your opinion, was it justified?" Witness 142 paused and then said, "yes," referencing the scuffle in the SUV. However, he then stated that Wilson should not have shot at Brown while Brown was "fleeing the scene," an opinion that would be inadmissible in federal court and a misstatement of applicable federal law.

SLCPD detectives recognized Witness 142's voice on the podcast from their initial canvass of Canfield Drive, when Witness 142 denied seeing anything. Therefore, an SLCPD detective and an FBI agent interviewed Witness 142 again in an effort to determine what he actually saw. However, during that interview, Witness 142 again changed his account from what he stated on the podcast. Witness 142 told the SLCPD detective and the FBI agent that he was inside his apartment and heard one gunshot. He looked out his patio sliding glass door and saw the driver's side of a police SUV, where Brown was "tussling" with Wilson, who was inside the SUV. Witness 142 stated that Wilson was tugging on Brown's shirt collar. Even though Brown's back was to him, Witness 142 saw Brown's hands against the SUV and Wilson's hands grabbing Brown's shirt. He denied seeing any part of Brown's body inside the SUV. Brown then pushed away from the SUV and "sprinted" east on Canfield Drive. Wilson, with his gun on his hip, immediately got out of the SUV and chased Brown. After that, Witness 142 does not know what happened, claiming that a concrete barrier obstructed his view.

Witness 142 admitted that on the podcast, he stated that Brown's head was inside the SUV, but claimed that he lied, though he could offer no explanation for doing so. He recalled saying that Wilson shot Brown as Brown was running away, though he admitted to law enforcement that he did not see that happen. Witness 142 clarified that he thought Wilson was shooting at Brown because everything happened in a matter of seconds. He also acknowledged that he told the podcast announcer that he saw Brown stop, turn around, and come back at Wilson. However, he told the SLCPD detective and the FBI agent that he only assumed that Brown did those things, based on Brown's body facing west in the street. Witness 142 told law enforcement that he stayed outside in the street for hours after the shooting, hearing people say that Brown had his hands up. However, he did not see Brown with his hands up. Witness 142 stood by his initial statement that the shooting was justified, though he stated that he did not actually see what happened. He further told law enforcement that he originally lied to SLCPD detectives on the day of the shooting, when he claimed to not have seen anything. Witness 142 explained that he was afraid and did not want to get involved.

Witness 142 has no criminal history. Witness 142 changed his account and could offer no explanation as to why he did so, and his most recent account is inconsistent with credible witness accounts and inconsistent with forensic and physical evidence. Accordingly, federal prosecutors determined that they could not credit either one of his accounts. Regardless, his accounts do not inculpate Darren Wilson and therefore do not support a prosecution.

xv. Witness 138

Witness 138 is a 22-year-old black male. The SLCPD first interviewed Witness 138 about five hours after the shooting. The interview was very brief and federal prosecutors and agents sought to interview him to obtain more detailed information. Witness 138 repeatedly ignored attempts by federal authorities to meet with him when he lived in St. Louis. He then moved out of state. Again, Witness 138 failed to respond to messages left by county and federal authorities, and refused to appear before the county grand jury. Finally, an FBI agent and federal prosecutor tracked down Witness 138 outside of his mother's house in Kentucky. Witness 138's account to federal authorites stood in stark contrast to what he initially told the SLCPD.

Witness 138 told SLCPD that on the day of the shooting, he was watching television in his apartment when he heard one gunshot, causing him to run outside. Brown had kicked off his flip flops and started running away from Wilson, who had emerged from his SUV with his gun drawn. Wilson ran east after Brown, past Witness 101 who was by a white Monte Carlo. Wilson shot Brown as he was running away. Brown then turned around, "threw his hands up," and said something. Initially, Witness 138 stated that he could not hear what Brown said. Then he explained that Brown said something with the word "shoot" in it. By the end of the interview, Witness 138 stated that Brown said, "Please don't shoot." Brown then fell to his knees, and Wilson shot him again. Other police officers arrived on the scene, and Wilson got into a different police vehicle than the one in which he arrived, and left the scene.

Witness 138 told federal authorities that Brown and Witness 101 came to his house the morning of the shooting, prior to their walk to Ferguson Market. They made plans to smoke marijuana later in the day and Brown and Witness 101 told Witness 138 that they were going to get cigarillos and would return. Thereafter, Witness 120 arrived at Witness 138's house. While Witness 138 and Witness 120 were talking in the doorway, Witness 138 heard two gunshots. He ran toward the gunshots, while Witness 120 ran in a different direction. Witness 138 saw Wilson "walk quickly" toward Brown. Unlike what he told the SLCPD detective, Witness 138 said that while going after Brown, Wilson was yelling "stop" or "freeze." Also contrary to his initial account, Witness 138 said that he did not hear Brown say anything. He saw Brown stop and put his hands up, shoulder height at 90 degree angles. Because he heard gunfire, Witness 138 ducked for cover, face-first in the dirt where two white contractors were working. Witness 138 remained in that position until the incident was over, and he looked up and saw Brown dead on the ground.

Witness 138 told federal authorities that Brown fell to the ground in the exact place where he first turned around and did not move forward toward Wilson. Because this is inconsistent with the physical evidence and other credible accounts, federal authorities asked Witness 138 if it was possible that Brown moved toward Wilson. Witness 138 explained that Brown could have moved forward, could have put his arms down, and in fact, he did not know what Brown did for the majority of the shooting because he was face-first in the dirt. He did not look up until Brown was already dead. Witness 138 described the position of Brown's body as having his hands at right angles next to his head, contrary to photographic evidence and the observations of the SLCME medicolegal investigator.

After Brown was killed, Witness 101 ran over to Witness 138 in shock. Witness 101 left the scene to change his clothes, and then returned. According to Witness 138, at the insistence of Witness 101's uncle and pastor, Witness 101 gave an interview to the media. Witness 138 explained that he was "stupid" to stand next to Witness 101 as he appeared on camera.

In response to federal authorities questioning about Wilson's description of Brown as "Hulk Hogan," Witness 138 said that Brown was more like the World Wrestling Federation wrestler

"Big Show" in stature, but not in personality. Brown was intimidating because of his size, and Witness 138 understood how Wilson could generally perceive him as a threat. Witness 138 explained that he was friendly with Brown, and although it would surprise him if Brown attacked a police officer, it also surprised him to see the surveillance video of Brown shoving a store clerk, as it was uncharacteristic of him. In the days leading up to his death, Brown was acting out of character, speaking about his desire to get away from the struggles of life.

Witness 138 has no criminal history. There are significant inconsistencies between his two accounts, with the physical and forensic evidence, and with credible witness accounts. Accordingly, after a thorough review of the evidence, federal prosecutors determined this witness's first account to lack credibility. His second account, regardless of credibility, does not inculpate Wilson. Therefore, these accounts do not support a prosecution of Darren Wilson.

xvi. Witness 132

Witness 132 is a 25-year-old black male. He spoke with FBI agents on three occasions. First, Witness 132 met with FBI agents during their canvass on August 16, 2014. At that time, Witness 132 stated that he did not see the shooting or hear the gunshots. However, he stated that his wife may have seen some of the incident. Ten days later, two other FBI agents followed up with his wife. She indicated that she did not see anything, but Witness 132, contrary to what he stated before, claimed to have witnessed the shooting of Brown. Finally, Witness 132 spoke again to the FBI, claiming her memory of the shooting was "blurry."

During her second encounter with the FBI, contrary to all accounts that Wilson was driving westbound, Witness 132 said that he, Witness 132, was driving eastbound behind two FPD marked SUVs. Each SUV had two police officers, all of whom were white. According to Witness 132, the first SUV stopped in the middle of the street, cutting off Brown and running over his feet. Brown then "punched into the police car" because he was angry. In return, the police officer, to whom Witness 132 referred as "Ears," reached down and shot Brown. Witness 132 explained that Brown tried to run, but again, the officer shot Brown right where he stood, about five feet from the SUV. Brown half-turned, fell to his knees, and put his hands up. The officer shot Brown eight or nine more times. This all occurred on the passenger side of the vehicle.

After that interview with the FBI, Witness 132 actively and successfully evaded service of a county grand jury subpoena. Federal and county prosecutors independently and repeatedly tried to contact Witness 132 to no avail in an effort to reconcile the inconsistencies in his statements. However, Witness 132 ignored phone calls, hung up on the prosecutors, and pretended he was not at home. Witness 132 moved out of state and the FBI tracked him down in Georgia. Witness 132 refused to meet with federal prosecutors and told the FBI that the events of August 9, 2014 were "blurry," he could not remember what happened, and he was starting a new chapter in his life.

Witness 132 has no criminal history. Witness 132's second statement is starkly inconsistent with what he initially told law enforcement, is inconsistent with forensic and physical evidence, and is inconsistent with credible witness accounts. Federal prosecutors determined his account to inherently lack credibility, and did not consider it when making a prosecutive decision.

xvii. Witness 121

Witness 121 is a 36-year-old black female who twice spoke to federal authorities, and then testified before the county grand jury.

FBI agents initially interviewed Witness 121 in the presence of three other people during the FBI canvass on August 16, 2014. Her account was confusing and hard to follow, made more confusing by the three other individuals who interjected their thoughts into her account. Nonetheless, Witness 121 initially told the FBI that she saw Brown and Witness 101 walking in the street and she also saw an SUV with two police officers. The police officer on the driver's side of the SUV reached out from within the vehicle and grabbed Brown by the collar. She assumed that the officer had his hand on his gun when he grabbed Brown. She heard a gunshot which struck Brown in the upper chest, leaving a red spot on Brown's shirt. Witness 121 explained that the officer then immediately fired a second shot. Witness 121 seemed to suggest that the second shot happened while Brown was still by the SUV, prompting him to run; at another point during the same interview, Witness 121 suggested that the second shot occurred as Brown was running. She did not know whether that second shot struck Brown. She also explained that the second police officer emerged from the vehicle, though Witness 121 could not provide a description of him, nor be specific about when he emerged. Witness 121 explained that after Brown took off running, Brown put his hands up, walked toward Wilson, and then Wilson shot him. She further stated that Wilson walked over to Brown and "emptied" his gun into Brown, and that Brown "finally fell" after the last shot.

In contrast, however, during her follow up interview with federal prosecutors, Witness 121 explained that based on her vantage point, she did not see the initial interaction between Wilson and Brown. She explained that she had been standing by a dumpster, smoking a cigarette and talking on her phone when a gunshot drew her attention to the SUV. Once she heard the first shot, she became terrified and got ready to run, but instead watched Brown run from the SUV. Witness 121 made no mention of the second shot during her second interview. Likewise, Witness 121 denied that the second officer got out of the vehicle.

As before, Witness 121 explained that after Brown took off running, he put his hands up, walked toward Wilson, and then Wilson shot Brown. However, unlike in her first interview, Witness 121 denied that Wilson walked over to Brown and "emptied his gun" into him. Although she admitted making that prior statement, Witness 121 could offer no explanation for saying something that was inconsistent with the physical evidence and the accounts of almost all other witnesses. Instead, she described a chaotic scene and broke down in tears, acknowledging that she did not know what led up to the shooting. Witness 121 tearfully stated that she "didn't see that young man do anything wrong," empathizing with Brown's mother because her own mother lost a child.

Witness 121 confirmed during her interview with federal authorities that Wilson did not fire any shots while Brown was running way. According to Witness 121, the only shots fired were the first one and the volley of shots as Brown was walking toward the officer with his hands up in surrender. Contrary to how Brown's body was found and photographed when he fell to his death, Witness 121 was certain that Brown's body landed in the same position that his hands were in when he was standing, at right angles adjacent to his head.

Contrary to every other witness account and mobile phone video taken in the immediate aftermath of the shooting, Witness 121 explained that Wilson then checked Brown's pulse while his body lay on the ground. When federal prosecutors pressed her on this, Witness 121 acknowledged that perhaps she was mistaken. She stated that she was unsure which police officer checked his pulse and it likely happened after the police tape went up.

When asked about Witness 101's presence, Witness 121 explained that she had been looking back and forth between Brown and Witness 101 during the shooting. However, Witness 101's whereabouts were unclear throughout both of her accounts. During her first interview, Witness 121 stated that Witness 101 took off running when the initial shots were fired. During the second interview, she first stated that Witness 101 stood by the SUV and vomited on the street. When federal prosecutors asked if crime scene investigators would find vomit on the street to corroborate her claim, Witness 121 admitted that she did not see, but rather heard from others, that Witness 101 vomited on the street. Federal prosecutors and agents repeatedly urged Witness 121 to describe what she herself witnessed. It was then that she stated that Witness 101 had been crouched down, below car level, before he ran from the scene.

When Witness 121 appeared before the county grand jury, she again testified inconsistently. She testified that while she witnessed the shooting, she was standing next to Witness 126. As detailed below, Witness 126's account was internally inconsistent and inconsistent with physical evidence. She also claimed that Witness 137 tossed a cigarette down to her from a balcony above. Witness 137, as detailed below, admitted to being untruthful when he was first interviewed by the FBI, giving an account inconsistent with the physical evidence.

Reverting back to her initial account, Witness 121 testified before the county grand jury that even though her view was of the passenger side of the SUV, contrary to the physical evidence and other credible witnesses, Brown's hands were never inside the SUV. She also added that she heard Witness 101 tell Wilson that he and Brown "weren't that far" from where they were going.

Further, even though she admitted to federal prosecutors that she never heard Brown say anything, Witness 121 told the county grand jury that Brown screamed, "I give up!" as Wilson faced him in the roadway, gun drawn. However, she claimed that she was too far away to hear Wilson say anything.

Witness 121 has no criminal history. Witness 121 admittedly made false statements during her initial interview, her accounts are inconsistent with each other, inconsistent with the physical and forensic evidence, inconsistent with credible accounts, and she demonstrated bias in favor of Brown's family. Accordingly, after a thorough review of all of the evidence, federal prosecutors determined this witness's accounts to lack credibility and therefore do not support a prosecution of Darren Wilson.

xviii. Witness 126

Witness 126 is a 53-year-old black female. She is the godmother of Witness 137. Witness 126 gave two statements, first to the FBI and then to the county grand jury. During the course of her interview with the FBI, Witness 126 stated that her godson had been shot by police.

According to Witness 126, she suffers from memory loss and is under psychiatric care. Her account to the FBI was brief and is inconsistent with the autopsy results. She claimed that she was outside of her apartment during the shooting, never mentioning Witness 121 who claimed to be with Witness 126 at the time. Witness 126 saw Brown on his knees with his hands up, as Wilson was coming toward him and shooting at him. Brown then fell face down to the ground. Wilson went over to him, and similar to what her godson, Witness 137, said, "finished him off." When the FBI told Witness 126 that her account was contrary to the evidence, she became belligerent, grabbed the recording device, shut it off, and would not return it to the agents.

When the agents retrieved it, and turned the recording device back on, Witness 126 admitted that she initially lied. She stated that she never saw Wilson inflict gunshot wounds on Brown. Rather, she saw him running from behind, and then fall to his knees with his hands in the air. She then saw Wilson walking toward Brown, followed by a "click click" sound. Wilson had bruising and redness on the right side of his face. Someone then tapped her on the shoulder and she turned away. She heard nine gunshots in total, and by the time she turned back around, Brown was dead on the ground.

Witness 126 stated that she had spoken with Brown before. They discussed college and helping senior citizens. Brown told her that "everything he used to do, he wouldn't do it anymore."

Witness 126 telephoned the FBI the day after her interview to schedule an interview because she did not remember meeting with the agents and giving her account.

When Witness 126 testified before the county grand jury, she claimed to suffer from memory loss, but then recounted everything she had eaten for breakfast and every pill she had taken on the morning of August 9, 2014. Then she testified that she heard several shots, came out onto the parking lot, and saw Brown on his knees as Wilson fired shots into his head. She denied being untruthful to the FBI, and denied that she admitted to being untruthful to the FBI.

After Witness 126 testified before the county grand jury, she told the state prosecutor that she recorded the shooting on her mobile phone. However, she had since dropped the phone in the toilet. When the state prosecutor told her that forensic experts may still be able to recover the data, Witness 126 stated that she got mad and threw the phone in the junk yard.

Witness 126 has several felony arrests and a misdemeanor conviction that likely would be inadmissible in federal court as impeachment evidence. However, Witness 126 was admittedly untruthful to the FBI, suffers from memory loss, and provided internally inconsistent accounts that are also inconsistent with the physical and forensic evidence and credible witness accounts.

Her account would be subject to extensive cross examination. Accordingly, federal prosecutors determined this witness's account to lack credibility and therefore it does not support a prosecution of Darren Wilson.

xix. Witness 137

Witness 137 is 40-year-old black male. After the shooting, Witness 137 had learned that Brown was his nephew's friend. He is the godson of Witness 126. He gave two law enforcement statements and testified before the county grand jury. Witness 137 first met with FBI agents on August 16, 2014, during their neighborhood canvass. Witness 137 also gave an interview to the media which was widely circulated throughout various media outlets. The account to the media and to the FBI was both internally inconsistent and inconsistent with the physical evidence. Therefore, federal agents and prosecutors subsequently met with Witness 137 in an attempt to assess inconsistencies and clarify his statement.

In his initial account during the neighborhood canvass, Witness 137 stated that he was on his porch using his mobile phone when he heard a gunshot. He looked out from his porch and saw Brown running away from a police officer who was chasing him. The police officer shot Brown in the back. "Realiz[ing] he was shot," Brown turned around with his hands up in surrender. Brown walked toward the officer and as he did so, the officer "closed in on him" until they were less than an arm's length apart. The officer fired "every round" into Brown, killing him "execution" style. Witness 137 explained that the officer shot Brown in the lower abdomen, chest, and then the "head shot." Witness 137 stated that after Brown fell forward, "the officer stood over him and finished him off." Witness 137 stated that the officer shot Brown in the head both when he was still standing and then when he was on the ground. Although Witness 137 stated that Brown fell to his knees for the final shots, and the last words Brown said were "Don't shoot," he also stated that Brown was lying on the ground when the final bullets were fired. Witness 137 referred to how clear the "visual" of events was to him.

Throughout the interview, Witness 137 also referred to events that preceded the initial gunshots even though he admitted that he did not see those events. He also discussed the interaction at the SUV, the location of recovered bullets, and the type of clip in the officer's gun.

During their follow-up interview with Witness 137, federal prosecutors and agents asked Witness 137 to describe only what he saw. Witness 137 once again stated that the sound of a gunshot drew his attention. When he moved further onto his porch, he said that he heard another shot, and saw Brown turn around with his hands up. Referencing the arm graze wound that was widely reported in the news after the privately-commissioned autopsy, Witness 137 stated that he believed that wound caused Brown to turn around. He then saw the officer backing up while firing shots as Brown walked at a "steady pace" of about ten steps in total toward him. According to Witness 137, there was no pause in the succession of shots, and Brown kept walking, even after he was shot in the torso. Witness 137 stated, "that's all I seen," explaining that he did not see Brown fall to the ground because that occurred in a blind spot. However, he was able to see the officer walk away, call for back up, and appear to be discombobulated. It was then that Witness 137 walked over to the scene where Brown's body lay in the street.

Contrary to his previous statement, Witness 137 denied that the officer shot Brown from less than an arm's length away, denied that he saw the officer shoot Brown execution-style; denied that the officer shot Brown when he was on the ground; denied that the officer "finished him off," and denied that Brown's last words while on his knees were "Don't shoot." Witness 137 explained that he initially told the FBI that the officer stood over Brown and shot him execution-style while on his knees because he "assumed" that to be true. Witness 137 based his assumptions on the sound of the bullets and "common sense" from living in the community, despite claiming to have a "clear visual" of events.

Witness 137 also identified his voice on the aforementioned video taken in the aftermath of the shooting depicting the two contractors. As mentioned, Witness 137 was one of two people who claimed to be off camera shouting, "He wasn't no threat at all," because he did not perceive

Brown to be a threat. However, Witness 137 acknowledged that contrary to what he originally told the FBI, the only part he saw was Brown moving back toward the officer. He did not witness what transpired at the SUV, did not witness Brown run from the SUV, and he did not witness Brown fall to his death. Therefore, Witness 137 agreed that he did not know whether Brown was a physical threat before or after the portion that Witness 137 claimed to see.

Witness 137 has previously been convicted of second-degree murder and armed criminal action which likely would be admissible in federal court as impeachment evidence. Additionally, Witness 137 was untruthful to the FBI during his initial interview, and untruthful in his media accounts. Although he later recanted most of what he claimed to have seen, he was unable to offer a credible explanation as to why he was not truthful at the outset, leaving federal prosecutors to question what, if anything, he actually did witness. His accounts are inconsistent with each other, inconsistent with the physical and forensic evidence, and inconsistent withcredible witness accounts. Accordingly, after a thorough review of the evidence, federal prosecutors determined this witness's accounts not to be credible and therefore do not support a prosecution of Darren Wilson.

xx. Witness 128

Witness 128 is a 23-year-old black male who has made three different statements to law enforcement and testified before the county grand jury. He initially had a telephone interview with an investigator from the St. Louis County Prosecutor's Office and then an additional interview with that same investigator and the FBI. Both interviews were materially inconsistent with the physical evidence. Federal agents and prosecutors interviewed Witness 128 again in an effort to evaluate some of the inconsistencies.

According to Witness 128's initial accounts, he was driving east on Canfield Drive when he witnessed the shooting. It is unclear what Witness 128 initially saw because in one interview, he stated that he saw the police vehicle quickly back up. In another interview, he stated that by the time he pulled up, Wilson had already stopped his vehicle. Witness 128 stated that he then saw Brown struggling to get away from Wilson, who was choking Brown with both hands, while Witness 101 stood behind Brown. Witness 128 then heard a gunshot and saw the impact of the bullet, initially giving little detail but subsequently adding that Wilson held the gun out the window with his right hand while holding Brown with his left hand, and firing the gun into Brown's left chest.

Brown broke free and ran about 15 feet while Witness 101 ducked down between the police vehicle and the car right behind it. Witness 128 explained that while Wilson was still seated in the vehicle with the door closed, Wilson "let more shots go." Brown appeared to get hit by four rounds in the middle of his back. Brown "slowed up" and turned around, although Witness 128 later stated that Brown continued running another 20 or 25 feet before he turned around.

Wilson then emerged from the SUV about five seconds after he fired four or five rounds, and "patiently" walked toward Brown in "lazy pursuit." Brown "threw his hands up, clean in the air." Initially, Witness 128 stated that Brown said, "Don't kill me," but later admitted that he did not actually hear Brown or Wilson say anything. Wilson then fired two shots at "point blank range" from within two feet. The shots hit Brown in the face and Brown fell to the ground. Wilson then fired four or five shots into Brown's back after Brown was already dead, face first on the ground. Witness 128 then drove by Wilson and asked him why he shot Brown. Wilson told Witness 128 to "shut the fuck up," "mind [his] own business," and "keep going." Witness 128 then pulled into his complex and parked, staying away because he did not want to get shot himself. According to Witness 128, there were no other people or cars on the street, except for a white pick-up truck behind him.

Federal prosecutors and agents met with Witness 128 and challenged him on internal inconsistencies and statements he made that were inconsistent with physical evidence. Contrary to his previous account, he stated that when he pulled up on Canfield Drive, he saw Brown in the driver's side window of the SUV from his mid-chest up. He stated that Brown and Wilson were pulling on each other's shirts until Brown backed up. Wilson then held his gun out the window and fired a shot. As a result, Brown ran from the vehicle. Contrary to his previous statement to the FBI, Witness 128 told federal prosecutors that although he heard additional shots, he did not see them because he ducked down in his vehicle. For the first time, Witness 128 mentioned the presence of a female passenger in his vehicle. He could not identify the passenger, but explained that during the shooting, his attention was diverted to her because he was trying to keep her calm, as she had become hysterical.

Witness 128 explained that when he stopped ducking for cover, he saw Brown coming back toward Wilson with his hands up. Witness 128 stated that Wilson shot Brown, causing him to fall face down to the ground. He maintained that Wilson then stood over Brown and shot into his back. When federal prosecutors asked him to reconcile those final shots with the autopsy report that shows that Brown was not shot in the back, Witness 128 said he may have hallucinated but could not offer more of an explanation. He also admitted that much of what he initially said was assumption.

As mentioned, Witness 128 was one of two witnesses who identified his voice on the aforementioned video taken in the aftermath of the shooting depicting the two contractors. Witness 128 claimed to be the person off camera shouting, "He wasn't no threat at all," because he did not perceive Brown to be a threat. However, Witness 128 acknowledged that he did not know what happened at the SUV. Contrary to what he originally told the FBI, he did not see Brown run from the SUV, was mistaken about the final shots fired, and therefore did not know whether Brown was a threat to Wilson.

Witness 128 also admitted that he spoke to Brown's mother on the day of the shooting and shared details of the shooting. Witness 128 told Brown's mother that Wilson shot Brown at point blank range while his hands were up, and that even after Brown fell to his death, Wilson stood over Brown and fired several more times. Witness 128 also told several neighbors his inaccurate version of what happened, as they were gathering in the minutes and hours after the shooting. Several individuals identified Witness 128 through description as someone who was going around spreading a narrative that Brown was shot with his hands up in surrender.

Witness 128 has been convicted of multiple felonies including crimes of dishonesty, all of which would be admissible in federal court as impeachment evidence. Witness 128's accounts are inconsistent with each other, inconsistent with the forensic and physical evidence, and inconsistent with credible witness accounts. Accordingly, after a thorough review of the evidence, federal prosecutors determined this witness's accounts to lack credibility and therefore do not support a prosecution of Darren Wilson.

xxi. Witness 140

Witness 140 is a 45-year-old white female who gave two statements to law enforcement and testified before the county grand jury. Witness 140 contacted SLCPD detectives in September 2014, claiming to have been a witness to the shooting of Brown, but too fearful to come forward when it happened. She explained that she decided it was time to come forward because she knew the case was being presented to the county grand jury and she was "tired of hearing that the officer is guilty." SLCPD and the FBI jointly interviewed Witness 140, who completely corroborated Wilson's account. Although the physical and forensic evidence was consistent with her account, the timing of her disclosure and the details of her narrative caused investigators to question her veracity. Therefore, federal prosecutors and agents conducted a follow-up interview.

During her follow-up interview, as in her initial account, Witness 140 claimed that she inadvertently ended up on Canfield Drive because she got lost on her way to visit a friend in Florissant, whom she had not seen in about 25 years. Witness 140 explained that she did not have a cell phone or a GPS, and was prone to getting lost. She pulled into the Canfield Green apartment complex to ask for directions, getting out of her car to do so. When federal prosecutors asked her why, as a woman, she would get out of her car in an unfamiliar neighborhood, she explained that she wanted to smoke a cigarette. Thereafter, while standing on the sidewalk, smoking a cigarette with a man from whom she was getting directions, she saw Wilson's SUV drive in the opposite direction of Brown and Witness 101, who were walking in the middle of the street. Witness 140 explained that she saw Wilson stop, speak to Brown and Witness 101, pull forward, and then back up. Wilson then tried to open the door of the SUV, but Brown punched it shut. Witness 101 grabbed the rearview mirror, bending it inward and catching his bracelet which broke and fell to the ground.

The specificity of this description initially caused SLCPD detectives concern because it mimicked an obscure media article which offered theories about how the SUV rearview mirror came to be folded inward and how beaded bracelets, found at the scene, landed on the ground. During Witness 140's follow-up interview, federal prosecutors asked her about this online article and Witness 140 acknowledged reading it prior to meeting with SLCPD detectives, possibly using it to fill in gaps in her memory.

According to Witness 140, she saw a struggle by the SUV, explaining that Brown was bent forward such that the top portion of his body, starting at the navel, was in the SUV. She described "childish wrestling" or "fist fighting" that ensued. She heard one gunshot from within the SUV, and then saw Brown run away, as Wilson shouted, "Stop. Freeze. I'm gonna shoot." Wilson fired a second gunshot as he got out of the SUV. Witness 140 described it as a possible "warning shot" because Brown did not "even flinch," indicating to her that he was not hit. Wilson then pursued Brown, who "made it further than where he got shot." Brown then turned around as Brown's arms flew upward, and Wilson stopped pursuing him. Brown bent forward in a "football-type" mode, hands balled up in fists, and "started charging." Witness 140 explained that Brown looked like "he was on something." Wilson looked panicked as he repeatedly shot Brown in the arm. Brown, however, kept coming at Wilson, who backed up as Brown closed the distance. Witness 140 heard a volley of four shots, a pause, and then two more shots before Brown fell to his death and "it got gross."

Witness 140 explained that she did not see Witness 101 after the initial interaction at the SUV until he reappeared five to 10 minutes after the shooting with his black t-shirt draped over his "wife-beater" tank top. This description matched how Witness 101 appeared in media interviews in the aftermath of the shooting. Also, seeing Witness 101 reappear conflicted with Witness 140's explanation that she immediately left Canfield Drive after the last shots because she was the only white woman in a neighborhood that was quickly growing hostile.

Investigators also questioned Witness 140 about the route she took out of the complex, which looks navigable on a map, but in reality is blocked by a concrete street barrier. Witness 140 responded that she is not good with directions, and was unsure the route she took. Since the shooting incident, she has acquired both a GPS and a mobile phone.

Witness 140 stated that she went immediately home and told no one about what she witnessed except her ex-husband. However, when SLCPD detectives attempted to verify this, Witness 140's ex-husband reported that Witness 140 has a tendency to lie. Witness 140's response was that her ex-husband was distrustful that the detectives were who they claimed to be. Nonetheless, Witness 140 acknowledged that she suffers from bouts of mania because she does not take her medicine for bipolar disorder and she suffered traumatic brain injury from a car crash several years ago.

Witness 140 also admitted to federal prosecutors that although she told no one about what she had witnessed, she posted comments on websites and Facebook about the shooting. Her comments were blatantly profane and racist. Furthermore, she was involved in developing a fundraising organization for first responders, and had a picture of a "thin blue line" as her Facebook profile picture.

During her testimony before the county grand jury, Witness 140 admitted that she did not get lost on Canfield Drive while en route to visit a high school friend, but rather she purposely went to Canfield Drive that day because she fears black people and was attempting to conquer her fears. However, in an effort to bolster he testimony, Witness 140 provided county prosecutors with a daily journal she claimed to keep, with one entry that documented the events of August 9. While that entry was detailed, all of the other entries were generic and sporadic.

Witness 140 was twice convicted of passing bad checks, felonies that are crimes of dishonesty and likely admissible in federal court as impeachment evidence. Although Witness 140's account of this incident is consistent with physical and forensic evidence and with credible witness accounts, large parts of her narrative have been admittedly fabricated from media accounts, and her bias in favor of Wilson is readily apparent. Accordingly, while her account likely is largely accurate, federal prosecutors determined that the account as a whole was not reliable and therefore did not consider it when making a prosecutive decision.

xxii. Witness 139

Witness 139 is 50-year-old black female. She made two statements, including her county grand jury testimony. As detailed below, Witness 139's initial account was riddled with inconsistencies from one sentence to the next. She was unable to provide a coherent narrative, and when she was asked to clarify, Witness 139 would respond with "you know what I mean," answer with a non sequitur, or break down in sobs. The details that she did provide were largely inconsistent with the physical evidence. Witness 139 was similarly incoherent and inconsistent when she testified before the county grand jury, unable to provide any sort of linear narrative.

Witness 139 reluctantly came to the NAACP office in St. Louis to meet with SLCPD detectives, FBI agents, and federal prosecutors. Through hysterical tears, she expressed fear in speaking with law enforcement because she felt pressured by the community to make a statement about what she had purportedly witnessed. She explained that ever since she gave a media interview,[25] people have been anonymously calling her. Witness 139 explained that these calls made her feel threatened, though she could not articulate how or why she felt threatened.

According to Witness 139, at about 2:30 to 3:00 p.m., she was driving eastbound on Canfield Drive, in the same direction she claimed Wilson's "four door car" was traveling, and the same direction in which Brown and Witness 101 were walking. She had difficulty distinguishing between Brown and Witness 101. Witness 139 stated that she was behind the police car, but pulled over to let him pass. Wilson then stopped his car to speak with Brown and Witness 101, though Witness 139 was inconsistent about whether two or three cars pulled past her and drove off or whether there were two or three cars in front of her when Wilson stopped. Witness 139 stated that Wilson told Brown and Witness 101 to use the sidewalk, but then said that she could not actually hear words. Rather, she just heard a deep voice. Either Brown or Witness 101 then walked toward the front of the police car and Wilson grabbed that person. Witness 139 could not be more descriptive, explaining that she had answered her mobile phone while this was happening.

Witness 139 explained that Wilson reached for his gun and held it straight out of the driver's side window, firing one or two shots. Later in her interview, she described Wilson holding the gun on the window frame when firing. Either way, Witness 139 explained that while this was happening, Witness 101 ran behind the police car. Brown was standing by the driver's side window, close enough to touch the car. However, she later described Brown being closer to the headlights of the car. When she saw those first gunshots, Witness 139 put her head down on the steering wheel, covering her eyes. Wilson then got out of his car, stood over Brown, and kept shooting. If Witness 139 was initially driving behind Wilson, she would have had the same vantage point as Witness 123 and Witness 133 in the white Monte Carlo, and therefore, would have been unable to see the driver's side of Wilson's vehicle and much of what she described.

Also inconsistent with what she initially described, Witness 139 said that Brown ran from the police car after the first two shots. She first claimed that Wilson shot Brown in the back as Brown was running, which caused Brown to turn around. Witness 139 also stated that Wilson was still getting out of his car when Brown turned around, making it unclear if Wilson shot at Brown as he was running away. To that end, Witness 139 also stated that she was not sure if the bullet struck him in the back. Regardless, Brown turned around, never moving forward from where he stood. According to Witness 139, Brown fell to the ground dead with his hands next to his head at right angles because his hands had been up. Wilson then fired at least three shots as Brown was lying face down on the ground. Witness 139 saw that Brown was bleeding from his back. When asked how she was able to witness the final shots if she had her head down in her arms, Witness 139 explained that she put her head down in her arms after the first two shots, but she could still see because she was peeking. Witness 139 claimed that when she asked Wilson if she could check on Brown because she is a nurse, he told her to "get the fuck on."

Witness 139 has no criminal history. Witness 139's account was incoherent and inconsistent throughout, markedly inconsistent with the physical and forensic evidence, and inconsistent with credible witness accounts. Wilson was driving an SUV westbound at noon, not a car eastbound at 2:30 p.m.; Wilson fired the first shot inside the SUV, not straight out the window; Brown moved toward Wilson and did not fall to his death where he turned around, nor did he die within an arm's length of the police vehicle; and Wilson did not stand over Brown and shoot him causing him to bleed from the back. Accordingly, federal prosecutors determined this witness's account not to be credible and therefore it does not support a prosecution of Darren Wilson.

xxiii. Witness 120

Witness 120 is a 19-year-old black male who said he was Brown's best friend and Witness 101's "cousin." Brown was staying with Witness 120 the night before the shooting occurred, during which time they did "a whole lot of talking about God" and "about the problems that [they have] been going through." Witness 120 explained that it seemed like Brown was "going through a phase."

Witness 120 gave three statements, including his testimony before the county grand jury. FBI agents and SCLPD detectives initially interviewed Witness 120 in the presence of his lawyer and his uncle. Witness 120 gave an internally inconsistent account that was also inconsistent with physical evidence. Federal prosecutors and agents interviewed Witness 120, with his lawyer present, in an attempt to determine what he actually witnessed.

According to Witness 120's initial account, he was on the phone on the third floor of his sister's apartment when he heard a gunshot. He instantly hopped up to look out the window because he knew that Brown and Witness 101 were walking to the store to get cigarillos to smoke marijuana later that day. When he looked out the window, Witness 120 saw Brown, who was facing the window, drop to his knees with his hands in the air, blood coming from his left shoulder and ribcage.[26] Brown's back was to the police vehicle. Witness 101 was next to Brown. Brown told Witness 101 to "run for your life." However, later in the same interview, Witness 120 stated that Witness 101 told him (Witness 120) that he, Witness 101, ran away after that first shot. When Witness 120 testified before the county grand jury, he said that he did not see Witness 101 until after the shooting was over.

According to Witness 120, Wilson then got out of the police cruiser, and positioned himself "a step away" from Brown, who stated, "Please don't shoot me." Wilson then shot Brown "point blank" in the head and Brown fell on his side. Wilson then fired eight more shots while Brown was on the ground, one of which grazed his arm.[27]

During his follow-up interview with federal prosecutors and federal agents, Witness 120 stated that he was asleep when Brown and Witness 101 left to go to the store. He woke to the sound of a gunshot. Witness 120 then repeated the same account as before: He went to the window and saw Brown on his knees with his hands up, situated about five feet from the police vehicle. Brown said, "Please don't shoot me," and Wilson fired a shot into Brown's head at "point blank" range. However, during the second interview, Witness 120 acknowledged that he never saw Wilson emerge from his vehicle and never saw any injury on Brown. Instead, he claimed that after that second shot, he ran downstairs and heard two volleys of four shots each with a pause in between. By the time he got downstairs, the gunfire had ended. Witness 120 explained that although he did not see the shots, common sense dictates that those eight shots struck Brown. He also explained that he based most of his recanted account on what people "in the community told [him]."

Although Witness 120 recanted most of his original statement, his version to federal prosecutors was still inconsistent with the autopsy results. Likewise, Witness 120 gave an inconsistent account to the county grand jury, admittedly based on rumor and hearsay, and motivated by his allegiance to his friend. When grand jurors questioned Witness 120 about inconsistencies with physical evidence, he dismissed the question, stating that Brown "was assassinated for what reason."

Witness 120's claim that Brown's body was found five feet from the police vehicle is inconsistent with the crime scene; Witness 120's description that Wilson shot Brown at point blank range is inconsistent with the autopsy results; Witness 120's description that he was at home at the time the first shots were fired is inconsistent with Witness 138's description that Witness 120 was at Witness 138's house when the shots were fired.

Witness 120 has a felony arrest that likely would be inadmissible in federal court as impeachment evidence. In addition to his accounts being riddled with inconsistencies with each other, the physical and forensic evidence, and credible witness accounts, Witness 120's account is driven by apparent bias for his friend. Accordingly, federal prosecutors determined his account to lack credibility and it does not therefore support a prosecution of Darren Wilson.

xxiv. Witness 148

Witness 148 is a 26-year-old black female who did not report to federal authorities that she witnessed the shooting until late February, 2015. Witness 148 briefly spoke to federal prosecutors via telephone to provide a summary of what she witnessed on August 9, 2014. Based on that description, federal prosecutors and agents subsequently met with Witness 148 in person.

According to Witness 148, she was driving eastbound on Canfield Drive, traveling in the same direction as Brown and Witness 101. She drove past Wilson, who was driving his SUV, and Brown and Witness 101 who were walking in the street, but right next to the curb of the sidewalk. Contrary to all other evidence, they were not in the middle of the street. She heard Wilson say, "Get the fuck on the sidewalk," and she heard either Brown or Witness 101 respond that they were near their "destination." Suspecting something was going to happen between Wilson and Brown and Witness 101 because she is from Chicago and is used to bad interactions with police, she slowed down and watched over her right shoulder, out her back window. She heard tires "screech" and saw the SUV reverse back.

Witness 148 pulled her vehicle into a nearby parking lot and parked because she wanted to see what would happen next. She told her four-year-old son to wait in her car while she got out of her vehicle and watched as Brown and Wilson engaged in a struggle on the driver side of the SUV. Witness 148 stated her that her vantage point was of the passenger side of the SUV, but she could nonetheless see Brown using his hands to push off the driver's door as Wilson pulled Brown toward the SUV. She heard Brown repeatedly state, "I didn't do anything," as Wilson stated, "Stop resisting." Despite being in a parking lot and on the opposite side of the SUV as Brown, Witness 148 stated that Brown "looked scared and it's not like he's a giant or anything." Witness 148 also stated that Brown never put his hands inside the SUV window, despite forensic and physical evidence to the contrary. However, she ultimately acknowledged to prosecutors that because she could not see the driver's side of the SUV, she did not know whether Brown put his hands inside the SUV window.

According to Witness 148, her son then got out of her vehicle because he wanted to watch what was happening. Witness 148 heard a gunshot. Witness 148 got down on the grass and covered her child's body with her own to protect him. While doing so, she watched Witness 101 and then Brown run from the SUV. After that, Witness 101 disappeared and she never saw him again. Wilson then emerged from the SUV and fired at least two shots. Brown flinched, arching his body back as though the bullet had "grazed" him. Brown then turned around and put his hands up in right angles at shoulder-height in a sign of surrender. He then dropped to his knees, and started to say something like, "I don't have a -," but was cut off as Wilson walked toward Brown firing at least six shots, killing Brown. Witness 148 described Wilson as "possessed" based on the "look in his eyes," as though "he wasn't human." It is unclear based on Witness 148's description how she was able to see both the look in Wilson's eyes and Brown trying to speak as he was surrendering, all at the same time.

Witness 148 was initially adamant that, contrary to DNA evidence in the roadway and credible witness accounts that establish otherwise, Brown never moved forward from the spot where he turned around to face Wilson. When prosecutors specifically asked her about this, Witness 148 acknowledged that because he son was squirming on the ground and she feared for his safety, her attention may have been diverted during the shooting, and therefore she may have missed parts of it. Nonetheless, she repeated that Wilson shot Brown as he was "surrendering."

When prosecutors and agents pressed Witness 148 as to why it took her nearly seven months to come forward and report what she witnessed, she explained that she feared the FPD. She maintained that she did not tell anyone – "not one living soul" – about what she witnessed on August 9, 2014. Witness 148 stated however, that she was she was not going to live in fear and therefore went to Ferguson every day since the shooting until the day of the county grand jury's decision on November 24, 2014. She protested and marched, but never shared with anyone what she witnessed, including her god-daughter who started a "Michael Brown movement." However, Witness 148 met a close friend of the Brown family after a Martin Luther King Day protest. Several weeks after that, she told the friend what she had witnessed and ultimately met with Brown's mother. Witness 148 explained that as a mother herself, she wanted to share with Brown's mother what happened to Brown.

Federal prosecutors asked Witness 148 why she chose not report to the FBI or the SLCPD, since her distrust was specific to the FPD. Witness 148 explained that she did not know that either of those agencies was investigating, despite the fact that she went to Ferguson everyday for three months and admittedly, read media reports about the shooting in the hours, days, and weeks after it occurred.

Witness 148 has felony convictions including conviction for a crime of dishonesty that would be admissible in federal court as impeachment evidence. Her account is inconsistent with the physical and forensic evidence, inconsistent with undisputed facts, *i.e.* Brown and Witness 101 were in fact walking in the middle of the street, and she admittedly did not see portions of the incident based on her vantage point and because she was protecting her child from gunfire. Similar to Witness 140, even if Witness 148 was present on Canfield Drive on August 14, 2014, and saw parts of the incident, Witness 148's account is inherently unreliable and subject to extensive cross-examination based on how she obtained her information and what motivated her to come forward. She did not report what she witnessed for nearly seven months without any reasonable explanation for the delay, giving her ample opportunity to research the facts in the form of media stories and county grand jury transcripts; she has an apparent distrust of the police (she told federal prosecutors at the outset of her interview that she "didn't trust police at all"); she is upset that "Darren Wilson got away" with what she believes to be a crime and then subsequently engaged in months of protests, but yet she failed to report it to the FBI, not because of distrust, but because she was unaware of the federal investigation. This is difficult to reconcile in light of both her daily visits to Ferguson while the FBI was canvassing the area and her regular internet searches about the shooting. For these reasons, federal prosecutors did not credit her account and could not rely upon it to support a prosecution of Darren Wilson.

xxv. Other Individuals Who Did Not Witness the Shootings

Throughout the course of the two investigations, FBI agents and SLCPD detectives both jointly and independently monitored social media, print media, and local and national television broadcasts and news reports in an effort to locate potential witnesses and sources of information. Investigators tracked down several individuals who, via the aforementioned media, claimed to have witnessed Wilson shooting Brown as Brown held his hands up in clear surrender. All of these purported witnesses, upon being interviewed by law enforcement, acknowledged that they did not actually witness the shooting, but rather repeated what others told them in the immediate aftermath of the shooting.

For example, one individual publicly posted a description of the shooting during a Facebook chat, explaining that Brown "threw his hands up in the air" as Wilson shot him dead. A Twitter user took a screenshot of the description and "tweeted" it throughout the social media site.

When the SLCPD and the FBI interviewed the individual who made the initial post, he explained that he "gave a brief description of what [he] was hearing from the people that were outside" on Canfield Drive, but he did not witness the incident itself. Similarly, another individual publicly "tweeted" about the shooting as though he had just witnessed it, even though he had not.

Likewise, another individual appeared on a television program and discussed the shooting as if he had seen it firsthand. When law enforcement interviewed him, he explained that it was a "misconception" that he witnessed the shooting. He spoke to the host of the show because he was asked if he wanted to talk about the shooting. In so doing, he was inaccurately portrayed as a witness.

Another individual recorded the aforementioned video of the contractors taken in the aftermath of the shootings. When an FBI agent and federal prosecutor met with that individual, he explained that because the video had been widely circulated in the media, many people incorrectly believed that he had witnessed the shooting. He did not witness the shootings, and was initially unsurprised to hear gunshots because it was not uncommon to hear gunfire in the neighborhood. He started recording after the gunshots abated by placing his iPad in the ground-level window of his basement apartment. He provided federal authorities with that video and other videos taken minutes after the shooting. Several videos captured conversations of bystanders on Canfield Drive, standing by police tape as paramedics covered Brown's body with two more sheets in addition to the one that was already covering him. During those conversations, bystanders discussed what transpired, although none of what was recorded was consistent with the physical evidence or credible accounts from other witnesses. For example, one woman stated that the officer shot at Brown from inside his vehicle while the SUV was still moving and then the "officer stood over [Brown] and pow-pow-pow."

Because none of these individuals actually witnessed the shooting incident and admitted so to law enforcement, federal prosecutors did not consider their inaccurate postings, tweets, media interviews, and the like when making a prosecutive decision.

IV. Legal Analysis

The evidence discussed above does not meet the standards for presentation of an indictment set forth in the USAM and in the governing federal law. The evidence is insufficient to establish probable cause or to prove beyond a reasonable doubt a violation of 18 U.S.C. § 242 and would not be likely to survive a defense motion for acquittal at trial pursuant to Federal Rule of Criminal Procedure 29(a). This is true for all six to eight shots that struck Brown. Witness accounts suggesting that Brown was standing still with his hands raised in an unambiguous signal of surrender when Wilson shot Brown are inconsistent with the physical evidence, are otherwise not credible because of internal inconsistencies, or are not credible because of inconsistencies with other credible evidence. In contrast, Wilson's account of Brown's actions, if true, would establish that the shootings were not objectively unreasonable under the relevant Constitutional standards governing an officer's use of deadly force. Multiple credible witnesses corroborate virtually every material aspect of Wilson's account and are consistent with the physical evidence. Even if the evidence established that Wilson's actions were unreasonable, the government would also have to prove that Wilson acted willfully, *i.e.* that he acted with a specific intent to violate the law. As discussed above, Wilson's stated intent for shooting Brown was in response to a perceived deadly threat. The only possible basis for prosecuting Wilson under Section 242 would therefore be if the government could prove that his account is not true – *i.e.*, that Brown never punched and grabbed Wilson at the SUV, never struggled with Wilson over the gun, and thereafter clearly surrendered in a way that no reasonable officer could have failed to perceive. Not only do eyewitnesses and physical evidence corroborate Wilson's account, but there is no credible evidence to disprove Wilson's perception that Brown posed a threat to Wilson as Brown advanced toward him. Accordingly, seeking his indictment is not permitted by Department of Justice policy or the governing law.

A. Legal Standard

To obtain a conviction of Darren Wilson at trial for his actions in shooting Michael Brown, the government must prove the following elements beyond a reasonable doubt: (1) that Wilson was acting under color of law; (2) that he acted willfully; (3) that he deprived Brown of a right protected by the Constitution or laws of the United States; and (4) that the deprivation resulted in bodily injury or death. The Constitutional right at stake depends on Brown's custodial status at the time Wilson shot him. *See Graham*, 490 U.S. at 395; *Loch v. City of Litchfield*, 689 F.3d 961, 965 (8th Cir. 2012). In this case, Wilson had attempted to stop and possibly arrest Brown. The rights of an arrestee are governed by the Fourth Amendment's prohibition against unreasonable searches and seizures, which includes the right to be free from excessive force during the course of an arrest. *See Nelson v. County of Wright*, 162 F.3d 986, 990 (8th Cir. 1998). Under the Fourth Amendment, an officer's use of force must be "objectively reasonable" under the facts and circumstances known to the officer at the time he made the decision to use physical force. *Id.* Establishing that the intent behind a Constitutional violation is "willful" requires proof that the officer acted with the purpose "to deprive a person of a right which has been made specific either by the express terms of the Constitution or laws of the United States or by decisions interpreting them." *See United States v. Lanier*, 520 U.S. 259, 267 (1997), *citing Screws v. United States*, 325 U.S. 91 (1945). While the officer need not be "thinking in Constitutional terms" when deciding to use force, he must know what he is doing is wrong and decide to do it anyway. *Screws* at 106-07. Mistake, panic, misperception, or even poor judgment by a police officer does not provide a basis for prosecution under Section 242. *See*

United States v. McClean, 528 F.2d 1250, 1255 (2d Cir. 1976) (inadvertence or mistake negates willfulness for purposes of 18 U.S.C. § 242).

There is no dispute that Wilson, who was on duty and working as a patrol officer for the FPD, acted under color of law when he shot Brown, or that the shots resulted in Brown's death. The determination of whether criminal prosecution is appropriate rests on whether there is sufficient evidence to establish that any of the shots fired by Wilson were unreasonable given the facts known to Wilson at the time, and if so, whether Wilson fired the shots with the requisite "willful" criminal intent, which, in this case, would require proof that Wilson shot Brown under conditions that no reasonable officer could have perceived as a threat.

B. Uses of Force

Under the Fourth Amendment, a police officer's use of physical force against an arrestee must be objectively reasonable under the circumstances. *Graham*, 490 U.S. at 396-97 (1989). "The 'reasonableness' of a particular use of force must be judged from the perspective of a reasonable officer on the scene, rather than with the 20/20 vision of hindsight." *Id.* at 396. "Careful attention" must be paid "to the facts and circumstances of each particular case, including the severity of the crime at issue, whether the suspect poses an immediate threat to the safety of the officers or others, and whether he is actively resisting arrest or attempting to evade arrest by flight." *Id.* Allowance must be made for the fact that law enforcement officials are often forced to make split-second judgments in circumstances that are tense, uncertain, and rapidly evolving. *Id.* at 396-97.

The use of deadly force is justified when the officer has "probable cause to believe that the suspect pose[s] a threat of serious physical harm, either to the officer or to others." *Tennessee v. Garner*, 471 U.S. 1, 11 (1985); *see Nelson*, 162 F.3d at 990; *O'Bert ex. rel. Estate of O'Bert v. Vargo*, 331 F.3d 29, 36 (2d Cir. 2003) (same as *Garner*); *Deluna v. City of Rockford*, 447 F.3d 1008, 1010 (7th Cir. 2006), *citing Scott v. Edinburg*, 346 F.3d 752, 756 (7th Cir. 2003) (deadly force can be reasonably employed where an officer believes that the suspect's actions place him, or others in the immediate vicinity, in imminent danger of death or serious bodily injury). An officer may use deadly force under certain circumstances even if the suspect is fleeing. "Where the officer has probable cause to believe that the suspect poses a threat of serious physical harm, either to the officer or to others, it is not constitutionally unreasonable to prevent escape by using deadly force. Thus, if the suspect threatens the officer with a weapon or there is probable cause to believe that he has committed a crime involving the infliction or threatened infliction of serious physical harm, deadly force may be used if necessary to prevent escape, and if, where feasible, some warning has been given." *See Garner*, 471 U.S. at 11-12.

An officer may not, on the other hand, use physical force, deadly or otherwise, once a threat has been neutralized. This is true even if the suspect threatened an officer's life – or that of another – prior to being brought under control. *See Moore v. Indehar*, 514 F.3d 756, 762 (8th Cir. 2008); *Nelson*, 162 F.3d at 990. For that reason, every instance in which Wilson shot Brown could potentially be prosecuted if the deployment of deadly force was objectively unreasonable in the particular circumstance. We must therefore determine whether, each time he fired his weapon, the available evidence could prove that Wilson acted reasonably or unreasonably in light of the facts available to him at the time. In particular, we must examine whether the available evidence shows that Wilson reasonably believed that Brown posed a threat of serious bodily harm to Wilson himself or others in the community, or whether Brown clearly attempted to surrender, prior to any of the shots fired by Wilson.

1. Shooting at the SUV

The evidence establishes that the shots fired by Wilson while he was seated in his SUV were in self-defense and thus were not objectively unreasonable under the Fourth Amendment. According to Wilson, when he backed up his SUV and attempted to get out to speak with Brown, Brown blocked him from opening the door. Brown then reached through the window and began to punch Wilson in the face, after which he reached for and gained control of Wilson's firearm by putting his hand over Wilson's hand. As Brown was struggling for the gun and pointing it into Wilson's hip, Wilson gained control of the firearm and fired it just over his lap at Brown's hand. The physical evidence corroborates Wilson's account in that the bullet was recovered from the door panel just over Wilson's lap, the base of Brown's hand displayed injuries consistent with it being within inches of the muzzle of the gun, and Wilson had injuries to his jaw consistent with being struck. Witnesses 102, 103, and 104 all state that they saw Brown with the upper portion of his body and/or arms inside the SUV as he struggled with Wilson. These witnesses have given consistent statements, and their statements are also consistent with the physical evidence.

In contrast, the two primary witnesses who state that Wilson instigated the encounter by grabbing Brown and pulling him toward the SUV and that Brown's hands were never inside the vehicle are Witnesses 101 and 127. Both of those witnesses have given accounts that are inconsistent with the forensic and physical evidence. For example, both witnesses insisted that Wilson shot Brown in the back as he fled and that they saw shots hit Brown in the back. These statements are contradicted by all three autopsies, which concluded that Brown had no entry wounds to his back. Both witnesses also insist that, after he turned to face Wilson, Brown raised his hands, never moved forward, and never reached for his waistband. While Brown might well have briefly raised his hands in some fashion (see below), the physical evidence in the form of the blood on the ground establishes that he did move forward and that he fell to the ground with his left hand near his waistband. Both of these accounts are further undermined by the witnesses' physical inability to perceive what they claim to have seen. Witness 101 was hiding behind a vehicle for significant portions of the incident and Witness 127 was looking at her cell phone, attempting to make a video recording of the encounter, and driving her car. Given the deficiencies in the accounts of these two witnesses, federal prosecutors credited the accounts of Witnesses 102, 103, 104, and Wilson and concluded that Brown did in fact reach for and attempt to grab Wilson's gun, that Brown could have overpowered Wilson, which was acknowledged even by Witness 101, and that Wilson fired his weapon just over his own lap in an attempt to regain control of a dangerous situation.

Under well-established Fourth Amendment precedent, it is not objectively unreasonable for a law enforcement officer to use deadly force in response to being physically assaulted by a subject who attempts to take his firearm. *See, e.g., Nelson,* 162 F.3d at 990-91 (holding that it was not objectively unreasonable for officer to shoot at a suspect through a closet door after suspect attempted to grab his gun, hit him in the head with an asp, and pushed him into closet). The government therefore cannot meet its burden of establishing probable cause to a grand jury or proving beyond a reasonable doubt to twelve trial jurors that the shots fired by Wilson at the SUV were unreasonable. These shots are thus not prosecutable violations of 18 U.S.C. § 242.

2. Wilson's Subsequent Pursuit of Brown and Shots Allegedly Fired as Brown Was Running Away

The evidence does not support concluding that Wilson shot Brown while Brown's back was toward Wilson. Witnesses, such as Witness 118, Witness 128, Witness 139 and others, who claim to have seen Wilson fire directly into Brown's back, gave accounts that lack credibility because the physical evidence establishes that there were no entry wounds to Brown's back, although there was a wound to the anatomical back of Brown's right arm, and a graze wound to Brown's right arm. Also, other witnesses who say that Wilson fired at Brown as he ran have given accounts that are not credible because significant aspects of their statements are irreconcilable with the physical evidence, such as Witness 101 and 127, whose statements are suspect for the reasons noted above. Similarly, Witness 124 claims to have seen Wilson following behind Brown while steadily firing at him. However, Witness 124 dramatically changed her accounts of what she saw between the time of her first statement to the SLCPD and second statement to the FBI. She refused to meet with the federal prosecutors to clarify her varying accounts. Also, her account was dramatically different from that of her husband, Witness 115, who was standing next to her during the incident. Witness 115 stated that he thought he saw Wilson fire once at Brown as he was running away, but other aspects of his account lack credibility for the reasons set forth above, *i.e.* he did not witness significant parts of the shooting and based parts of his account on assumption. Witnesses 128 and 137 initially claimed that Wilson fired at Brown while he was running away, but then acknowledged that they did not see what Wilson and Brown were doing at this point and thus do not know whether Wilson fired at Brown as he was running away. Witnesses 105 and 106 thought they saw Wilson fire at Brown as he was running, but describe seeing Brown hit in the leg and back in a manner that does not match the autopsy findings. Accordingly, there is no credible evidence that establishes that Wilson fired at or struck Brown's back as Brown fled.

3. Shots Fired After Brown Turned to Face Wilson

The evidence establishes that the shots fired by Wilson after Brown turned around were in self-defense and thus were not objectively unreasonable under the Fourth Amendment. The physical evidence establishes that after he ran about 180 feet away from the SUV, Brown turned and faced Wilson, then moved toward Wilson until Wilson finally shot him in the head and killed him. According to Wilson, Brown balled or clenched his fists and "charged" forward, ignoring commands to stop. Knowing that Brown was much larger than him and that he had previously attempted to overpower him and take his gun, Wilson stated that he feared for his safety and fired at Brown. Again, even Witness 101's account supports this perception. Brown then reached toward his waistband, causing Wilson to fear that Brown was reaching for a weapon. Wilson stated that he continued to fear for his safety at this point and fired at Brown again. Wilson finally shot Brown in the head as he was falling or lunging forward, after which Brown immediately fell to the ground. Wilson did not fire any additional shots. Wilson's version of events is corroborated by the physical evidence that indicates that Brown moved forward toward Wilson after he ran from the SUV, by the fact that Brown went to the ground with his left hand at (although not inside) his waistband, and by credible eyewitness accounts.

Wilson's version is further supported by disinterested eyewitnesses Witness 102, Witness 104, Witness 105, Witness 108, and Witness 109, among others. These witnesses all agree that Brown ran or charged toward Wilson and that Wilson shot at Brown only as Brown moved toward him. Although some of the witnesses stated that Brown briefly had his hands up or out at about waist-level, none of these witnesses perceived Brown to be attempting to surrender at any point when Wilson fired upon him. To the contrary, several of these witnesses stated that they would have felt threatened by Brown and would have responded in the same way Wilson did. For example, Witness 104 stated that as Wilson ran after Brown yelling "stop, stop, stop," Brown finally turned around and raised his hands "for a second." However, Brown then immediately balled his hands into fists and "charged" at Wilson in a "tackle run." Witness 104 stated that Wilson fired only when Brown moved toward him and that she "would have fired sooner." Likewise, Witness 105 stated that Brown turned around and put his hands up "for a brief moment," then refused a command from Wilson to "get down" and instead put his hands "in running position" and started running toward Wilson. Witness 105 stated that Wilson shot at Brown only when Brown was moving toward him. These witnesses' accounts are consistent with prior statements they have given, consistent with the forensic and physical evidence, and consistent with each other's accounts. Accordingly, we conclude that these accounts are credible.

Furthermore, there are no witnesses who could testify credibly that Wilson shot Brown while Brown was clearly attempting to surrender. The accounts of the witnesses who have claimed that Brown raised his hands above his head to surrender and said "I don't have a gun," or "okay, okay, okay" are inconsistent with the physical evidence or can be challenged in other material ways, and thus cannot be relied upon to form the foundation of a federal prosecution.[28] The two most prominent witnesses who have stated that Brown was shot with his hands up in surrender are Witness 101 and Witness 127, both of whom claim that Brown turned around with his hands raised in surrender, that he never reached for his waistband, that he never moved forward toward Wilson after turning to face him with his hands up, and that he fell to the ground with his hands raised. These and other aspects of their statements are contradicted by the physical evidence. Crime scene photographs establish that Brown fell to the ground with his left hand at his waistband and his right hand at his side. Brown's blood in the roadway demonstrates that Brown came forward at least 21.6 feet from the time he turned around toward Wilson. Other aspects of the accounts of Witness 101 and Witness 127 would render them not credible in a prosecution of Wilson, namely their accounts of what happened at the SUV. Both claim that Wilson fired the first shot out the SUV window, Witness 101 claims that the shot hit Brown at close range in the torso, and both claim that Brown did not reach inside the vehicle. These claims are irreconcilable with the bullet in the SUV door, the close-range wound to Brown's hand, Brown's DNA inside Wilson's car and on his gun, and the injuries to Wilson's face.

Other witnesses who have suggested that Brown was shot with his hands up in surrender have either recanted their statements, such as Witnesses 119 and 125, provided inconsistent statements, such as Witness 124, or have provided accounts that are verifiably untrue, such as Witnesses 121, 139, and 132. Witness 122 recanted significant portions of his statement by acknowledging that he was not in a position to see what either Brown or Wilson were doing, and who falsely insisted that three police officers pursued Brown and that the shooter was heavy set (in contrast to the slimly-built Wilson). Similar to Witness 128, Witness 122 told Brown's family that Brown had been shot execution-style. Witness 120 initially told law enforcement that he saw Brown shot at point-blank range as he was on his knees with his hands up. Similar to Witness 138, Witness 120 subsequently acknowledged that he did not see Brown get shot but "assumed" he had been executed while on his knees with his hands up based on "common sense" and what others "in the community told [him.]" There is no witness who has stated that Brown had his hands up in surrender whose statement is otherwise consistent with the physical evidence. For example, some witnesses say that Wilson only fired his weapon out of the SUV, (*e.g.* Witnesses 128, 101, and 127) or that Wilson stood next to the SUV and killed Brown right there (*e.g.* Witnesses 139, 132, 120). Some witnesses insist that Wilson shot Brown in the back as he lay on the ground. (*e.g.* Witnesses 128 and 139). Some witnesses say that Wilson shot Brown and he went to the ground immediately upon turning to face Wilson. (*e.g.* Witnesses 138, 101, 118, and 127). Some say Wilson went to the ground with his hands raised at right angles. (*e.g.* Witnesses 138, 118, and 121). Again, all of these statements are contradicted by the physical and forensic evidence, which also undermines the credibility of their accounts of other aspects of the incident, including their assertion that Brown had his hands up in a surrender position when Wilson shot him.

When the shootings are viewed, as they must be, in light of all the surrounding circumstances and what Wilson knew at the time, as established by the credible physical evidence and eyewitness testimony, it was not unreasonable for Wilson to fire on Brown until he stopped moving forward and was clearly subdued. Although, with hindsight, we know that Brown was not armed with a gun or other weapon, this fact does not render Wilson's use of deadly force objectively unreasonable. Again, the key question is whether Brown could reasonably have been perceived to pose a deadly threat to Wilson at the time he shot him regardless of whether Brown was armed. Sufficient credible evidence supports Wilson's claim that he reasonably perceived Brown to be posing a deadly threat. First, Wilson did not know that Brown was not armed at the time he shot him, and had reason to suspect that he might be when Brown reached into the waistband of his pants as he advanced toward Wilson. *See Loch v. City of Litchfield*, 689 F.3d 961, 966 (8th Cir. 2012) (holding that "[e]ven if a suspect is ultimately 'found to be unarmed, a police officer can still employ deadly force if objectively reasonable.'") (quoting *Billingsley v. City of Omaha*, 277 F.3d 990, 995 (8th Cir. 2002)); *Reese v. Anderson*, 926 F.2d 494, 501 (5th Cir. 1991) ("Also irrelevant is the fact that [the suspect] was actually unarmed. [The officer] did not and could not have known this."); *Smith v. Freland*, 954 F.2d 343, 347 (noting that "unarmed" does not mean "harmless) (6th Cir. 1992). While Brown did not use a gun on Wilson at the SUV, his aggressive actions would have given Wilson reason to at least question whether he might be armed, as would his subsequent forward advance and reach toward his waistband. This is especially so in light of the rapidly-evolving nature of the incident. Wilson did not have time to determine whether Brown had a gun and was not required to risk being shot himself in order to make a more definitive assessment.

Moreover, Wilson could present evidence that a jury likely would credit that he reasonably perceived a deadly threat from Brown even if Brown's hands were empty and he had never reached into his waistband because of Brown's actions in refusing to halt his forward movement toward Wilson. The Eighth Circuit Court of Appeals' decision in *Loch v. City of Litchfield* is dispositive on this point. There, an officer shot a suspect eight times as he advanced toward the officer. Although the suspect's "arms were raised above his head or extended at his sides," the Court of Appeals held that a reasonable officer could have perceived the suspect's forward advance in the face of the officer's commands to stop as resistance and a threat. As the Court of Appeals explained:

> Although [the suspect] had by this time thrown his firearm in the snow,...[the officer] did not observe that action. Instead of complying with [the officer's] command to get on the ground, [the suspect] turned and moved toward the officer. [Plaintiffs], noting that [the suspect's] arms were raised above his head or extended at his sides, suggest that [the suspect] was simply trying to find a suitable place to get on the ground, because his truck sat near a tree and snowbank. But even if [the suspect's] motives were innocent, a reasonable officer on the scene could have interpreted [the suspect's] actions as resistance. *It is undisputed that [the suspect] continued toward [the officer] despite the officer's repeated orders to get on the ground.... Thus, a reasonable officer could believe that [the suspect's] failure to comply was a matter of choice rather than necessity.*

Loch, 689 F.3d 961, 966 (8th Cir. 2012) (emphasis added).

Were the government to prosecute Wilson, the court would instruct the jury using *Loch* as a foundation. Given the evidence in this matter, jurors would likely conclude that Wilson had reason to be concerned that Brown was a threat to him as he continued to advance, just as did the officer in *Loch*.

In addition, even assuming that Wilson definitively knew that Brown was not armed, Wilson was aware that Brown had already assaulted him once and attempted to gain control of his gun. Wilson could thus present evidence that he reasonably feared that, if left unimpeded, Brown would again assault Wilson, again attempt to overpower him, and again attempt to take his gun. Under the law, Wilson has a strong argument that he was justified in firing his weapon at Brown as he continued to advance toward him and refuse commands to stop, and the law does not require Wilson to wait until Brown was close enough to physically assault Wilson. Even if, with hindsight, Wilson could have done something other than shoot Brown, the Fourth Amendment does not second-guess a law enforcement officer's decision on how to respond to an advancing threat. The law gives great deference to officers for their necessarily split-second judgments, especially in incidents such as this one that unfold over a span of less than two minutes. "Thus, under *Graham,* we must avoid substituting our personal notions of proper police procedure for the instantaneous decision of the officer at the scene. We must never allow the theoretical, sanitized world of our imagination to replace the dangerous and complex world that policemen face every day." *Smith*, 954 F.2d at 347 (6th Cir. 1992). *See also Ryburn v. Huff,* 132 S. Ct. 987, 991-92 (2012) (courts "should be cautious about second-guessing a police officer's assessment, made on the scene, of the danger presented by a particular situation"); *Estate of Morgan v. Cook*, 686 F.3d 494, 497 (8th Cir. 2012) ("The Constitution ...requires only that the seizure be objectively reasonable, not that the officer pursue the most prudent course of conduct as judged by 20/20 hindsight vision." (citing *Cole v. Bone*, 993 F.2d 1328, 1334 (8th Cir. 1993)) "It may appear, in the calm aftermath, that an officer could have taken a different course, but we do not hold the police to such a demanding standard." (citing *Gardner v. Buerger,* 82 F.3d 248, 251 (8th Cir. 1996) (same))). Rather, where, as here, an officer points his gun at a suspect to halt his advance, that suspect should be on notice that "escalation of the situation would result in the use of the firearm." *Estate of Morgan* at 498. An officer is permitted to continue firing until the threat is neutralized. *See Plumhoff v. Rickard*, 134 S.Ct. 2012, 2022 (2014) ("Officers need not stop shooting until the threat has ended").

For all of the reasons stated, Wilson's conduct in shooting Brown as he advanced on Wilson, and until he fell to the ground, was not objectively unreasonable and thus not a violation of 18 U.S.C. § 242.

C. Willfulness

Even if federal prosecutors determined there were sufficient evidence to convince twelve jurors beyond a reasonable doubt that Wilson used unreasonable force, federal law requires that the government must also prove that the officer acted willfully, that is, with the purpose to violate the law. *Screws v. United States*, 325 U.S. 91, 101-107 (1945) (discussing willfulness element of 18 U.S.C. § 242). The Supreme Court has held that an act is done willfully if it was "committed" either "in open defiance or in reckless disregard of a constitutional requirement which has been made specific and definite." *Screws*, 325 U.S. at 105. The government need not show that the defendant knew a federal statute or law protected the right with which he intended to interfere. *Id*. at 106-07 ("[t]he fact that the defendants may not have been thinking in constitutional terms is not material where their aim was not to enforce local law but to deprive a citizen of a right and that right was protected"); *United States v. Walsh*, 194 F.3d 37, 52-53 (2d Cir. 1999) (holding that jury did not have to find defendant knew of the particular Constitutional provision at issue but that it had to find intent to invade interest protected by Constitution). However, we must prove that the defendant intended to engage in the conduct that violated the Constitution and that he did so knowing that it was a wrongful act. *Id*.

"[A]ll the attendant circumstance[s]" should be considered in determining whether an act was done willfully. *Screws*, 325 U.S. at 107. Evidence regarding the egregiousness of the conduct, its character and duration, the weapons employed and the provocation, if any, is therefore relevant to this inquiry. *Id*. Willfulness may be inferred from blatantly wrongful conduct. *See id*. at 106; *see also United States v. Reese*, 2 F.3d 870, 881 (9th Cir. 1993) ("Intentionally wrongful conduct, because it contravenes a right definitely established in law, evidences a reckless disregard for that right; such reckless disregard, in turn, is the legal equivalent of willfulness."); *United States v. Dise*, 763 F.2d 586, 592 (3d Cir. 1985) (holding that when defendant invades personal liberty of another, knowing that invasion is violation of state law, defendant has demonstrated bad faith and reckless disregard for federal constitutional rights). Mistake, fear, misperception, or even poor judgment do not constitute willful conduct prosecutable under the statute. *See United States v. McClean*, 528 F.2d 1250, 1255 (2d Cir. 1976) (inadvertence or mistake negates willfulness for purposes of 18 U.S.C. § 242).

As discussed above, Darren Wilson has stated his intent in shooting Michael Brown was in response to a perceived deadly threat. The only possible basis for prosecuting Wilson under section 242 would therefore be if the government could prove that his account is not true – *i.e.*, that Brown never assaulted Wilson at the SUV, never attempted to gain control of Wilson's gun, and thereafter clearly surrendered in a way that no reasonable officer could have failed to perceive. Given that Wilson's account is corroborated by physical evidence and that his perception of a threat posed by Brown is corroborated by other eyewitnesses, to include aspects of the testimony of Witness 101, there is no credible evidence that Wilson willfully shot Brown as he was attempting to surrender or was otherwise not posing a threat. Even if Wilson was mistaken in his interpretation of Brown's conduct, the fact that others interpreted that conduct the same way as Wilson precludes a determination that he acted with a bad purpose to disobey the law. The same is true even if Wilson could be said to have acted with poor judgment in the manner in which he first interacted with Brown, or in pursuing Brown after the incident at the SUV. These are matters of policy and procedure that do not rise to the level of a Constitutional violation and thus cannot support a criminal prosecution. *Cf. Gardner v. Howard*, 109 F.3d 427, 430-31 (8th Cir. 1997) (violation of internal policies and procedures does not in and of itself rise to violation of Constitution).

Because Wilson did not act with the requisite criminal intent, it cannot be proven beyond reasonable doubt to a jury that he violated 18 U.S.C. § 242 when he fired his weapon at Brown.

VI. Conclusion

For the reasons set forth above, this matter lacks prosecutive merit and should be closed.

Investigation into the Policing Practices of the Ferguson Police Department

I. REPORT SUMMARY

The Civil Rights Division of the United States Department of Justice opened its investigation of the Ferguson Police Department ("FPD") on September 4, 2014. This investigation was initiated under the pattern-or-practice provision of the Violent Crime Control and Law Enforcement Act of 1994, 42 U.S.C. § 14141, the Omnibus Crime Control and Safe Streets Act of 1968, 42 U.S.C. § 3789d("Safe Streets Act"), and Title VI of the Civil Rights Act of 1964, 42 U.S.C. § 2000d ("Title VI"). This investigation has revealed a pattern or practice of unlawful conduct within the Ferguson Police Department that violates the First, Fourth, and Fourteenth Amendments to the United States Constitution, and federal statutory law.

Over the course of the investigation, we interviewed City officials, including City Manager John Shaw, Mayor James Knowles, Chief of Police Thomas Jackson, Municipal Judge Ronald Brockmeyer, the Municipal Court Clerk, Ferguson's Finance Director, half of FPD's sworn officers, and others. We spent, collectively, approximately 100 person-days onsite in Ferguson. We participated in ride-alongs with on-duty officers, reviewed over 35,000 pages of police records as well as thousands of emails and other electronic materials provided by the police department. Enlisting the assistance of statistical experts, we analyzed FPD's data on stops, searches, citations, and arrests, as well as data collected by the municipal court. We observed four separate sessions of Ferguson Municipal Court, interviewing dozens of people charged with local offenses, and we reviewed third-party studies regarding municipal court practices in Ferguson and St. Louis County more broadly. As in all of our investigations, we sought to engage the local community, conducting hundreds of in-person and telephone interviews of individuals who reside in Ferguson or who have had interactions with the police department. We contacted ten neighborhood associations and met with each group that responded to us, as well as several other community groups and advocacy organizations. Throughout the investigation, we relied on two police chiefs who accompanied us to Ferguson and who themselves interviewed City and police officials, spoke with community members, and reviewed FPD policies and incident reports.

We thank the City officials and the rank-and-file officers who have cooperated with this investigation and provided us with insights into the operation of the police department, including the municipal court.Notwithstanding our findings about Ferguson's approach to law enforcement and the policing culture it creates, we found many Ferguson police officers and other City employees to be dedicated public servants striving each day to perform their duties lawfully and with respect for all members of the Ferguson community. The importance of their often-selfless work cannot be overstated.

We are also grateful to the many members of the Ferguson community who have met with us to share their experiences. It became clear during our many conversations with Ferguson residents from throughout the City that many residents, black and white, genuinely embrace Ferguson's diversity and want to reemerge from the events of recent months a truly inclusive, united community. This Report is intended to strengthen those efforts by recognizing the harms caused by Ferguson's law enforcement practices so that those harms can be better understood and overcome.

Ferguson's law enforcement practices are shaped by the City's focus on revenue rather than by public safety needs. This emphasis on revenue has compromised the institutional character of Ferguson's police department, contributing to a pattern of unconstitutional policing, and has also shaped its municipal court, leading to procedures that raise due process concerns and inflict unnecessary harm on members of the Ferguson community. Further, Ferguson's police and municipal court practices both reflect and exacerbate existing racial bias, including racial stereotypes.Ferguson's own data establish clear racial disparities that adversely impact African Americans. The evidence shows that discriminatory intent is part of the reason for these disparities. Over time, Ferguson's police and municipal court practices have sown deep mistrust between parts of the community and the police department, undermining law enforcement legitimacy among African Americans in particular.

Focus on Generating Revenue

The City budgets for sizeable increases in municipal fines and fees each year, exhorts police and court staff to deliver those revenue increases, and closely monitors whether those increases are achieved. City officials routinely urge Chief Jackson to generate more revenue through enforcement. In March 2010, for instance, the City Finance Director wrote to Chief Jackson that "unless ticket writing ramps up significantly before the end of the year, it will be hard to significantly raise collections next year... . Given that we are looking at a substantial sales tax shortfall, it's not an insignificant issue." Similarly, in March 2013, the Finance Director wrote to the City Manager:"Court fees are anticipated to rise about 7.5%. I did ask the Chief if he thought the PD could deliver 10% increase. He indicated they could try." The importance of focusing on revenue generation is communicated to FPD officers. Ferguson police officers from all ranks told us that revenue generation is stressed heavily within the police department, and that the message comes from City leadership. The evidence we reviewed supports this perception.

Police Practices

The City's emphasis on revenue generation has a profound effect on FPD's approach to law enforcement. Patrol assignments and schedules are geared toward aggressive enforcement of Ferguson's municipal code, with insufficient thought given to whether enforcement strategies promote public safety or unnecessarily undermine community trust and cooperation. Officer evaluations and promotions depend to an inordinate degree on "productivity," meaning the number of citations issued. Partly as a consequence of City and FPD priorities, many officers appear to see some residents, especially those who live in Ferguson's predominantly African-American neighborhoods, less as constituents to be protected than as potential offenders and sources of revenue.

This culture within FPD influences officer activities in all areas of policing, beyond just ticketing. Officers expect and demand compliance even when they lack legal authority. They are inclined to interpret the exercise of free-speech rights as unlawful disobedience, innocent movements as physical threats, indications of mental or physical illness as belligerence. Police supervisors and leadership do too little to ensure that officers act in accordance with law and policy, and rarely respond meaningfully to civilian complaints of officer misconduct. The result is a pattern of stops without reasonable suspicion and arrests without probable cause in violation of the Fourth Amendment; infringement on free expression, as well as retaliation for protected expression, in violation of the First Amendment; and excessive force in violation of the Fourth Amendment.

Even relatively routine misconduct by Ferguson police officers can have significant consequences for the people whose rights are violated. For example, in the summer of 2012, a 32-year-old African-American man sat in his car cooling off after playing basketball in a Ferguson public park. An officer pulled up behind the man's car, blocking him in, and demanded the man's Social Security number and identification. Without any cause, the officer accused the man of being a pedophile, referring to the presence of children in the park, and ordered the man out of his car for a pat-down, although the officer had no reason to believe the man was armed. The officer also asked to search the man's car. The man objected, citing his constitutional rights. In response, the officer arrested the man, reportedly at gunpoint, charging him with eight violations of Ferguson's municipal code. One charge, Making a False Declaration, was for initially providing the short form of his first name (e.g., "Mike" instead of "Michael"), and an address which, although legitimate, was different from the one on his driver's license.

Another charge was for not wearing a seat belt, even though he was seated in a parked car. The officer also charged the man both with having an expired operator's license, and with having no operator's license in his possession. The man told us that, because of these charges, he lost his job as a contractor with the federal government that he had held for years.

Municipal Court Practices

Ferguson has allowed its focus on revenue generation to fundamentally compromise the role of Ferguson's municipal court. The municipal court does not act as a neutral arbiter of the law or a check on unlawful police conduct. Instead, the court primarily uses its judicial authority as the means to compel the payment of fines and fees that advance theCity's financial interests. This has led to court practices that violate the Fourteenth Amendment's due process and equal protectionrequirements. The court's practices also impose unnecessary harm, overwhelmingly on African-American individuals, and run counter to public safety.

Most strikingly, the court issues municipal arrest warrants not on the basis of public safety needs, but rather as a routine response to missed court appearances and required fine payments. In 2013 alone, the court issued over 9,000 warrants on cases stemming in large part from minor violations such as parking infractions, traffic tickets, or housing code violations. Jail time would be considered far too harsh a penalty for the great majority of these code violations, yet Ferguson's municipal court routinely issues warrants for people to be arrested and incarcerated for failing to timely pay related fines and fees. Under state law, a failure to appear in municipal court on a traffic charge involving a moving violation also results in a license suspension. Ferguson has made this penalty even more onerous by only allowing the suspension to be lifted after payment of an owed fine is made in full. Further, until recently, Ferguson also added charges, fines, and fees for each missed appearance and payment. Many pending cases still include such charges that were imposed before the court recently eliminated them, making it as difficult as before for people to resolve these cases.

The court imposes these severe penalties for missed appearances and payments even as several of the court's practices create unnecessary barriers to resolving a municipal violation. The court often fails to provide clear and accurate information regarding a person's charges or court obligations. And the court's fine assessment procedures do not adequately provide for a defendant to seek a fine reduction on account of financial incapacity or to seek alternatives to payment such as community service. City and court officials have adhered to these court practices despite acknowledging their needlessly harmful consequences. In August 2013, for example, one City Councilmember wrote to the City Manager, the Mayor, and other City officials lamenting the lack of a community service option and noted the benefits of such a program, including that it would "keep those people that simply don't have the money to pay their fines from constantly being arrested and going to jail, only to be released and do it all over again."

Together, these court practices exacerbate the harm of Ferguson's unconstitutional police practices. They impose a particular hardship upon Ferguson's most vulnerable residents, especially upon those living in or near poverty. Minor offenses can generate crippling debts, result in jail time because of an inability to pay, and result in the loss of a driver's license, employment, or housing.

We spoke, for example, with an African-American woman who has a still-pending case stemming from 2007, when, on a single occasion, she parked her car illegally. She received two citations and a $151 fine, plus fees. The woman, who experienced financial difficulties and periods of homelessness over several years, was charged with seven Failure to Appear offenses for missing court dates or fine payments on her parking tickets between 2007 and 2010. For each Failure to Appear, the court issued an arrest warrant and imposed new fines and fees. From 2007 to 2014, the woman was arrested twice, spent six days in jail, and paid $550 to the court for the events stemming from this single instance of illegal parking. Court records show that she twice attempted to make partial payments of $25 and $50, but the court returned those payments, refusing to accept anything less than payment in full. One of those payments was later accepted, but only after the court's letter rejecting payment by money order was returned as undeliverable. This woman is now making regular payments on the fine. As of December 2014, over seven years later, despite initially owing a $151 fine and having already paid $550, she still owed $541.

Racial Bias

Ferguson's approach to law enforcement both reflects and reinforces racial bias, including stereotyping. The harms of Ferguson's police and court practices are borne disproportionately by African Americans, and there is evidence that this is due in part to intentional discrimination on the basis of race.

Ferguson's law enforcement practices overwhelmingly impact African Americans. Data collected by the Ferguson Police Department from 2012 to 2014 shows that African Americans account for 85% of vehicle stops, 90% of citations, and 93% of arrests made by FPD officers, despite comprising only 67% of Ferguson's population. African Americans are more than twice as likely as white drivers to be searched during vehicle stops even after controlling for non-race based variables such as the reason the vehicle stop was initiated, but are found in possession of contraband 26% less often than white drivers, suggesting officers are impermissibly considering race as a factor when determining whether to search. African Americans are more likely to be cited and arrested following a stop regardless of why the stop was initiated and are more likely to receive multiple citations during a single incident. From 2012 to 2014, FPD issued four or more citations to African Americans on 73 occasions, but issued four or more citations to non-African Americans only twice. FPD appears to bring certain offenses almost exclusively against African Americans. For example, from 2011 to 2013, African Americans accounted for 95% of Manner of Walking in Roadway charges, and 94% of all Failure to Comply charges. Notably, with respect to speeding charges brought by FPD, the evidence shows not only that African Americans are represented at disproportionately high rates overall, but also that the disparate impact of FPD's enforcement practices on African Americans is 48% larger when citations are issued not on the basis of radar or laser, but by some other method, such as the officer's own visual assessment.

These disparities are also present in FPD's use of force. Nearly 90% of documented force used by FPD officers was used against African Americans. In every canine bite incident for which racial information is available, the person bitten was African American.

Municipal court practices likewise cause disproportionate harm to African Americans. African Americans are 68% less likely than others to have their cases dismissed by the court, and are more likely to have their cases last longer and result in more required court encounters. African Americans are at least 50% more likely to have their cases lead to an arrest warrant, and accounted for 92% of cases in which an arrest warrant was issued by the Ferguson Municipal Court in 2013. Available data show that, of those actually arrested by FPD only because of an outstanding municipal warrant, 96% are African American.

Our investigation indicates that this disproportionate burden on African Americans cannot be explained by any difference in the rate at which people of different races violate the law. Rather, our investigation has revealed that these disparities occur, at least in part, because of unlawful bias against and stereotypes about African Americans. We have found substantial evidence of racial bias among police and court staff in Ferguson. For example, we discovered emails circulated by police supervisors and court staff that stereotype racial minorities as criminals, including one email that joked about an abortion by an African-American woman being a means of crime control.

City officials have frequently asserted that the harsh and disparate results of Ferguson's law enforcement system do not indicate problems with police or court practices, but instead reflect a pervasive lack of "personal responsibility" among "certain segments" of the community. Our investigation has found that the practices about which area residents have complained are in fact unconstitutional and unduly harsh. But the City's personal-responsibility refrain is telling: it reflects many of the same racial stereotypes found in the emails between police and court supervisors. This evidence of bias and stereotyping, together with evidence that Ferguson has long recognized but failed to correct the consistent racial disparities caused by its police and court practices,demonstrates that the discriminatory effects of Ferguson's conduct are driven at least in part by discriminatory intent in violation of the Fourteenth Amendment.

Community Distrust

Since the August 2014 shooting death of Michael Brown, the lack of trust between the Ferguson Police Department and a significant portion of Ferguson's residents, especially African Americans, has become undeniable. The causes of this distrust and division, however, have been the subject of debate. Police and other City officials, as well as some Ferguson residents, have insisted to us that the public outcry is attributable to "outside agitators" who do not reflect the opinions of "real Ferguson residents." That view is at odds with the facts we have gathered during our investigation. Our investigation has shown that distrust of the Ferguson Police Department is longstanding and largely attributable to Ferguson's approach to law enforcement. This approach results in patterns of unnecessarily aggressive and at times unlawful policing; reinforces the harm of discriminatory stereotypes; discourages a culture of accountability; and neglects community engagement. In recent years, FPD has moved away from the modest community policing efforts it previously had implemented, reducing opportunities for positive police-community interactions, and losing the little familiarity it had with some African-American neighborhoods. The confluence of policing to raise revenue and racial bias thus has resulted in practices that not only violate the Constitution and cause direct harm to the individuals whose rights are violated, but also undermine community trust, especially among many African Americans. As a consequence of these practices, law enforcement is seen as illegitimate, and the partnerships necessary for public safety are, in some areas, entirely absent.

Restoring trust in law enforcement will require recognition of the harms caused by Ferguson's law enforcement practices, and diligent, committed collaboration with the entire Ferguson community. At the conclusion of this report, we have broadly identified the changes that are necessary for meaningful and sustainable reform. These measures build upon a number of other recommended changes we communicated verbally to the Mayor, Police Chief, and City Manager in September so that Ferguson could begin immediately to address problems as we identified them. As a result of those recommendations, the City and police department have already begun to make some changes to municipal court and police practices. We commend City officials for beginning to take steps to address some of the concerns we have already raised. Nonetheless, these changes are only a small part of the reform necessary. Addressing the deeply embedded constitutional deficiencies we found demands an entire reorientation of law enforcement in Ferguson. The City must replace revenue-driven policing with a system grounded in the principles of community policing and police legitimacy, in which people are equally protected and treated with compassion, regardless of race.

II. BACKGROUND

The City of Ferguson is one of 89 municipalities in St. Louis County, Missouri.[29] According to United States Census Data from 2010, Ferguson is home to roughly 21,000 residents.[30] While Ferguson's total population has stayed relatively constant in recent decades, Ferguson's racial demographics have changed dramatically during that time. In 1990, 74% of Ferguson's population was white, while 25% was black.[31] By 2000, African Americans became the new majority, making up 52% of the City's population.[32] According to the 2010 Census, the black population in Ferguson has grown to 67%, whereas the white population has decreased to 29%.[33] According to the 2009-2013 American Community Survey, 25% of the City's population lives below the federal poverty level.[34]

Residents of Ferguson elect a Mayor and six individuals to serve on a City Council. The City Council appoints a City Manager to an indefinite term, subject to removal by a Council vote. *See* Ferguson City Charter § 4.1. The City Manager serves as chief executive and administrative officer of the City of Ferguson, and is responsible for all affairs of the City. The City Manager directs and supervises all City departments, including the Ferguson Police Department.

The current Chief of Police, Thomas Jackson, has commanded the police department since he was appointed by the City Manager in 2010. The department has a total of 54 sworn officers divided among several divisions. The patrol division is the largest division; 28 patrol officers are supervised by four sergeants, two lieutenants, and a captain. Each of the four patrol squads has a canine officer. While all patrol officers engage in traffic enforcement, FPD also has a dedicated traffic officer responsible for collecting traffic stop data required by the state of Missouri. FPD has two School Resource Officers ("SROs"), one who is assigned to the McCluer South-Berkeley High School and one who is assigned to the Ferguson Middle School. FPD has a single officer assigned to be the "Community Resource Officer," who attends community meetings,serves as FPD's public relations liaison, and is charged with collecting crime data. FPD operates its own jail, which has ten individual cells and a large holding cell. The jail is staffed by three non-sworn correctional officers. Of the 54 sworn officers currently serving in FPD, four are African American.

FPD officers are authorized to initiate charges — by issuing citations or summonses, or by making arrests — under both the municipal code and state law. Ferguson's municipal code addresses nearly every aspect of civic life for those who live in Ferguson, and regulates the conduct of all who work, travel through, or otherwise visit the City. In addition to mirroring some non-felony state law violations, such as assault, stealing, and traffic violations, the code establishes housing violations, such as High Grass and Weeds; requirements for permits to rent an apartment or use the City's trash service; animal control ordinances, such as Barking Dog and Dog Running at Large; and a number of other violations, such as Manner of Walking in Roadway. *See, e.g.*, Ferguson Mun. Code §§ 29-16 *et seq.*; 37-1 *et seq.et seq.* 344.

FPD files most charges as municipal offenses, not state violations, even when an analogous state offense exists. Between July 1, 2010, and June 30, 2014, the City of Ferguson issued approximately 90,000 citations and summonses for municipal violations. Notably, the City issued nearly 50% more citations in the last year of that time period than it did in the first. This increase in enforcement has not been driven by a rise in serious crime. While the ticketing rate has increased dramatically, the number of charges for many of the most serious offenses covered by the municipal code — e.g., Assault, Driving While Intoxicated, and Stealing — has remained relatively constant.[35]

Because the overwhelming majority of FPD's enforcement actions are brought under the municipal code, most charges are processed and resolved by the Ferguson Municipal Court, which has primary jurisdiction over all code violations. Ferguson Mun. Code § 13-2. Ferguson's municipal court operates as part of the police department. The court is supervised by the Ferguson Chief of Police, is considered part of the police department for City organizational purposes, and is physically located within the police station. Court staff report directly to the Chief of Police. Thus, if the City Manager or other City officials issue a court-related directive, it is typically sent to the Police Chief's attention. In recent weeks, City officials informed us that they are considering plans to bring the court under the supervision of the City Finance Director.

A Municipal Judge presides over court sessions. The Municipal Judge is not hired or supervised by the Chief of Police, but is instead nominated by the City Manager and elected by the City Council. The Judge serves a two-year term, subject to reappointment. The current Municipal Judge, Ronald Brockmeyer, has presided in Ferguson for approximately ten years. The City's Prosecuting Attorney and her assistants officially prosecute all actions before the court, although in practice most cases are resolved without trial ora prosecutor's involvement. The current Prosecuting Attorney was appointed in April 2011. At the time of her appointment, the Prosecuting Attorney was already serving as City Attorney, and she continues to serve in that separate capacity, which entails providing general counsel and representation to the City. The Municipal Judge, Court Clerk, Prosecuting Attorney, and all assistant court clerks are white.

While the Municipal Judge presides over court sessions, the Court Clerk, who is employed under the Police Chief's supervision, plays the most significant role in managing the court and exercises broad discretion in conducting the court's daily operations. Ferguson's municipal code confers broad authority on the Court Clerk, including the authority to collect all fines and fees, accept guilty pleas, sign and issue subpoenas, and approve bond determinations. Ferguson Mun. Code § 13-7. Indeed, the Court Clerk and assistant clerks routinely perform duties that are, for all practical purposes, judicial. For example, documents indicate that court clerks have disposed of charges without the Municipal Judge's involvement.

The court officially operates subject to the oversight of the presiding judge of the St. Louis County Circuit Court (21ˢᵗ Judicial Circuit) under the rules promulgated by that Circuit Court and the Missouri Supreme Court. Notwithstanding these rules, the City of Ferguson and the court itself retain considerable power to establish and amend court practices and procedures. The Ferguson municipal code sets forth a limited number of protocols that the court must follow, but the code leaves most aspects of court operations to the discretion of the court itself. *See* Ferguson Mun. Code Ch. 13, Art. III. The code also explicitly authorizes the Municipal Judge to "make and adopt such rules of practice and procedure as are necessary to hear and decide matters pending before the municipal court." Ferguson Mun. Code § 13-29.

The Ferguson Municipal Court has the authority to issue and enforce judgments, issue warrants for search and arrest, hold parties in contempt, and order imprisonment as a penalty for contempt. The court may conduct trials, although it does so rarely, and most charges are resolved without one. Upon resolution of a charge, the court has the authority to impose fines, fees, and imprisonment when violations are found. Specifically, the court can impose imprisonment in the Ferguson City Jail for up to three months, a fine of up to $1,000, or a combination thereof. It is rare for the court to sentence anyone to jail as a *penalty* for a violation of the municipal code; indeed, the Municipal Judge reports that he has done so only once. Rather, the court almost always imposes a monetary penalty payable to the City of Ferguson, plus court fees. Nonetheless, as discussed in detail below, the court issues arrest warrants when a person misses a court appearance or fails to timely pay a fine. As a result, violations that would normally not result in a penalty of imprisonment can, and frequently do, lead to municipal warrants, arrests, and jail time.

As the number of charges initiated by FPD has increased in recent years, the size of the court's docket has also increased. According to data the City reported to the Missouri State Courts Administrator, at the end of fiscal year 2009, the municipal court had roughly 24,000 traffic cases and 28,000 non-traffic cases pending. As of October 31, 2014, both of those figures had roughly doubled to 53,000 and 50,000 cases, respectively. In fiscal year 2009, 16,178 new cases were filed, and 8,727 were resolved. In 2014, by contrast, 24,256 new offenses were filed, and 10,975 offenses were resolved.

The court holds three or four sessions per month, and each session lasts no more than three hours. It is not uncommon for as many as 500 people to appear before the court in a single session, exceeding the court's physical capacity and leading individuals to line up outside of court waiting to be heard. Many people have multiple offenses pending; accordingly, the court typically considers 1,200-1,500 offenses in a single session, and has in the past considered over 2,000 offenses during one sitting. Previously there was a cap on the number of offenses that could be assigned to a particular docket date. Given that cap, and the significant increase in municipal citations in recent years, a problem developed in December 2011 in which more citations were issued than court sessions could timely accommodate. At one point court dates were initially scheduled as far as six months after the date of the citation. To address this problem, court staff first raised the cap to allow 1,000 offenses to be assigned to a single court date and later eliminated the cap altogether. To handle the increasing caseload, the City Manager also requested and secured City Council approval to fund additional court positions, noting in January 2013 that "each month we are setting new all-time records in fines and forfeitures," that this was overburdening court staff, and that the funding for the additional positions"will be more than covered by the increase in revenues."

III. FERGUSON LAW ENFORCEMENT EFFORTS ARE FOCUSED ON GENERATING REVENUE

City officials have consistently set maximizing reven ue as the priority for Ferguson's law enforcement activity. Ferguson generates a significant and increasing amount of revenue from the enforcement of code provisions. The City has budgeted for, and achieved, significant increases in revenue from municipal code enforcement over the last several years, and these increases are projected to continue. Of the $11.07 million in general fund revenue the City collected in fiscal year 2010, $1.38 million came from fines and fees collected by the court; similarly, in fiscal year 2011, the City's general fund revenue of $11.44 million included $1.41 million from fines and fees. In its budget for fiscal year 2012, however, the City predicted that revenue from municipal fines and fees would increase over 30% from the previous year's amount to $1.92 million; the court exceeded that target, collecting $2.11 million. In its budget for fiscal year 2013, the City budgeted for fines and fees to yield $2.11 million; the court exceeded that target as well, collecting $2.46 million. For 2014, the City budgeted for the municipal court to generate $2.63 million in revenue. The City has not yet made public the actual revenue collected that year, although budget documents forecasted lower revenue than was budgeted. Nonetheless, for fiscal year 2015, the City's budget anticipates fine and fee revenues to account for $3.09 million of a projected $13.26 million in general fund revenues.[36]

City, police, and court officials for years have worked in concert to maximize revenue at every stage of the enforcement process, beginning with how fines and fine enforcement processes are established. In a February 2011 report requested by the City Council at a Financial Planning Session and drafted by Ferguson's Finance Director with contributions from Chief Jackson, the Finance Director reported on "efforts to increase efficiencies and maximize collection" by the municipal court. The report included an extensive comparison of Ferguson's fines to those of surrounding municipalities and noted with approval that Ferguson's fines are "at or near the top of the list." The chart noted, for example, that while other municipalities' parking fines generally range from $5 to $100, Ferguson's is $102. The chart noted also that the charge for "Weeds/Tall Grass" was as little as $5 in one city but, in Ferguson, it ranged from $77 to $102. The report stated that the acting prosecutor had reviewed the City's "high volume offenses" and "started recommending higher fines on these cases, and recommending probation only infrequently." While the report stated that this recommendation was because of a "large volume of non-compliance," the recommendation was in fact emphasized as one of several ways that the code enforcement system had been honed to produce more revenue.

In combination with a high fine schedule, the City directs FPD to aggressively enforce the municipal code. City and police leadership pressure officers to write citations, independent of any public safety need, and rely on citation productivity to fund the City budget. In an email from March 2010, the Finance Director wrote to Chief Jackson that "unless ticket writing ramps up significantly before the end of the year, it will be hard to significantly raise collections next year. What are your thoughts? Given that we are looking at a substantial sales tax shortfall, it's not an insignificant issue." Chief Jackson responded that the City would see an increase in fines once more officers were hired and that he could target the $1.5 million forecast. Significantly, Chief Jackson stated that he was also "looking at different shift schedules which will place more officers on the street, which in turn will increase traffic enforcement per shift." Shortly thereafter, FPD switched to the 12-hour shift schedule for its patrol officers, which FPD continues to use. Law enforcement experience has shown that this schedule makes community policing more difficult — a concern that we have also heard directly from FPD officers. Nonetheless, while FPD heavily considered the revenue implications of the 12-hour shift and certain other factors such as its impact on overtime and sick time usage, we have found no evidence that FPD considered the consequences for positive community engagement. The City's 2014 budget itself stated that since December 2010, "the percent of [FPD] resources allocated to traffic enforcement has increased," and "[a]s a result, traffic enforcement related collections increased" in the following two years. The 2015 budget added that even after those initial increases, in fiscal year 2012-2013,FPD was once again "successful in increasing their proportion of resources dedicated to traffic enforcement" and increasing collections.

As directed, FPD supervisors and line officers have undertaken the aggressive code enforcement required to meet the City's revenue generation expectations. As discussed below in Part III.A., FPD officers routinely conduct stops that have little relation to public safety and a questionable basis in law. FPD officers routinely issue multiple citations during a single stop, often for the same violation. Issuing three or four charges in one stop is not uncommon in Ferguson. Officers sometimes write six, eight, or, in at least one instance, fourteen citations for a single encounter. Indeed, officers told us that some compete to see who can issue the largest number of citations during a single stop.

The February 2011 report to the City Council notes that the acting prosecutor — with the apparent approval of the Police Chief — "talked with police officers about ensuring all necessary summonses are written for each incident, i.e. when DWI charges are issued, are the correct companion charges being issued, such as speeding, failure to maintain a single lane, no insurance, and no seat belt, etc." The prosecutor noted that "[t]his is done to ensure that a proper resolution to all cases is being achieved and that the court is maintaining the correct volume for offenses occurring within the city." Notably, the "correct volume" of law enforcement is uniformly presented in City documents as related to revenue generation, rather than in terms of what is necessary to promote public safety.[37] Each month, the municipal court provides FPD supervisors with a list of the number of tickets issued by each officer and each squad. Supervisors have posted the list inside the police station, a tactic officers say is meant to push them to write more citations.

The Captain of FPD's Patrol Division regularly communicates with his Division commanders regarding the need to increase traffic "productivity," and productivity is a common topic at squad meetings. Patrol Division supervisors monitor productivity through monthly "self-initiated activity reports" and instruct officers to increase production when those reports show they have not issued enough citations. In April 2010, for example, a patrol supervisor criticized a sergeant for his squad only issuing 25 tickets in a month, including one officer who issued "a grand total" of 11 tickets to six people on three days "devoted to traffic stops." In November 2011, the same patrol supervisor wrote to his patrol lieutenants and sergeants that "[t]he monthly self-initiated activity totals just came out," and they "may want to advise [their] officers who may be interested in the open detective position that one of the categories to be considered when deciding on the eligibility list will be self-initiated activity." The supervisor continued:"Have any of you heard comments such as, why should I produce when I know I'm not getting a raise? Well, some people are about to find out why." The email concludes with the instruction to "[k]eep in mind, productivity (self-initiated activity) cannot decline for next year."

FPD has communicated to officers not only that they must focus on bringing in revenue, but that the department has little concern with how officers do this. FPD's weak systems of supervision, review, and accountability, discussed below in Part III.A., have sent a potent message to officers that their violations of law and policy will be tolerated, provided that officers continue to be "productive" in making arrests and writing citations. Where officers fail to meet productivity goals, supervisors have been instructed to alter officer assignments or impose discipline. In August 2012, the Captain of the Patrol Division instructed other patrol supervisors that,"[f]or those officers who are not keeping up an acceptable level of productivity and they have already been addressed at least once if not multiple times, take it to the next level." He continued: "As we have discussed already, regardless of the seniority and experience take the officer out of the cover car position and assign them to prisoner pick up and bank runs... . Failure to perform *can*result in disciplinary action not just a bad evaluation." Performance evaluations also heavily emphasize productivity. A June 2013 evaluation indicates one of the "Performance-Related Areas of Improvements" as "Increase/consistent in productivity, the ability to maintain an average ticket [sic]of 28 per month."

Not all officers within FPD agree with this approach. Several officers commented on the futility of imposing mounting penalties on people who will never be able to afford them. One member of FPD's command staff quoted an old adage, asking: "How can you get blood from a turnip?" Another questioned why FPD did not allow residents to use their limited resources to fix equipment violations, such as broken headlights, rather than paying that money to the City, as fixing the equipment violation would more directly benefit public safety.[38]

However, enough officers — at all ranks — have internalized this message that a culture of reflexive enforcement action, unconcerned with whether the police action actually promotes public safety, and unconcerned with the impact the decision has on individual lives or community trust as a whole, has taken hold within FPD. One commander told us, for example, that when he admonished an officer for writing too many tickets, the officer challenged the commander, asking if the commander was telling him not to do his job. When another commander tried to discipline an officer for over-ticketing, he got the same response from the Chief of Police: "No discipline for doing your job."

The City closely monitors whether FPD's enforcement efforts are bringing in revenue at the desired rate. Consistently over the last several years, the Police Chief has directly reported to City officials FPD's successful efforts at raising revenue through policing, and City officials have continued to encourage those efforts and request regular updates. For example, in June 2010, at the request of the City, the Chief prepared a report comparing court revenues in Ferguson to court revenues for cities of similar sizes. The Chief's email sending the report to the City Manager notes that,"of the 80 St. Louis County Municipal Courts reporting revenue, only 8, including Ferguson, have collections greater than one million dollars." In the February 2011 report referenced above, Chief Jackson discussed various obstacles to officers writing tickets in previous months, such as training, injury leave, and officer deployment to Iraq, but noted that those factors had subsided and that, as a result, revenues were increasing. The acting prosecutor echoed these statements, stating "we now have several new officers writing tickets, and as a result our overall ticket volume is increasing by 400-700 tickets per month. This increased volume will lead to larger dockets this year and should have a direct effect in increasing overall revenue to the municipal court."

Similarly, in March 2011, the Chief reported to the City Manager that court revenue in February was $179,862.50,and that the total "beat our next biggest month in the last four years by over $17,000," to which the City Manager responded: "Wonderful!" In a June 2011 email from Chief Jackson to the Finance Director and City Manager, the Chief reported that "May is the 6th straight month in which court revenue (gross) has exceeded the previous year." The City Manager again applauded the Chief's efforts, and the Finance Director added praise, noting that the Chief is "substantially in control of the outcome." The Finance Director further recommended in this email greater police and judicial enforcement to"have a profound effect on collections." Similarly, in a January 2013 email from Chief Jackson to the City Manager, the Chief reported: "Municipal Court gross revenue for calendar year 2012 passed the $2,000,000 mark for the first time in history, reaching $2,066,050 (not including red light photo enforcement)." The City Manager responded: "Awesome! Thanks!" In one March 2012 email, the Captain of the Patrol Division reported directly to the City Manager that court collections in February 2012 reached $235,000, and that this was the first month collections ever exceeded $200,000. The Captain noted that "[t]he [court clerk] girls have been swamped all day with a line of people paying off fines today. Since 9:30 this morning there hasn't been less than 5 people waiting in line and for the last three hours 10 to 15 people at all times." The City Manager enthusiastically reported the Captain's email to the City Council and congratulated both police department and court staff on their "great work."

Even as officers have answered the call for greater revenue through code enforcement, the City continues to urge the police department to bring in more money. In a March 2013 email, the Finance Director wrote: "Court fees are anticipated to rise about 7.5%. I did ask the Chief if he thought the PD could deliver 10% increase. He indicated they could try." Even more recently, the City's Finance Director stated publicly that Ferguson intends to make up a 2014 revenue shortfall in 2015 through municipal code enforcement, stating to Bloomberg News that "[t]here's about a million-dollar increase in public-safety fines to make up the difference."[39] The City issued a statement to "refute[]" the Bloomberg article in part because it"insinuates" an "over reliance on municipal court fines as a primary source of revenues when in fact they represented less than 12% of city revenues for the last fiscal year." But there is no dispute that the City budget does, in fact, forecast an increase of nearly a million dollars in municipal code enforcement fines and fees in 2015 as reported in the Bloomberg News report.

The City goes so far as to direct FPD to develop enforcement strategies and initiatives, not to better protect the public, but to raise more revenue. In an April 2014 communication from the Finance Director to Chief Jackson and the City Manager, the Finance Director recommended immediate implementation of an "I-270 traffic enforcement initiative" in order to "begin to fill the revenue pipeline." The Finance Director's email attached a computation of the net revenues that would be generated by the initiative, which required paying five officers overtime for highway traffic enforcement for a four-hour shift. The Finance Director stated that"there is nothing to keep us from running this initiative 1,2,3,4,5,6, or even 7 days a week. Admittedly at 7 days per week[] we would see diminishing returns." Indeed, in a separate email to FPD supervisors, the Patrol Captain explained that "[t]he plan behind this [initiative] is to PRODUCE traffic tickets, not provide easy OT." There is no indication that anyone considered whether community policing and public safety would be better served by devoting five overtime officers to neighborhood policing instead of a"revenue pipeline" of highway traffic enforcement. Rather, the only downsides to the program that City officials appear to have considered are that "this initiative requires 60 to 90 [days] of lead time to turn citations into cash," and that Missouri law caps the proportion of revenue that can come from municipal fines at 30%, which limits the extent to which the program can be used. *See* Mo. Rev. Stat. § 302.341.2. With regard to the statewide-cap issue, the Finance Director advised: "As the RLCs [Red Light Cameras] net revenues ramp up to whatever we believe its annualized rate will be, then we can figure out how to balance the two programs to get their total revenues as close as possible to the statutory limit of 30%."[40]

The City has made clear to the Police Chief and the Municipal Judge that revenue generation must also be a priority in court operations. The Finance Director's February 2011 report to the City Council notes that "Judge Brockmeyer was first appointed in 2003, and during this time has been successful in significantly increasing court collections over the years." The report includes a list of "what he has done to help in the areas of court efficiency and revenue." The list, drafted by Judge Brockmeyer, approvingly highlights the creation of additional fees, many of which are widely considered abusive and may be unlawful, including several that the City has repealed during the pendency of our investigation. These include a $50 fee charged each time a person has a pending municipal arrest warrant cleared, and a "failure to appear fine," which the Judge noted is "increased each time the Defendant fails to appear in court or pay a fine." The Judge also noted increasing fines for repeat offenders, "especially in regard to housing violations, [which] have increased substantially and will continue to be increased upon subsequent violations." The February 2011 report notes Judge Brockmeyer's statement that "none of these changes could have taken place without the cooperation of the Court Clerk, the Chief of Police, and the Prosecutor's Office." Indeed, the acting prosecutor noted in the report that "I have denied defendants' needless requests for continuance from the payment docket in an effort to aid in the court's efficient collection of its fines."

Court staff are keenly aware that the City considers revenue generation to be the municipal court's primary purpose. Revenue targets for court fines and fees are created in consultation not only with Chief Jackson, but also the Court Clerk. In one April 2010 exchange with Chief Jackson entitled "2011 Budget," for example, the Finance Director sought and received confirmation that the Police Chief and the Court Clerk would prepare targets for the court's fine and fee collections for subsequent years. Court staff take steps to ensure those targets are met in operating court. For example, in April 2011, the Court Clerk wrote to Judge Brockmeyer (copying Chief Jackson) that the fines the new Prosecuting Attorney was recommending were not high enough. The Clerk highlighted one case involving three Derelict Vehicle charges and a Failure to Comply charge that resulted in $76 in fines, and noted this "normally would have brought a fine of all three charges around $400." After describing another case that she believed warranted higher fines, the Clerk concluded: "We need to keep up our revenue." There is no indication that ability to pay or public safety goals were considered.

The City has been aware for years of concerns about the impact its focus on revenue has had on lawful police action and the fair administration of justice in Ferguson. It has disregarded those concerns — even concerns raised from within the City government — to avoid disturbing the court's ability to optimize revenue generation. In 2012, a Ferguson City Councilmember wrote to other City officials in opposition to Judge Brockmeyer's reappointment, stating that "[the Judge] does not listen to the testimony, does not review the reports or the criminal history of defendants, and doesn't let all the pertinent witnesses testify before rendering a verdict." The Councilmember then addressed the concern that "switching judges would/could lead to loss of revenue," arguing that even if such a switch did "lead to a slight loss, I think it's more important that cases are being handled properly and fairly." The City Manager acknowledged mixed reviews of the Judge's work but urged that the Judge be reappointed, noting that "[i]t goes without saying the City cannot afford to lose any efficiency in our Courts, nor experience any decrease in our Fines and Forfeitures."

IV. FERGUSON LAW ENFORCEMENT PRACTICES VIOLATE THE LAW AND UNDERMINE COMMUNITY TRUST, ESPECIALLY AMONG AFRICAN AMERICANS

Ferguson's strategy of revenue generation through policing has fostered practices in the two central parts of Ferguson's law enforcement system — policing and the courts — that are themselves unconstitutional or that contribute to constitutional violations. In both parts of the system, these practices disproportionately harm African Americans. Further, the evidence indicates that this harm to African Americans stems, at least in part, from racial bias, including racial stereotyping. Ultimately, unlawful and harmful practices in policing and in the municipal court system erode police legitimacy and community trust, making policing in Ferguson less fair, less effective at promoting public safety, and less safe.

A.Ferguson's Police Practices

FPD's approach to law enforcement, shaped by the City's pressure to raise revenue, has resulted in a pattern and practice of constitutional violations. Officers violate the Fourth Amendment in stopping people without reasonable suspicion, arresting them without probable cause, and using unreasonable force. Officers frequently infringe on residents' First Amendment rights, interfering with their right to record police activities and making enforcement decisions based on the content of individuals' expression.

FPD's lack of systems to detect and hold officers responsible for misconduct reflects the department's focus on revenue generation at the expense of lawful policing and helps perpetuate the patterns of unconstitutional conduct we found. FPD fails to adequately supervise officers or review their enforcement actions. While FPD collects vehicle-stop data because it is required to do so by state law, it collects no reliable or consistent data regarding pedestrian stops, even though it has the technology to do so.[41] In Ferguson, officers will sometimes make an arrest without writing a report or even obtaining an incident number, and hundreds of reports can pile up for months without supervisors reviewing them. Officers' uses of force frequently go unreported, and are reviewed only laxly when reviewed at all. As a result of these deficient practices, stops, arrests, and uses of force that violate the law or FPD policy are rarely detected and often ignored when they are discovered.

1. FPD Engages in a Pattern of Unconstitutional Stops and Arrests in Violation of the Fourth Amendment

FPD's approach to law enforcement has led officers to conduct stops and arrests that violate the Constitution. We identified several elements to this pattern of misconduct. Frequently, officers stop people without reasonable suspicion or arrest them without probable cause. Officers rely heavily on the municipal "Failure to Comply" charge, which appears to be facially unconstitutional in part, and is frequently abused in practice. FPD also relies on a system of officer-generated arrest orders called "wanteds" that circumvents the warrant system and poses a significant risk of abuse. The data show, moreover, that FPD misconduct in the area of stops and arrests disproportionately impacts African Americans.

a. FPD Officers Frequently Detain People Without Reasonable Suspicion and Arrest People Without Probable Cause

The Fourth Amendment protects individuals from unreasonable searches and seizures. Generally, a search or seizure is unreasonable "in the absence of individualized suspicion of wrongdoing." *City of Indianapolis v. Edmond*, 531 U.S. 32, 37 (2000). The Fourth Amendment permits law enforcement officers to briefly detain individuals for investigative purposes if the officers possess reasonable suspicion that criminal activity is afoot. *Terry v. Ohio*, 392 U.S. 1, 21 (1968). Reasonable suspicion exists when an "officer is aware of particularized, objective facts which, taken together with rational inferences from those facts, reasonably warrant suspicion that a crime is being committed." *United States v. Givens*, 763 F.3d 987, 989 (8th Cir. 2014) (internal quotation marks omitted). In addition, if the officer reasonably believes the person with whom he or she is dealing is armed and dangerous, the officer may conduct a protectivesearch or frisk of the person's outer clothing. *United States v. Cotter*, 701 F.3d 544, 547 (8th Cir. 2012). Such a search is not justified on the basis of "inchoate and unparticularized suspicion;" rather, the "issue is whether a reasonably prudent man in the circumstances would be warranted in the belief that his safety or that of others was in danger." *Id.* (quoting *Terry*, 392 U.S. at 27). For an arrest to constitute a reasonable seizure under the Fourth Amendment, it must be supported by probable cause, which exists only if "the totality of facts based on reasonably trustworthy information would justify a prudent person in believing the individual arrested had committed an offense at the time of the arrest." *Stoner v. Watlingten*, 735 F.3d 799, 803 (8th Cir. 2013).

Under Missouri law, when making an arrest, "[t] he officer must inform the defendant by what authority he acts, and must also show the warrant if required." Mo. Rev. Stat. § 544.180. In reviewing FPD records, we found numerous incidents in which — based on the officer's own description of the detention — an officer detained an individual without articulable reasonable suspicion of criminal activity or arrested a person without probable cause. In none of these cases did the officer explain or justify his conduct.

For example, in July 2013 police encountered an African-American man in a parking lot while on their way to arrest someone else at an apartment building. Police knew that the encountered man was not the person they had come to arrest. Nonetheless, without even reasonable suspicion, they handcuffed the man, placed him in the back of a patrol car, and ran his record. It turned out he was the intended arrestee's landlord. The landlord went on to help the police enter the person's unit to effect the arrest, but he later filed a complaint alleging racial discrimination and unlawful detention. Ignoring the central fact that they had handcuffed a man and put him in a police car despite having no reason to believe he had done anything wrong, a sergeant vigorously defended FPD's actions, characterizing the detention as "minimal" and pointing out that the car was air conditioned. Even temporary detention, however, constitutes a deprivation of liberty and must be justified under the Fourth Amendment. *Whren v. United States*, 517 U.S. 806, 809-10 (1996).

Many of the unlawful stops we found appear to have been driven, in part, by an officer's desire to check whether the subject had a municipal arrest warrant pending. Several incidents suggest that officers are more concerned with issuing citations and generating charges than with addressing community needs. In October 2012, police officers pulled over an African-American man who had lived in Ferguson for 16 years, claiming that his passenger-side brake light was broken. The driver happened to have replaced the light recently and knew it to be functioning properly. Nonetheless, according to the man's written complaint, one officer stated, "let's see how many tickets you'regoing to get," while a second officer tapped his Electronic Control Weapon("ECW") on the roof of the man's car. The officers wrote the man a citation for "tail light/reflector/license plate light out." They refused to let the man show them that his car's equipment was in order, warning him, "don't you get out of that car until you get to your house." The man, who believed he had been racially profiled, was so upset that he went to the police station that night to show a sergeant that his brakes and license plate light worked.

At times, the constitutional violations are even more blatant. An African-American man recounted to us an experience he had while sitting at a bus stop near Canfield Drive. According to the man, an FPD patrol car abruptly pulled up in front of him. The officer inside, a patrol lieutenant, rolled down his window and addressed the man:

> Lieutenant: Get over here.
> Bus Patron: Me?
> Lieutenant: Get the f*** over here. Yeah, you.
> Bus Patron: Why? What did I do?
> Lieutenant: Give me your ID.
> Bus Patron: Why?
> Lieutenant: Stop being a smart ass and give me your ID.

The lieutenant ran t he man's name for warrants. Finding none, he returned the ID and said, "get the hell out of my face." These allegations are consistent with other, independent allegations of misconduct that we heard about this particular lieutenant, and reflect the routinely disrespectful treatment many African Americans say they have come to expect from Ferguson police. That a lieutenant with supervisory responsibilities allegedly engaged in this conduct is further cause for concern.

This incident is also consistent with a pattern of suspicionless, legally unsupportable stops we found documented in FPD's records, described by FPD as "ped checks" or "pedestrian checks." Though at times officers use the term to refer to reasonable-suspicion-based pedestrian stops, or "*Terry* stops," they often use it when stopping a person with no objective, articulable suspicion. For example, one night in December 2013, officers went out and "ped. checked those wandering around" in Ferguson's apartment complexes. In another case, officers responded to a call about a man selling drugs by stopping a group of six African-American youths who, due to their numbers, did not match the facts of the call. The youths were "detained and ped checked." Officers invoke the term "ped check" as though it has some unique constitutional legitimacy. It does not. Officers may not detain a person, even briefly, without articulable reasonable suspicion. *Terry*, 392 U.S. at 21. To the extent that the words "ped check" suggest otherwise, the terminology alone is dangerous because it threatens to confuse officers' understanding of the law. Moreover, because FPD does not track or analyze pedestrian *Terry* stops — whether termed "ped checks" or something else — in any reliable way, they are especially susceptible to discriminatory or otherwise unlawful use.

As with its pattern of unconstitutional stops, FPD routinely makes arrests without probable cause. Frequently, officers arrest people for conduct that plainly does not meet the elements of the cited offense. For example, in November 2013, an officer approached five African-American young people listening to music in a car. Claiming to have smelled marijuana, the officer placed them under arrest for disorderly conduct based on their "gathering in a group for the purposes of committing illegal activity." The young people were detained and charged — some taken to jail, others delivered to their parents — despite the officer finding no marijuana, even after conducting an inventory search of the car. Similarly, in February 2012, an officer wrote an arrest notification ticket for Peace Disturbance for"loud music" coming from a car. The arrest ticket appears unlawful as the officer did not assert, and there is no other indication, that a third party was disturbed by the music — an element of the offense. *See See* 82 (prohibiting certain conduct that "unreasonably and knowingly disturbs or alarms another person or persons"). Nonetheless, a supervisor approved it. These warrantless arrests violated the Fourth Amendment because they were not based on probable cause. *See Virginia v. Moore*, 553 U.S. 164, 173 (2008).

While the record demonstrates a pattern of stops that are improper from the beginning, it also exposes encounters that start as constitutionally defensible but quickly cross the line. For example, in the summer of 2012, an officer detained a 32-year-old African-American man who was sitting in his car cooling off after playing basketball. The officer arguably had grounds to stop and question the man, since his windows appeared more deeply tinted than permitted under Ferguson's code. Without cause, the officer went on to accuse the man of being a pedophile, prohibit the man from using his cell phone, order the man out of his car for a pat-down despite having no reason to believe he was armed, and ask to search his car. When the man refused, citing his constitutional rights, the officer reportedly pointed a gun at his head, and arrested him. The officer charged the man with eight different counts, including making a false declaration for initially providing the short form of his first name (e.g., "Mike" instead of "Michael") and an address that, although legitimate, differed from the one on his license. The officer also charged the man both with having an expired operator's license, and with having no operator's license in possession. The man told us he lost his job as a contractor with the federal government as a result of the charges.

b. FPD Officers Routinely Abuse the "Failure to Comply" Charge

One area of FPD activity deserves special attention for its frequency of Fourth[42] Amendment violations: enforcement of Ferguson's Failure to Comply municipal ordinance. Ferguson Mun. Code § 29-16. Officers rely heavily on this charge to arrest individuals who do not do what they ask, even when refusal is not a crime. The offense is typically charged under one of two subsections. One subsection prohibits disobeying a lawful order in a way that hinders an officer's duties, § 29-16(1); the other requires individuals to identify themselves, § 29-16(2). FPD engages in a pattern of unconstitutional enforcement with respect to both, resulting in many unlawful arrests.

i. Improper Enforcement of Code Provision Prohibiting Disobeying a Lawful Order

Officers frequently arrest individuals under Section 29-16(1) on facts that do not meet the provision's elements. Section 29-16(1)makes it unlawful to "[f]ail to comply with the lawful order or request of a police officer in the discharge of the officer's official duties where such failure interfered with, obstructed or hindered the officer in the performance of such duties." Many cases initiated under this provision begin with an officer ordering an individual to stop despite lacking objective indicia that the individual is engaged in wrongdoing. The order to stop is not a "lawful order" under those circumstances because the officer lacks reasonable suspicion that criminal activity is afoot. *See United States v. Brignoni-Ponce*, 422 U.S. 873, 882-83 (1975); *United States v. Jones*, 606 F.3d 964, 967-68 (8th Cir. 2010). Nonetheless, when individuals do not stop in those situations, FPD officers treat that conduct as a failure to comply with a lawful order, and make arrests. Such arrests violate the Fourth Amendment because they are not based on probable cause that the crime of Failure to Comply has been committed. *Dunaway v. New York*, 442 U.S. 200, 208 (1979).

FPD officers apply Section 29-16(1) remarkably broadly. In an incident from August 2010, an officer broke up an altercation between two minors and sent them back to their homes. The officer ordered one to stay inside her residence and the other not to return to the first's residence. Later that day, the two minors again engaged in an altercation outside the first minor's residence. The officer arrested both for Failure to Comply with the earlier orders. But Section 29-16(1) does not confer on officers the power to confine people to their homes or keep them away from certain places based solely on their verbal orders. At any rate, the facts of this incident do not satisfy the statute for another reason: there was no evidence that the failure to comply "interfered with, obstructed or hindered the officer in the performance" of official duties. § 29-16(1). The officer's arrest of the two minors for Failure to Comply without probable cause of all elements of the offense violated the Fourth Amendment.

ii. Improper Enforcement of Code Provision Requiring Individuals to Identify Themselves to a Police Officer

FPD's charging under Section 29-16(2) also violates the Constitution. Section 29-16(2) makes it unlawful to "[f]ail to give information requested by a police officer in the discharge of his/her official duties relating to the identity of such person." This provision, a type of "stop-and-identify" law, is likely unconstitutional under the void-for-vagueness doctrine. It is also unconstitutional as typically applied by FPD.

As the Supreme Court has explained, the void-for-vagueness doctrine "requires that a penal statute define the criminal offense with sufficient definiteness that ordinary people can understand what conduct is prohibited and in a manner that does not encourage arbitrary and discriminatory enforcement." *Kolender v. Lawson*, 461 U.S. 352, 357 (1983). In *Kolender*, the Supreme Court invalidated a California stop-and-identify law as unconstitutionally vague because its requirement that detained persons give officers "credible and reliable" identification provided no standard for what a suspect must do to comply with it. Instead, the law "vest[ed] complete discretion in the hands of the police" to determine whether a person had provided sufficient identity information, which created a "potential for arbitrarily suppressing First Amendment liberties" and "the constitutional right to freedom of movement." *Id.* at 358. The Eighth Circuit has applied the doctrine numerous times. In *Fields v. City of Omaha*, 810 F.2d 830 (8th Cir. 1987), the court struck down a city ordinance that required a person to "identify himself" because it did not make definite what would suffice for identification and thereby provided no "standard to guide the police officer's discretionary assessment" or "prevent arbitrary and discriminatory law enforcement." *Id.* at 833-34; *see also Stahl v. City of St. Louis*, 687 F.3d 1038, 1040 (8th Cir. 2012) (holding that an ordinance prohibiting conduct that would impede traffic was unconstitutionally vague under the Due Process Clause because it "may fail to provide the kind of notice that will enable ordinary people to understand what conduct it prohibits") (internal quotation marks omitted).

Under these binding precedents, Ferguson's stop -and-identify law appears to be unconstitutionally vague because the term "information ... relating to the identity of such person" in Section 29-16(2) is not defined. Neither the ordinance nor any court has narrowed that language. *Cf. Hiibel v. Sixth Judicial Dist. Ct. of Nevada*, 542 U.S. 177, 188-89 (2004) (upholding stop-and-identify law that was construed by the state supreme court to require only that a suspect provide his name). As a consequence, the average person has no understanding of precisely how much identity information, and what kind, he or she must provide when an FPD officer demands it; nor do officers. Indeed, we are aware of several people who were asked to provide their Social Security numbers, including one man who was arrested after refusing to do provide their Social Security numbers, including one man who was arrested after refusing to do 16(2) is likely unconstitutional on its face.[43]

Even apart from the facial unconstitutionality of the statute, the evidence is clear that FPD's enforcement of Section 29-16(2) is unconstitutional in its application. Stop-and-identify laws stand in tension with the Supreme Court's admonition that a person approached by a police officer "need not answer any question put to him; indeed, he may decline to listen to the questions at all and may go on his way." *Florida v. Royer*, 460 U.S. 491, 497-98 (1983). For this reason, the Court has held that an officer cannot require a person to identify herself unless the officer first has reasonable suspicion to initiate the stop. *See Brown v. Texas*, 443 U.S. 47, 52-53 (1979) (holding that the application of a Texas statute that criminalized refusal to provide a name and address to a peace officer violated the Fourth Amendment where the officer lacked reasonable suspicion of criminal activity); *see also Hiibel*, 542 U.S. at 184 (deeming the reasonablesuspicion requirement a "constitutional limitation[]" on stop-and-identify statutes). FPD officers, however, routinely arrest individuals under Section 29-16(2) for failure to identify themselves despite lacking reasonable suspicion to stop them in the first place.

For example, in an October 2011 incident, an officer arrested two sisters who were backing their car into their driveway. The officer claimed that the car had been idling in the middle of the street, warranting investigation, while the women claim they had pulled up outside their home to drop someone off when the officer arrived. In any case, the officer arrested one sister for failing to provide her identification when requested. He arrested the other sister for getting out of the car after being ordered to stay inside. The two sisters spent the next three hours in jail. In a similar incident from December 2011, police officers approached two people sitting in a car on a public street and asked the driver for identification. When the driver balked, insisting that he was on a public street and should not have to answer questions, the officers ordered him out of the car and ultimately charged him with Failure to Comply.

In another case, from March 2013, officers responded to the police station to take custody of a person wanted on a state warrant. When they arrived, they encountered a different man — not the subject of the warrant — who happened to be leaving the station. Having nothing to connect the man to the warrant subject, other than his presence at the station, the officers nonetheless stopped him and asked that he identify himself. The man asserted his rights, asking the officers "Why do you need to know?" and declining to be frisked. When the man then extended his identification toward the officers, at their request, the officers interpreted his hand motion as an attempted assault and took him to the ground. Without articulating reasonable suspicion or any other justification for the initial detention, the officers arrested the man on two counts of Failure to Comply and two counts of Resisting Arrest.

In our conversations with FPD officers, one officer admitted that when he conducts a traffic stop, he asks for identification from all passengers as a matter of course. If any refuses, he considers that to be "furtive and aggressive" conduct and cites — and typically arrests — the person for Failure to Comply. The officer thus acknowledged that he regularly exceeds his authority under the Fourth Amendment by arresting passengers who refuse, as is their right, to provide identification. *See Hiibel*, 542 U.S. at 188 ("[A]n officer may not arrest a suspect for failure to identify himself if the request for identification is not reasonably related to the circumstances justifying the stop."); *Stufflebeam v. Harris*, 521 F.3d 884, 887-88 (8th Cir. 2008) (holding that the arrest of a passenger for failure to identify himself during a traffic stop violated the Fourth Amendment where the passenger was not suspected of other criminal activity and his identification was not needed for officer safety). Further, the officer told us that he was trained to arrest for this violation.

Good supervision would correct improper arrests by an officer before they became routine. But in Ferguson, the same dynamics that lead officers to make unlawful stops and arrests cause supervisors to conduct only perfunctory review of officers' actions — when they conduct any review at all. FPD supervisors are more concerned with the number of citations and arrests officers produce than whether those citations and arrests are lawful or promote public safety. Internal communications among command staff reveal that FPD for years has failed to ensure even that officers write their reports and first-line supervisors approve them. In 2010, a senior police official complained to supervisors that every week reports go unwritten, and hundreds of reports remain unapproved. "It is time for you to hold your officers accountable," he urged them. In 2014, the official had the same complaint, remarking on 600 reports that had not been approved over a six-month period. Another supervisor remarked that coding errors in the new records management system is set up "to hide, do away with, or just forget reports," creating a heavy administrative burden for supervisors who discover incomplete reports months after they are created. In practice, not all arrests are given incident numbers, meaning supervisors may never know to review them. These systemic deficiencies in oversight are consistent with an approach to law enforcement in which productivity and revenue generation, rather than lawful policing, are the priority. Thus, even as commanders exhort line supervisors to more closely supervise officer activity, they perpetuate the dynamics that discourage meaningful supervision.

c. FPD's Use of a Police-run "Wanted" System Circumvents Judicial Review and Poses the Risk of Abuse

FPD and other law enforcement agencies in St. Louis County use a system of "wanteds" or "stop orders" as a substitute for seeking judicial approval for an arrest warrant. When officers believe a person has committed a crime but are not able to immediately locate that person, they can enter a "wanted" into the statewide law enforcement database, indicating to all other law enforcement agencies that the person should be arrested if located. While wanteds are supposed to be based on probable cause, *see* FPD General Order 424.01, they operate as an end-run around the judicial system. Instead of swearing out a warrant and seeking judicial authorization from a neutral and detached magistrate, officers make the probable cause determination themselves and circumvent the courts. Officers use wanteds for serious state-level crimes and minor code violations alike, including traffic offenses.

FPD command staff express support for the wanted system, extolling the benefits of being able to immediately designate a person for detention. But this expedience carries constitutional risks. If officers enter wanteds into the system on less than probable cause, then the subsequent arrest would violate the Fourth Amendment. Our interviews with command staff and officers indicate that officers do not clearly understand the legal authority necessary to issue a wanted. For example, one veteran officer told us he will put out a wanted "if I do not have enough probable cause to arrest you." He gave the example of investigating a car theft. Upon identifying a suspect, he would put that suspect into the system as wanted "because we do not have probable cause that he stole the vehicle." Reflecting the muddled analysis officers may employ when deciding whether to issue a wanted, this officer concluded, "you have to have reasonable suspicion and some probable cause to put out a wanted."

At times, FPD officers use wanteds not merely in spite of a lack of probable cause, but *because* they lack probable cause. In December 2014, a Ferguson detective investigating a shooting emailed a county prosecutor to see if a warrant for a suspect could be obtained, since "a lot of state agencies won't act on a wanted." The prosecutor responded stating that although "[c]hances are" the crime was committed by the suspect, "we just don't have enough for a warrant right now." The detective responded that he would enter a wanted.

There is evidence that the use of wanteds has resulted in numerous unconstitutional arrests in Ferguson. Internal communications reveal problems with FPD officers arresting individuals on wanteds without first confirming that the wanteds are still valid. In 2010, for instance, an FPD supervisor wrote that "[a]s of late we have had subjects arrested that were wanted for other agencies brought in without being verified first. You guessed it, come to find out they were no longer wanted by the agencies and had to be released." The same supervisor told us that in 2014 he cleared hundreds of invalid wanteds from the system, some of them over ten years old, suggesting that invalid wanteds have been an ongoing problem.

Wanteds can also be imprecise, leading officers to arrest in violation of the Fourth Amendment. For example, in June 2011, officers arrested a man at gunpoint because the car he was driving had an active wanted "on the vehicle and its occupants" in connection with an alleged theft. In fact, the theft was alleged to have been committed by the man's brother. Nonetheless, according to FPD's files, the man was arrested solely on the basis of the wanted.

This system creates the risk that wanteds could be used improperly to develop evidence necessary for arrest rather than to secure a person against whom probable cause already exists. Several officers described wanteds as an investigatory tool. According to Chief Jackson, "a wanted allows us to get a suspect in for booking and potential interrogation." One purpose, he said, is "to conduct an interview of that person." While it is perfectly legitimate for officers to try to obtain statements from persons lawfully detained, it is unconstitutional for them to jail individuals on less than probable cause for that purpose. *Dunaway*, 442 U.S. at 216. One senior supervisor acknowledged that wanteds could be abused. He agreed that the potential exists, for example, for an officer to pressure a subject into speaking voluntarily to avoid being arrested. These are risks that the judicially-reviewed warrant process is meant to avoid.

Compounding our concern is the minimal training and supervision provided on when to issue a wanted, and the lack of any meaningful oversight to detect and respond to improperly issued wanteds. Some officers told us that they may have heard about wanteds in the training academy. Others said that they received no formal training on wanteds and learned about them from their field training officers. As for supervision, officers are supposed to get authorization from their supervisors before entering a wanted into a law enforcement database. They purportedly do this by providing the factual basis for probable cause to their supervisors, orally or in their written reports. However, several supervisors and officers we spoke with acknowledged that this supervisory review routinely does not happen. Further, the supervisors we interviewed told us that they had never declined to authorize a wanted.

Finally, a Missouri appellate court has highlighted the constitutional risks of relying on a wanted as the basis for an arrest. In *State v. Carroll*, 745 S.W.2d 156 (Mo. Ct. App. 1987), the court held that a robbery suspect was arrested without probable cause when Ferguson and St. Louis police officers picked him up on a wanted for leaving the scene of an accident. *Id.* at 158. The officers then interrogated him three times at two different police stations, and he eventually made incriminating statements. Despite the existence of a wanted, the court deemed the initial arrest unconstitutional because "[t]he record…fail[ed] to show any *facts* known to the police at the time of the arrest to support a reasonable belief that defendant had committed a crime." *Id. Carroll* highlights the fact that wanteds do not confer an authority equal to a judicial arrest warrant. Rather, the *Carroll* court's holding suggests that wanteds may be of unknown reliability and thus insufficient to permit custodial detention under the Fourth Amendment. *See also* Steven J. Mulroy, *"Hold" On:* "Hold" On: Hour Hold, 63 Case W. Res. L. Rev. 815, 823, 842-45 (2013) (observing that one problem with police "holds" is that, although they require probable cause, "in practice they often lack it").

We received complaints from FPD officers that the County prosecutor's office is too restrictive in granting warrant requests, and that this has necessitated the wanted practice. This investigation did not determine whether the St. Louis County prosecutor is overly restrictive or appropriately cautious in granting warrant requests. What is clear, however, is that current FPD practices have resulted in wanteds being issued and executed without legal basis.

2. FPD Engages in a Pattern of First Amendment Violations

FPD's approach to enforcement results in violations of individuals' First Amendment rights. FPD arrests people for a variety of protected conduct: people are punished for talking back to officers, recording public police activities, and lawfully protesting perceived injustices.

Under the Constitution, what a person says generally should not determine whether he or she is jailed. Police officers cannot constitutionally make arrest decisions based on individuals' verbal expressions of disrespect for law enforcement, including use of foul language. *Buffkins v. City of Omaha*, 922 F.2d 465, 472 (8th Cir. 1990) (holding that officers violated the Constitution when they arrested a woman for disorderly conduct after she called one an "asshole," especially since "police officers are expected to exercise greater restraint in their response than the average citizen"); *Copeland v. Locke*, 613 F.3d 875, 880 (8th Cir. 2010) (holding that the First Amendment prohibited a police chief from arresting an individual who pointed at him and told him "move the f*****g car," even if the comment momentarily distracted the chief from a routine traffic stop); *Gorra v. Hanson*, 880 F.2d 95, 100 (8th Cir. 1989) (holding that arresting a person in retaliation for making a statement "constitutes obvious infringement" of the First Amendment). As the Supreme Court has held, "the First Amendment protects a significant amount of verbal criticism and challenge directed at police officers." *City of Houston, Tex. v. Hill*, 482 U.S. 451, 461 (1987) (striking down as unconstitutionally overbroad a local ordinance that criminalized interference with police by speech).

In Ferguson, however, officers frequently make enforcement decisions based on what subjects say, or how they say it. Just as officers reflexively resort to arrest immediately upon noncompliance with their orders, whether lawful or not, they are quick to overreact to challenges and verbal slights. These incidents — sometimes called "contempt of cop" cases — are propelled by officers' belief that arrest is an appropriate response to disrespect. These arrests are typically charged as a Failure to Comply, Disorderly Conduct, Interference with Officer, or Resisting Arrest.

For example, in July 2012, a police officer arrested a business owner on charges of Interfering in Police Business and Misuse of 911 because she objected to the officer's detention of her employee. The officer had stopped the employee for "walking unsafely in the street" as he returned to work from the bank. According to FPD records, the owner "became verbally involved," came out of her shop three times after being asked to stay inside, and called 911 to complain to the Police Chief. The officer characterized her protestations as interference and arrested her inside her shop.[44] The arrest violated the First Amendment, which "does not allow such speech to be made a crime." *Hill*, 482 U.S. at 462. Indeed, the officer's decision to arrest the woman after she tried to contact the Police Chief suggests that he may have been retaliating against her for reporting his conduct.

Officers in Ferguson also use their arrest power to retaliate against individuals for using language that, while disrespectful, is protected by the Constitution. For example, one afternoon in September 2012, an officer stopped a 20-year-old African-American man for dancing in the middle of a residential street. The officer obtained the man's identification and ran his name for warrants. Finding none, he told the man he was free to go. The man responded with profanities. When the officer told him to watch his language and reminded him that he was not being arrested, the man continued using profanity and was arrested for Manner of Walking in Roadway.

In February 2014, officers responded to a group of African-American teenage girls "play fighting" (in the words of the officer) in an intersection after school. When one of the schoolgirls gave the middle finger to a white witness who had called the police, an officer ordered her over to him.One of the girl's friends accompanied her. Though the friend had the right to be present and observe the situation — indeed, the offense reports include no facts suggesting a safety concern posed by her presence — the officers ordered her to leave and then attempted to arrest her when she refused. Officers used force to arrest the friend as she pulled away. When the first girl grabbed an officer's shoulder, they used force to arrest her, as well. Officers charged the two teenagers with a variety of offenses, including: Disorderly Conduct for giving the middle finger and using obscenities; Manner of Walking for being in the street; Failure to Comply for staying to observe; Interference with Officer; Assault on a Law Enforcement Officer; and Endangering the Welfare of a Child (themselves and their schoolmates) by resisting arrest and being involved in disorderly conduct. This incident underscores how officers' unlawful response to activity protected by the First Amendment can quickly escalate to physical resistance, resulting in additional force, additional charges, and increasing the risk of injury to officers and members of the public alike.

These accounts are drawn entirely from officers' own descriptions, recorded in offense reports. That FPD officers believe criticism and insolence are grounds for arrest, and that supervisors have condoned such unconstitutional policing, reflects intolerance for even lawful opposition to the exercise of police authority. These arrests also reflect that, in FPD, many officers have no tools for de-escalating emotionally charged scenes, even though the ability of a police officer to bring calm to a situation is a core policing skill.

FPD officers also routinely infringe on the public's First Amendment rights by preventing people from recording their activities. The First Amendment "prohibit[s] the government from limiting the stock of information from which members of the public may draw." *First Nat'l Bank v. Belloti*, 435 U.S. 765, 783 (1978). Applying this principle, the federal courts of appeal have held that the First Amendment "unambiguously" establishes a constitutional right to videotape police activities. *Glik v. Cunniffe*, 655 F.3d 78, 82 (1st Cir. 2011); *see also ACLU v. Alvarez*, 679 F.3d 583, 600 (7th Cir. 2012) (issuing a preliminary injunction against the use of a state eavesdropping statute to prevent the recording of public police activities); *Fordyce v. City of Seattle*, 55 F.3d 436, 439 (9th Cir. 1995) (recognizing a First Amendment right to film police carrying out their public duties); *Smith v. City of Cumming*, 212 F.3d 1332, 1333 (11th Cir. 2000) (recognizing a First Amendment right "to photograph or videotape police conduct"). Indeed, as the ability to record police activity has become more widespread, the role it can play in capturing questionable police activity, and ensuring that the activity is investigated and subject to broad public debate, has become clear. Protecting civilian recording of police activity is thus at the core of speech the First Amendment is intended to protect. *Cf. Branzburg v. Hayes*, 408 U.S. 665, 681 (1972) (First Amendment protects "news gathering"); *Mills v. Alabama*, 384 U.S. 214, 218 (1966) (news gathering enhances "free discussion of governmental affairs"). "In a democracy, public officials have no general privilege to avoid publicity and embarrassment by preventing public scrutiny of their actions." *Walker v. City of Pine Bluff*, 414 F.3d 989, 992 (8th Cir. 2005).

In Ferguson, however, officers claim without any factual support that the use of camera phones endangers officer safety. Sometimes, officers offer no rationale at all. Our conversations with community members and review of FPD records found numerous violations of the right to record police activity. In May 2014, an officer pulled over an African-American woman who was driving with her two sons. During the traffic stop, the woman's 16-year-old son began recording with his cell phone. The officer ordered him to put down the phone and refrain from using it for the remainder of the stop. The officer claimed this was "for safety reasons." The situation escalated, apparently due to the officer's rudeness and the woman's response. According to the 16 year old, he began recording again, leading the officer to wrestle the phone from him. Additional officers arrived and used force to arrest all three civilians under disputed circumstances that could have been clarified by a video recording.

In June 2014, an African-American couple who had taken their children to play at the park allowed their small children to urinate in the bushes next to their parked car. An officer stopped them, threatened to cite them for allowing the children to "expose themselves," and checked the father for warrants. When the mother asked if the officer had to detain the father in front of the children, the officer turned to the father and said, "you're going to jail because your wife keeps running her mouth." The mother then began recording the officer on her cell phone. The officerbecame irate, declaring, "you don't videotape me!" As the officer drove away with the father in custody for"parental neglect," the mother drove after them, continuing to record. The officer then pulled over and arrested her for traffic violations. When the father asked the officer to show mercy, he responded, "no more mercy, since she wanted to videotape," and declared "nobody videotapes me." The officer then took the phone, which the couple's daughter was holding. After posting bond, the couple found that the video had been deleted.

A month later, the same officer pulled over a truck hauling a trailer that did not have operating tail lights. The officer asked for identification from all three people inside, including a 54-year-old whiteman in the passenger seat who asked why. "You have to have a reason. This is a violation of my Fourth Amendment rights," he asserted. The officer, who characterized the man's reaction as "suspicious," responded, "the reason is, if you don't hand it to me, I'll arrest you." The man provided his identification. The officer then asked the man to move his cell phone from his lap to the dashboard, "for my safety." The man said, "okay, but I'm going to record this." Due to nervousness, he could not open the recording application and quickly placed the phone on the dash. The officer then announced that the man was under arrest for Failure to Comply. At the end of the traffic stop, the officer gave the driver a traffic citation, indicated at the other man, and said, "you're getting this ticket because of him." Upon bringing that man to the jail, someone asked the officer what offense the man had committed. The officer responded, "he's one of those guys who watches CNBC too much about his rights." The man did not say anything else, fearing what else the officer might be capable of doing. He later told us, "I never dreamed I could end up in jail for this. I'm scared of driving through Ferguson now."

The Ferguson Police Department's infringement of individuals' freedom of speech and right to record has been highlighted in recent months in the context of large-scale public protest. In November 2014, a federal judge entered a consent order prohibiting Ferguson officers from interfering with individuals' rights to lawfully and peacefully record public police activities. That same month, the City settled another suit alleging that it had abused its loitering ordinance, Mun. Code § 29-89, to arrest people who were protesting peacefully on public sidewalks.

Despite these lawsuits, it appears that FPD continues to interfere with individuals' rights to protest and record police activities. On February 9, 2015, several individuals were protesting outside the Ferguson police station on the six-month anniversary of Michael Brown's death. According to protesters, and consistent with several video recordings from that evening, the protesters stood peacefully in the police department's parking lot, on the sidewalks in front of it, and across the street. Video footage shows that two FPD vehicles abruptly accelerated from the police parking lot into the street. An officer announced,"everybody here's going to jail," causing the protesters to run. Video shows that as one man recorded the police arresting others, he was arrested for interfering with police action. Officers pushed him to the ground, began handcuffing him, and announced,"stop resisting or you're going to get tased." It appears from the video, however, that the man was neither interfering nor resisting. A protester in a wheelchair who was live streaming the protest was also arrested. Another officer moved several people with cameras away from the scene of the arrests, warning them against interfering and urging them to back up or else be arrested for Failure to Obey. The sergeant shouted at those filming that they would be arrested for Manner of Walking if they did not back away out of the street, even though it appears from the video recordings that the protesters and those recording were on the sidewalk at most, if not all, times. Six people were arrested during this incident. It appears that officers' escalation of this incident was unnecessary and in response to derogatory comments written in chalk on the FPD parking lot asphalt and on a police vehicle.

FPD's suppression of speech reflects a police culture that relies on the exercise of police power — however unlawful — to stifle unwelcome criticism. Recording police activity and engaging in public protest are fundamentally democratic enterprises because they provide a check on those "who are granted substantial discretion that may be misused to deprive individuals of their liberties." *Glik*, 655 F.3d at 82. Even profane backtalk can be a form of dissent against perceived misconduct. In thewords of the Supreme Court, "[t]he freedom of individuals verbally to oppose or challenge police action without thereby risking arrest is one of the principal characteristics by which we distinguish a free nation from a police state." *Hill*, 482 U.S. at 463. Ideally, officers would not encounter verbal abuse. Communities would encourage mutual respect, and the police would likewise exhibit respect by treating people with dignity. But, particularly where officers engage in unconstitutional policing, they only exacerbate community opposition by quelling speech.

3. FPD Engages in a Pattern of Excessive Force in Violation of the Fourth Amendment

FPD engages in a pattern of excessive force in violation of the Fourth Amendment. Many officers are quick to escalate encounters with subjects they perceive to be disobeying their orders or resisting arrest. They have come to rely on ECWs, specifically Tasers®, where less force — or no force at all — would do. They also release canines on unarmed subjects unreasonably and before attempting to use force less likely to cause injury. Some incidents of excessive force result from stops or arrests that have no basis in law. Others are punitive and retaliatory. In addition, FPD records suggest a tendency to use unnecessary force against vulnerable groups such as people with mental health conditions or cognitive disabilities, and juvenile students. Furthermore, as discussed in greater detail in Part III.C. of this report, Ferguson's pattern of using excessive force disproportionately harms African-American members of the community. The overwhelming majority of force — almost 90% — is used against African Americans.

The use of excessive force by a law enforcement officer violates the Fourth Amendment. *Graham v. Conner*, 490 U.S. 386, 394 (1989); *Atkinson v. City of Mountain View, Mo.*, 709 F.3d , 709 F.3d 09 (8th Cir. 2013). The constitutionality of an officer's use of force depends on whether the officer's conduct was "'objectively reasonable' in light of the facts and circumstances," which must be assessed "from the perspective of a reasonable officer on the scene, rather than with the 20/20 vision of hindsight." *Graham*, 490 U.S. at 396. Relevant considerations include "the severity of the crime at issue, whether the suspect poses an immediate threat to the safety of the officers or others, and whether he is actively resisting arrest or attempting to evade arrest by flight." *Id.*; *Johnson v. Caroll*, 658 F.3d 819, 826 (8th Cir. 2011).

FPD also imposes limits on officers' use of force through department policies. The useofforce policy instituted by Chief Jackson in 2010 states that "force may not be resorted to unless other reasonable alternatives have been exhausted or would clearly be ineffective under a particular set of circumstances." FPD General Order 410.01. The policy also sets out a use-offorce continuum, indicating the force options permitted in different circumstances, depending on the level of resistance provided by a suspect. FPD General Order 410.08.

FPD's st ated practice is to maintain use-of-force investigation files for all situations in which officers use force. We reviewed the entire set of force files provided by the department for the period of January 1, 2010 to September 8, 2014.[45] Setting aside the killing of animals (e.g., dogs, injured deer) and three instances in which the subject of the use of force was not identified, FPD provided 151 files. We also reviewed related documentation regarding canine deployments. Our finding that FPD force is routinely unreasonable and sometimes clearly punitive is drawn largely from FPD's documentation; that is, fromofficers' own words.

a. FPD's Use of Electronic Control Weapons Is Unreasonable

FPD's pattern of excessive force includes using ECWs in a manner that is unconstitutional, abusive, and unsafe. For example, in August 2010, a lieutenant used an ECW in drive-stun mode against an African-American woman in the Ferguson City Jail because she had refused to remove her bracelets.[46] The lieutenant resorted to his ECW even though there were five officers present and the woman posed no physical threat.

Similarly, in November 2013, a correctional officer fired an ECW at an African-American woman's chest because she would not follow his verbal commands to walk toward a cell. The woman, who had been arrested for driving while intoxicated, had yelled an insulting remark at the officer, but her conduct amounted to verbal noncompliance or passive resistance at most. Instead of attempting hand controls or seeking assistance from a state trooper who was also present, the correctional officer deployed the ECWbecause the woman was "not doing as she was told." When another FPD officer wrote up the formal incident report, the reporting officer wrote that the woman "approached [the correctional officer] in a threatening manner."

This "threatening manner" allegation appears nowhere in the statements of the correctional officer or witness trooper. The woman was charged with Disorderly Conduct, and the correctional officer soon went on to become an officer with another law enforcement agency.

These are not isolated incidents. In September 2012, an officer drive-stunned an African-American woman who he had placed in the back of his patrol car but who had stretched out her leg to block him from closing the door. The woman was in handcuffs. In May 2013, officers drive-stunned a handcuffed African-American man who verbally refused to get out of the back seat of a police car once it had arrived at the jail. The man did not physically resist arrest or attempt to assault the officers. According to the man, he was also punched in the face and head. That allegation was neither reported by the involved officers nor investigated by their supervisor, who dismissed it.

FPD officers seem to regard ECWs as an all-purpose tool bearing no risk. But an ECW —an electroshock weapon that disrupts a person's muscle control, causing involuntary contractions — can indeed be harmful. The Eighth Circuit Court of Appeals has observed that ECW-inflicted injuries are "sometimes severe and unexpected." *LaCross v. City of Duluth*, 713 F.3d 1155, 1158 (8th Cir. 2013). Electroshock "inflicts a painful and frightening blow, which temporarily paralyzes the large muscles of the body, rendering the victim helpless." *Hickey v. Reeder*, 12 F.3d 754, 757 (8th Cir. 1993). Guidance produced by the United States Department of Justice, Office of Community Oriented Policing Services, and the Police Executive Research Forum in 2011 warns that ECWs are "'less-lethal' and not 'nonlethal weapons'" and "have the potential to result in a fatal outcome." *2011 Electronic Control Weapon Guidelines* 12 (Police Executive Research Forum & U.S. Dep't of Justice Office of Community Oriented Policing Services, Mar. 2011) ("*2011 ECW Guidelines*").

FPD officers' swift, at times automatic , resort to using ECWs against individuals who typically have committed low-level crimes and who pose no immediate threat violates the Constitution. As the Eighth Circuit held in 2011, an officer uses excessive force and violates clearly established Fourth Amendment law when he deploys an ECW against an individual whose crime was minor and who is not actively resisting, attempting to flee, or posing any imminent danger to others. *Brown v. City of Golden Valley*, 574 F.3d 491, 497-99 (8th Cir. 2011) (upholding the denial of a qualified immunity claim made by an officer who drive-stunned a woman on her arm for two or three seconds when she refused to hang up her phone despite being ordered to do so twice); *cf. Hickey*, 12 F.3d at 759 (finding that the use of a stun gun against a prisoner for refusing to sweep his cell violated the more deferential Eighth Amendment prohibition against cruel and unusual punishment). Courts have found that even when a suspect resists but does so only minimally, the surrounding factors may render the use of an ECW objectively unreasonable. *See Mattos v. Agarano*, 661 F.3d 433, 444-46, 448-51 (9th Cir. 2011) (en banc) (holding in two consolidated cases that minimal defensive resistance — including stiffening the body to inhibit being pulled from a car, and raising an arm in defense — does not render using an ECW reasonable where the offense was minor, the subject did not attempt to flee, and the subject posed no immediate threat to officers); *Parker v. Gerrish*, 547 F.3d 1, 9-11 (1st Cir. 2008) (upholding a jury verdict of excessive use of force for an ECW use because the evidence supported a finding that the subject who had held his hands together was not actively resisting or posing an immediate threat); *Casey v. City of Fed. Heights*, 509 F.3d 1278, 1282-83 (10th Cir. 2007) (holding that the use of an ECW was not objectively reasonable when the subject pulled away from the officer but did not otherwise actively resist arrest, attempt to flee, or pose an immediate threat).

Indeed, officers' unreasonable ECW use violates FPD's own policies. The department prohibits the use of force unless reasonable alternatives have been exhausted or would clearly be ineffective. FPD General Order 410.01. A separate ECW policy describes the weapon as "designed to overcome active aggression or overt actions of assault." FPD General Order 499.00. The policy states that an ECW "will never be deployed punitively or for purposes of coercion. It is to be used as a way of averting a potentially injurious or dangerous situation." FPD General

Order 499.04. Despite the existence of clearly established Fourth Amendment case law and explicit departmental policies in this area, FPD officers routinely engage in the unreasonable use of ECWs, and supervisors routinely approve their conduct.

It is in part FPD officers' approach to policing that leads them to violate the Constitution and FPD's own policies. Officers across the country encounter drunkenness, passive defiance, and verbal challenges. But in Ferguson, officers have not been trained or incentivized to use deescalation techniques to avoid or minimize force in these situations. Instead, they respond with impatience, frustration, and disproportionate force. FPD's weak oversight of officer use of force, described in greater detail below, facilitates this abuse. Officers should be required to view the ECW as one tool among many, and "a weapon of need, not a tool of convenience." *2011 ECW Guidelines* at 11. Effective policing requires that officers not depend on ECWs, or any type of force, "at the expense of diminishing the fundamental skills of communicating with subjects and deescalating tense encounters." *Id.* at 12.

b. FPD's Use of Canines on Low-level, Unarmed Offenders Is Unreasonable

FPD engages in a pattern of deploying canines to bite individuals when the articulated facts do not justify this significant use of force. The department's own records demonstrate that, as with other types of force, canine officers use dogs out of proportion to the threat posed by the people they encounter, leaving serious puncture wounds to nonviolent offenders, some of them children. Furthermore, in every canine bite incident for which racial information is available, the subject was African American. This disparity, in combination with the decision to deploy canines in circumstances with a seemingly low objective threat, suggests that race may play an impermissible role in officers' decisions to deploy canines.

FPD currently has four canines, each assigned to a particular canine officer. Under FPD policy, canines are to be used to locate and apprehend "dangerous offenders." FPD General Order 498.00. When offenders are hiding, the policy states, "handlers will not allow their K-9 to engage a suspect by biting if a lower level of force could reasonably be expected to control the suspect or allow for the apprehension." *Id.* at 498.06. The policy also permits the use of a canine, however, when any crime — not just a felony or violent crime — has been committed. *Id.* at 498.05. This permissiveness, combined with the absence of meaningful supervisory review and an apparent tendency to overstate the threat based on race, has resulted in avoidable dog bites to low-level offenders when other means of control were available.

In December 2011, officers deployed a canine to bite an unarmed 14-year-old African-American boy who was waiting in an abandoned house for his friends. Four officers, including a canine officer, responded to the house mid-morning after a caller reported that people had gone inside. Officers arrested one boy on the ground level. Describing the offense as a burglary in progress even though the facts showed that the only plausible offense was trespassing, the canine officer's report stated that the dog located a second boy hiding in a storage closet under the stairs in the basement. The officer peekedinto the space and saw the boy, who was 5'5" and 140 pounds, curled up in a ball, hiding. According to the officer, the boy would not show his hands despite being warned that the officer would use the dog. The officer then deployed the dog, which bit the boy's arm, causing puncture wounds.

According to the boy, with whom we spoke, he never hid in a storage space and he never heard any police warnings. He told us that he was waiting for his friends in the basement of the house, a vacant building where they would go when they skipped school. The boy approached the stairs when he heard footsteps on the upper level, thinking his friends had arrived. When he saw the dog at the top of the steps, he turned to run, but the dog quickly bit him on the ankle and then the thigh, causing him to fall to the floor. The dog was about to bite his face or neck but instead got his left arm, which the boy had raised to protect himself. FPD officers struck him while he was on the ground, one of them putting a boot on the side of his head. He recalled the officers laughing about the incident afterward.

The lack of sufficient documentation or a supervisory force investigation prevents us from resolving which version of events is more accurate. However, even ifthe officer's version of the force used were accurate, the use of the dog to bite the boy was unreasonable. Though described as a felony, the facts as described by the officer, and the boy, indicate that this was a trespass — kids hanging out in a vacant building. The officers had no factual predicate to believe the boy was armed. The offense reports document no attempt to glean useful information about the second boy from the first, who was quickly arrested. By the canine officer's own account, he saw the boy in the closetand thus had the opportunity to assess the threat posed by this 5'5" 14 year old. Moreover, there were no exigent circumstances requiring apprehension by dog bite. Four officers were present and had control of the scene.

There is a recurring pattern of officers claiming they had to use a canine to extract a suspect hiding in a closed space. The frequency with which this particular rationale is used to justify dog bites, alongside the conclusory language in the reports, provides cause for concern. In December 2012, a 16-year-old African-American boy suspected of stealing a car fled from an officer, jumped several fences, and ran into a vacant house. A second officer arrived with a canine, which reportedly located the suspect hiding in a closet. Without providing a warning outside the closet, the officer opened the door and sent in the dog, which bit the suspect and dragged him out by the legs. This force appears objectively unreasonable. *See Kuha v. City of Minnetonka*, 365 F.3d 590, 598 (8th Cir. 2004), abrogated on other grounds by *Szabla v. City of Brooklyn Park, Minn.*, 486 F.3d 385, 396 (8th Cir. 2007) (en banc) (holding that "a jury could find it objectively unreasonable to use a police dog trained in the bite and hold method without first giving the suspect a warning and opportunity for peaceful surrender"). The first officer, who was also on the scene by this point, deployed his ECW against the suspect three times as the suspect struggled with the dog, which was still biting him. The offense reports provide only minimal explanation for why apprehension by dog bite was necessary. The pursuing officer claimed the suspect had "reached into the front section of his waist area," but the report does not say that he relayed this information to the canine officer, and no weapon was found. Moreover, given the lack of a warning at the closet, the use of the dog and ECW at the same time, and the application of three ECWstuns in quick succession, the officers' conduct raises the possibility that the force was applied in retaliation for leading officers on a chase.

In November 2013, an officer deployed a canine to bite and detain a fleeing subject even though the officer knew the suspect was unarmed. The officer deemed the subject, an African-American male who was walking down the street, suspicious because he appeared to walk away when he saw the officer. The officer stopped him and frisked him, finding no weapons. The officer then ran his name for warrants. When the man heard the dispatcher say over the police radio that he had outstanding warrants — the report does not specify whether the warrants were for failing to appear in municipal court or to pay owed fines, or something more serious — he ran. The officer followed him and released his dog, which bit the man on both arms. The officer's supervisor found the force justified because the officer released the dog "fearing that the subject was armed," even though the officer had already determined the man was unarmed.

As these incidents demonstrate, FPD officers' use of canines to bite people is frequently unreasonable. Officers command dogs to apprehend by biting even when multiple officers are present. They make no attempt to slow situations down, creating time to resolve the situation with lesser force. They appear to use canines not to counter a physical threat but to inflict punishment. They act as if every offender has a gun, justifying their decisions based on what might be possible rather than what the facts indicate is likely.Overall, FPD officers' use of canines reflects a culture in which officers choose not to use the skills and tactics that could resolve a situation without injuries, and instead deploy tools and methods that are almost guaranteed to produce an injury of some type.

FPD's use of canines is part of its pattern of excessive force in violation of the Fourth Amendment. In addition, FPD's use of dog bites only against African-American subjects is evidence of discriminatory policing in violation of the Fourteenth Amendment and other federal laws.

c. FPD's Use of Force Is Sometimes Retaliatory and Punitive

Many FPD uses of force appear entirely punitive. Officers often use force in response to behavior that may be annoying or distasteful but does not pose a threat. The punitive use of force by officers is unconstitutional and, in many cases, criminal. *See, e.g., Gibson v. County of Washoe, Nev.*, 290 F.3d 1175, 1197 (9th Cir. 2002) ("The Due Process clause protects pretrial detainees from the use of excessive force that amounts to punishment."); *see also* 18 U.S.C. § 242 (making willful deprivation of rights under color of law, such as by excessive force, a federal felony punishable by up to ten years in prison).

We reviewed many incidents in which it appeared that FPD officers used force not to counter a physical threat but to inflict punishment. The use of canines and ECWs, in particular, appear prone to such abuse by FPD. In April 2013, for example, a correctional officer deployed an ECW against an African-American prisoner, delivering a five-second shock, because the man had urinated out of his cell onto the jail floor. The correctional officer observed the man on his security camera feed inside the booking office. When the officer came out, some of the urine hit his pant leg and, he said,almost caused him to slip. "Due to the possibility of contagion," the correctional officer claimed, he deployed his ECW "to cease the assault." The ECW prongs, however, both struck the prisoner in the back. The correctional officer's claim that he deployed the ECW to stop the ongoing threat of urine is not credible, particularly given that the prisoner was in his locked cell with his back to the officer at the time the ECW was deployed. Using lesslethal force to counter urination, especially when done punitively as appears to be the case here, is unreasonable. *See Shumate v. Cleveland*, 483 F. App'x 112, 114 (6th Cir. 2012) (affirming denial of summary judgment on an excessive-force claim against an officer who punched a handcuffed arrestee in response to being spit on, when the officer could have protected himself from further spitting by putting the arrestee in the back of a patrol car and closing the door).

d. FPD Use of Force Often Results from Unlawful Arrest and Officer Escalation

A defining aspect of FPD's pattern of excessive force is the extent to which force r esults from unlawful stops and arrests, and from officer escalation of incidents. Too often, officers overstep their authority by stopping individuals without reasonable suspicion and arresting without probable cause. Officers frequently compound the harm by using excessive force to effect the unlawful police action. Individuals encountering police under these circumstances are confused and surprised to find themselves being detained. They decline to stop or try to walk away, believing it within their rights to do so. They pull away incredulously, or respond with anger. Officers tend to respond to these reactions with force.

In January 2013, a patrol sergeant stopped an African-American man after he saw the man talk to an individual in a truck and then walk away. The sergeant detained the man, although he did not articulate any reasonable suspicion that criminal activity was afoot. When the man declined to answer questions or submit to a frisk — which the sergeant sought to execute despite articulating no reason to believe the man was armed — the sergeant grabbed the man by the belt, drew his ECW, and ordered the man to comply. The man crossed his arms and objected that he had not done anything wrong. Video captured by the ECW's built-in camera shows that the man made no aggressive movement toward the officer. The sergeant fired the ECW, applying a five-second cycle of electricity and causing the man to fall to the ground. The sergeant almost immediately applied the ECW again, which he later justified in his report by claiming that the man tried to stand up. The video makes clear, however, that the man never tried to stand — he only writhed in pain on the ground. The video also shows that the sergeant applied the ECW nearly continuously for 20 seconds, longer than represented in his report. The man was charged with Failure to Comply and Resisting Arrest, but no independent criminal violation.

In a January 2014 incident, officers attempted to arrest a young African-American man for trespassing on his girlfriend's grandparents' property, even though the man had been invited into the home by the girlfriend. According to officers, he resisted arrest, requiring several officers to subdue him. Seven officers repeatedly struck and used their ECWs against the subject, who was 5'8" and 170 pounds. The young man suffered head lacerations with significant bleeding.

In the above examples, force resulted from temporary detentions or attempted arrests for which officers lacked legal authority. Force at times appeared to be used as punishment for noncompliance with an order that lacked legal authority. Even where FPD officers have legal grounds to stop or arrest, however, they frequently take actions that ratchet up tensions and needlessly escalate the situation to the point that they feel force is necessary. One illustrative instance from October 2012began as a purported check on a pedestrian's well-being and ended with the man being taken to the ground, drive-stunned twice, and arrested for Manner of Walking in Roadway and Failure to Comply. In that case, an African-American man was walking after midnight in the outer lane of West Florissant Avenue when an officer asked him to stop. The officer reported that he believed the man might be under the influence of an "impairing substance." When the man, who was 5'5" and 135 pounds, kept walking, the officer grabbed his arm; when the man pulled away, the officer forced him to the ground. Then, for reasons not articulated in the officer's report, the officer decided to handcuff the man, applying his ECW in drive-stun mode twice, reportedly because the man would not provide his hand for cuffing. The man was arrested but there is no indication in the report that he was in fact impaired or indeed doing anything other than walking down the street when approached by the officer.

In November 2011, officers stopped a car for speeding. The two African-American women inside exited the car and vocally objected to the stop. They were told to get back in the car. When the woman in the passenger seat got out a second time, an officer announced she was under arrest for Failure to Comply. This decision escalated into a use of force. According to the officers, the woman swung her arms and legs, although apparently not at anyone, and then stiffened her body. An officer responded by drive-stunning her in the leg. The woman was charged with Failure to Comply and Resisting Arrest.

As these examples demonstrate, a significant number of the documented use-of-force incidents involve charges of Failure to Comply and Resisting Arrest only. This means that officers who claim to act based on reasonable suspicion or probable cause of a crime either are wrong much of the time or do not have an adequate legal basis for many stops and arrests in the first place. *Cf. Lewis v. City of New Orleans*, 415 U.S. 130, 136 (1974) (Powell, J., concurring) (cautioning that an overbroad code ordinance "tends to be invoked only where there is no other valid basis for arresting an objectionable or suspicious person" and that the "opportunity for abuse... is self-evident"). This pattern is a telltale sign of officer escalation and a strong indicator that the use of force was avoidable.

e. FPD Officers Have a Pattern of Resorting to Force Too Quickly When Interacting with Vulnerable Populations

Another dimension of FPD's pattern of unreasonable force is FPD's overreliance on force when interacting with more vulnerable populations, such as people with mental health conditions or intellectual disabilities and juvenile students.

i. Force Used Against People with Mental Health Conditions or Intellectual Disabilities

The Fourth Amendment requires that an individual's mental health condition or intellectual disability be considered when determining the reasonableness of an officer's use of force. *See Champion v. Outlook Nashville, Inc.*, 380 F.3d 893, 904 (6th Cir. 2004) (explaining in case concerning use of force against a detainee with autismthat "[t]he diminished capacity of an unarmed detainee must be taken into account when assessing the amount of force exerted"); *see also Phillips v. Community Ins. Corp.*, 678 F.3d 513, 526 (7th Cir. 2012); *Deorle v. Rutherford*, 272 F.3d 1272, 1283 (9th Cir. 2001); *Giannetti v. City of Stillwater*, 216 F. App'x 756, 764 (10th Cir. 2007). This is because people with such disabilities "may be physically unable to comply with police commands." *Phillips*, 678 F.3d at 526. Our review indicates that FPD officers do not adequately consider the mental health or cognitive disability of those they suspect of wrongdoing when deciding whether to use force.

Ferguson is currently in litigation against the estate of a man with mental illness who died in September 2011 after he had an ECW deployed against him three times for allegedly running toward an officer while swinging his fist. *See Estate of Moore v. Ferguson Police Dep't*, No. 4:14-cv-01443 (E.D. Mo. filed Aug. 19, 2014). The man had been running naked through the streets and pounding on cars that morning while yelling "I am Jesus." The Eighth Circuit recently considered a similar set of allegations in *De Boise v. Taser Intern., Inc.*, 760 F.3d 892 (8th Cir. 2014). There, a man suffering from schizophrenia, who had run naked in and out of his house and claimed to be a god, died after officers used their ECWs against him multiple times because he would not stay on the ground. *Id.* at 897-98. Although the court resolved the case on qualified immunity grounds without deciding the excessive-force issue, the one judge who reached that issue opined that the allegations could be sufficient to establish a Fourth Amendment violation. *Id.* at 899-900 (Bye, J., dissenting).

In 2013, FPD stopped a man running with a shopping cart because he seemed "suspicious." According to the file, the man was "obviously mentally handicapped." Officers took the man to the ground and attempted to arrest him for Failure to Comply after he refused to submit to a pat-down. In the officers' view, the man resisted arrest by pulling his arms away. The officers drive-stunned him in the side of the neck. They charged him only with Failure to Comply and Resisting Arrest. In August 2011, officers used an ECW device against a man with diabetes who bit an EMT's hand without breaking the skin. The man had been having seizures when he did not comply with officer commands.

In August 2010, an officer responded to a call about an African-American man walking onto the highway and lying down on the pavement. Seeing that the man was sweating, acting jittery, and had dilated pupils, the officer believed he was on drugs. The man was cooperative at first but balked, pushing the officer back when the officer tried to handcuff him for safety reasons. The officer struck the man several times with his Asp® baton — including once in the head, a form of deadly force — causing significant bleeding. Two other officers then deployed their ECWs against the man a total of five times.

Jail staff have also reacted to people with mental health conditions by resorting to greater force than necessary. For example, in July 2011, a correctional officer used an ECW to drive-stun an African-American male inmate three times after he tried to hang himself with material torn from a medical dressing and banged his head on the cell wall. That same month, a correctional officer used an ECW against an African-American inmate with bipolar disorder who broke the overhead glass light fixture and tried to use it to cut his wrists. According to the correctional officer, the glass was "safety glass" and could not be used to cut the skin.

These incidents indicate a pattern of insufficient sensitivity to, and training about, the limitations of those with mental health conditions or intellectual disabilities. Officers view mental illness as narcotic intoxication, or worse, willful defiance. They apply excessive force to such subjects, not accounting for the possibility that the subjects may not understand their commands or be able to comply with them. And they have been insufficiently trained on tactics that would minimize force when dealing with individuals who are in mental health crisis or who have intellectual disabilities.

ii. Force Used Against Students

FPD's approach to policing impacts how its officers interact with students, as well, leading them to treat routine discipline issues as criminal matters and to use force when communication and de-escalation techniques would likely resolve the conflict.

FPD stations two School Resource Officers in the Ferguson-Florissant School District,[47] one at Ferguson Middle School and one at McCluer South-Berkeley High School. The stated mission of the SRO program, according to the memorandum of understanding between FPD and the school district, is to provide a safe and secure learning environment for students. But that agreement does not clearly define the SROs' role or limit SRO involvement in cases of routine discipline or classroom management. Nor has FPD established such guidance for its SROs or provided officers with adequate training on engaging with youth in an educational setting. The result of these failures, combined with FPD's culture of unreasonable enforcement actions more generally, is police action that is unreasonable for a school environment.

For example, in November 2013, an SRO charged a ninth grade girl with several violations after she refused to follow his orders to walk to the principal's office. The student and a classmate, both 15-year-old African-American girls, had gotten into a fight during class. When the officer responded, school staff had the two girls separated in a hallway. One refused the officer's order to walk to the principal's office, instead trying to push past staff toward the other girl. The officer pushed her backward toward a row of lockers and then announced that she was under arrest for Failure to Comply. Although the officer agreed not to handcuff her when she agreed to walk to the principals' office, he forwarded charges of Failure to Comply, Resisting Arrest, and Peace Disturbance to the county family court. The other student was charged with Peace Disturbance.

FPD officers respond to misbehavior common among students with arrest and force, rather than reserving arrest for cases involving safety threats. As one SRO told us, the arrests he made during the 2013-14 school year overwhelmingly involved minor offenses — Disorderly Conduct, Peace Disturbance, and Failure to Comply with instructions. In one case, an SRO decided to arrest a 14-year-old African-American student at the Ferguson Middle School for Failure to Comply when the student refused to leave the classroom after getting into a trivial argument with another student. The situation escalated, resulting in the student being drive-stunned with an ECW in the classroom and the school seeking a 180-day suspension for the student. SROs' propensity for arresting students demonstrates a lack of understanding of the negative consequences associated with such arrests. In fact, SROs told us that they viewed increased arrests in the schools as a positive result of their work. This perspective suggests a failure of training (including training in mental health, counseling, and the development of the teenage brain); a lack of priority given to de-escalation and conflict resolution; and insufficient appreciation for the negative educational and long-term outcomes that can result from treating disciplinary concerns as crimes and using force on students. *See* Dear Colleague Letter on the Nondiscriminatory Administration of School Discipline, U.S. Dep't of Justice & U.S. Dep't of Education, http://www.justice.gov/crt/about/edu/documents/dcl.pdf (2014) (citing research and providing guidance to public schools on how to comply with federal nondiscrimination law).

f. FPD's Weak Oversight of Use of Force Reflects its Lack of Concern for Whether Officer Conduct Is Consistent with the Law or Promotes Police Legitimacy

FPD's use-of-force review system is particularly ineffectual. Force frequently is not reported. When it is, there is rarely any meaningful review. Supervisors do little to no investigation; either do not understand or choose not to follow FPD's use-of-force policy in analyzing officer conduct; rarely correct officer misconduct when they find it; and do not see the patterns of abuse that are evident when viewing these incidents in the aggregate.

While Chief Jackson implemented new department policies when he joined FPD in 2010, including on use-of-force reporting and review, these policies are routinely ignored. Under FPD General Order 410.00, when an officer uses or attempts to use any force, a supervisor must respond to the scene to investigate. The supervisor must complete a two-page use-of-force report assessing whether the use of force complied with FPD's force policy. Additional forms are required for ECW uses and vehicle pursuits. According to policy and our interviews with Chief Jackson, a use-of-force packet is assembled — which should include the use-of-force report and supplemental forms, all police reports, any photographs, and any other supporting materials — and forwarded up the chain of command to the Chief. The force reporting and reviewsystem is intended to "help identify trends, improve training and officer safety, and provide timely information for the department addressing use-of-force issues with the public." FPD General Order 410.07. The policy even requires that a professional standards officer conduct an annual review of all force incidents. *Id.* These requirements are not adhered to in practice.

Perhaps the greatest deviation from FPD's use-of-force policies is that officers frequently do not report the force they use at all. There are many indications that this underreporting is widespread. First, we located information in FPD's internal affairs files indicating instances of force that were not included in the force files provided by FPD. Second, in reviewing randomly selected reports from FPD's records management system, we found several offense reports that described officers using force with no corresponding use-of-force report. Third, we found evidence that force had been used but not documented in officers' workers compensation claims. Of the nine cases between 2010 and 2014 in which officers claimed injury sustained from using force on the job, three had no corresponding use-of-force paperwork. Fourth, the set of force investigations provided by FPD contains lengthy gaps, including six stretches of time ranging from two to four months in which no incidents of force are reported. Otherwise, the files typically reflect between two and six force incidents per month. Fifth, we heard from community members about uses of force that do not appear within FPD's records, and we learned of many uses of force that were never officially reported or investigated from reviewing emails between FPD supervisors. Finally, FPD's force files reflect an overrepresentation of ECW uses — a type of force that creates a physical record (a spent ECW cartridge with discharged confetti) and that requires a separate form be filled out. It is much easier for officers to use physical blows and baton strikes without documenting them. Thus, the evidence indicates that a significant amount of force goes unreported within FPD. This in turn raises the possibility that the pattern of unreasonable force is even greater than we found.

Even when force is reported, the force review process falls so short of FPD's policy requirements that it is ineffective at improving officer safety or ensuring that force is used properly. First, and most significantly, supervisors almost never actually investigate force incidents. In almost every case, supervisors appear to view force investigations as a ministerial task, merely summarizing the involved officers' version of events and sometimes relying on the officers' offense report alone. The supervisory review starts and ends with the presumption that the officer's version of events is truthful and that the force was reasonable. As a consequence, though contrary to policy, supervisors almost never interview non-police witnesses, such as the arrestee or any independent witnesses. They do not review critical evidence even when it is readily available. For example, a significant portion of the documented uses of force occurs at the Ferguson jail, which employs surveillance cameras to monitor the area. Yet FPD records provide no indication that a supervisor has ever sought to review the footage for a jail incident. Nor do supervisors examine ECW camera video, even though it is available in FPD's newer model ECWs. Sometimes, supervisors provide no remarks on the use-of-force report, indicating simply, "see offense report."

Our review found the record to be replete with examples of this lack of meaningful supervisory review of force. For example, the use-of-force report for a May 2013 incident states that a suspect claims he had an ECW deployed against him and that he was punched in the head and face. The supervisor concludes simply, "other than the drive stun, no use of force was performed by the officers." The report does not clarify what investigation the supervisor did, if any, to assess the suspect's allegations, or how he determined that the allegations were false. Supervisors also fail to provide recommendations for how to ensure officer safety and minimize the need for force going forward. In January 2014, for instance, a correctional officer used force to subdue an inmate who tried to escape while the correctional officer was moving the inmate's cellmate to another cell without assistance. The supervisor missed the opportunity to recommend that correctional officers not act alone in such risky situations.

Second, supervisors either do not understand or choose not to follow FPD's use-of-force policy. As discussed above, in many of the force incidents we reviewed, it is clear from the officers' offense reports that the force used was, at the very least, contrary to FPD policy. Nonetheless, based on records provided by FPD, it appears that first-line supervisors and the command staff found all but one of the 151 incidents we reviewed to be within policy. This includes the instances of unreasonable ECW use discussed above. FPD policy advises that ECWs are to be used to "overcome active aggression or overt actions of assault." FPD General Order 499.00. They are to be used to "avert[] a potentially injurious or dangerous situation," and never "punitively or for purposes of coercion." FPD General Order 499.04. Simply referring back to these policies should have made clear to supervisors that the many uses of ECWs against subjects who were merely argumentative or passively resistant violated policy.

For example, in April 2014, an intoxicated jail detainee climbed up on the bars in his cell and refused to get down when ordered to by the arresting officer and the correctional officer on duty. The correctional officer then fired an ECW at him, from outside the closed cell door, striking the detainee in the chest and causing him to fall to the ground. In addition to being excessive, this force violated explicit FPD policy that "[p]roper consideration and care should be taken when deploying the X26 TASER on subjects who are in an elevated position or in other circumstance where a fall may cause substantial injury or death." FPD General Order 499.04. The reviewing supervisor deemed the use of force within policy.

Supervisors seem to believe that any level of resistance justifies any level of force. They routinely rely on boilerplate language, such as the statement that the subject took "a fighting stance," to justify force. Such language is not specific enough to understand the specific behavior the officer encountered and thus to determine whether the officer's response was reasonable. Indeed, a report from September 2010 shows how such terms may obscure what happened. In that case, the supervisor wrote that the subject "turned to [the officer] in a fighting stance" even though the officer's report makes clear that he chased and tackled the subject as the subject fled. That particular use of force may have been reasonable, but the use-of-force report reveals how little attention supervisors give to their force investigations. Another common justification, frequently offered by officers who use ECWs to subdue individuals who do not readily put their hands behind their back after being put on the ground, is to claim that a subject's hands were near his waist, where he might have a weapon. Supervisors tend to accept this justification without question.

Third, the review process breaks down even further when officers at the sergeant level or above use force. Instead of reporting their use of force to an official higher up the chain, who could evaluate it objectively, they complete the use-of-force investigation themselves. We found several examples of supervisors investigating their own conduct. When force investigations are conducted by the very officers involved in the incidents, the department is less likely to identify policy and constitutional violations, and the public is less likely to trust the department's commitment to policing itself.

Fourth, the failure of supervisors to investigate and the absence of analysis from their use-of-force reports frustrate review up the chain of command. Lieutenants, the assigned captain, and the Police Chief typically receive at most a one- or two-paragraph summary from supervisors; no witness statements, photographs, or video footage that should have been obtained during the investigation is included. These reviewers are left to rely only on the offense report and the sergeant's cursory summary. To take one example, 21 officers responded to a fight at the high school in March 2013, and several of them used force to take students into custody. FPD records contain only one offense report, which does not describe the actions of all officers who used force. The use-of-force report identifies the involved officers as "multiple" (without names) and provides only a one-paragraph summary stating that students "were grabbed, handcuffed, and restrained using various techniques of control." The offense report reflects that officers collected video from the school's security cameras, but the supervisor apparently never reviewed it. Further, while the offense report contains witness statements, those statements relate to the underlying fight, not the officer use of force, and there appear to be no statements from any of the 21 officers who responded to the fight. It is not possible for higher-level supervisors to adequately assess uses of force with so little information.

In fact, although a use-of-force packet is supposed to include all related documents, in practice only the two-page use-of-force report, that is, the supervisor's brief summary of the incident, goes to the Chief. In the example from the high school, then, the Chief would have known only that there was a fight at the school and that force was used — not which officers used force, what type of force was used, or what the students did to warrant the use of force. Offense reports are available in FPD's records management system, but Chief Jackson told us he rarely retrieves them when reviewing uses of force. The Chief also told us that he has never overturned a supervisor's determination of whether a use of force fell within FPD policy.

Finally, FPD does not perform any comprehensive review of force incidents sufficient to detect patterns of misconduct by a particular officer or unit, or patterns regarding a particular type of force. Indeed, FPD does not keep records in a manner that would allow for such a review. Within FPD's paper storage system, the two-page use-of-force reports (which are usually handwritten) are kept separately from all other documentation, including ECW and pursuit forms for the same incidents. Offense reports are attached to some use-of-force reports but not others. Some use-of-force reports have been removed from FPD's set of force files because the incidents became the subjects of an internal investigation or a lawsuit. As a consequence, when FPD provided us what it considers to be its force files — which, as described above, we have reason to believe do not capture all actual force incidents — a majority of those files were missing a critical document, such as an offense report, ECW report, or the use-of-force report itself. We had to make repeated requests for documents to construct force files amenable to fair review. There were some documents that FPD was unable to locate, even after repeated requests.

With its records incomplete and scattered, the department is unable to implement an early intervention system to identify officers who tend to use excessive force or the need for more training or better equipment — goals explicitly set out by FPD policy. It appears that no annual review of force incidents is conducted, as required by FPD General Order 410.07; indeed, a meaningful annual audit would be impossible. These recordkeeping problems also explain why Chief Jackson told us he could not remember ever imposing discipline for an improper use of force or ordering further training based on force problems.

These deficiencies in use-of-force review can have serious consequences. They make it less likely that officers will be held accountable for excessive force and more likely that constitutional violations will occur. They create potentially devastating liability for the City for failing to put in place systems to ensure officers operate within the bounds of the law. And they result in a police department that does not give its officers the supervision they need to do their jobs safely, effectively, and constitutionally.

B. Ferguson's Municipal Court Practices

The Ferguson municipal court handles most charges brought by FPD, and does so not with the primary goal of administering justice or protecting the rights of the accused, but of maximizing revenue. The impact that revenue concerns have on court operations undermines the court's role as a fair and impartial judicial body.[48] Our investigation has uncovered substantial evidence that the court's procedures are constitutionally deficient and function to impede a person's ability to challenge or resolve a municipal charge, resulting in unnecessarily prolonged cases and an increased likelihood of running afoul of court requirements. At the same time, the court imposes severe penalties when a defendant fails to meet court requirements, including added fines and fees and arrest warrants that are unnecessary and run counter to public safety. These practices both reflect and reinforce an approach to law enforcement in Ferguson that violates the Constitution and undermines police legitimacy and community trust.

Ferguson 's municipal court practices combine to cause significant harm to many individuals who have cases pending before the court. Our investigation has found overwhelming evidence of minor municipal code violations resulting in multiple arrests, jail time, and payments that exceed the cost of the original ticket many times over. One woman, discussed above, received two parking tickets for a single violation in 2007 that then totaled $151 plus fees. Over seven years later, she still owed Ferguson $541 — after already paying $550 in fines and fees, having multiple arrest warrants issued against her, and being arrested and jailed on several occasions. Another woman told us that when she went to court to try to pay $100 on a $600 outstanding balance, the Court Clerk refused to take the partial payment, even though the woman explained that she was a single mother and could not afford to pay more that month. A 90-year-old man had a warrant issued for his arrest after he failed to timely pay the five citations FPD issued to him during a single traffic stop in 2013. An 83-year-old man had a warrant issued against him when he failed to timely resolve his Derelict Auto violation. A 67-year-old woman told us she was stopped and arrested by a Ferguson police officer for an outstanding warrant for failure to pay a trash-removal citation. She did not know about the warrant until her arrest, and the court ultimately charged her $1,000 in fines, which she continues to pay off in $100 monthly increments despite being on a limited, fixed income. We have heard similar stories from dozens of other individuals and have reviewed court records documenting many additional instances of similarly harsh penalties, often for relatively minor violations.

Our review of police and court records suggests that much of the harm of Ferguson's law enforcement practices in recent years is attributable to the court's routine use of arrest warrants to secure collection and compliance when a person misses a required court appearance or payment. In a case involving a moving violation, procedural failures also result in the suspension of the defendant's license. And, until recently, the court regularly imposed a separate Failure to Appear charge for missed appearances and payments; that charge resulted in an additional fine in the amount of $75.50, plus $26.50 in court costs. *See* Ferguson Mun. Code § 13-58 (repealed Sept. 23, 2014). During the last three years, the court imposed roughly one Failure to Appear charge per every two citations or summonses issued by FPD. Since at least 2010, the court has collected more revenue for Failure to Appear charges than for any other charge. This includes $442,901 in fines for Failure to Appear violations in 2013, which comprised 24% of the total revenue the court collected that year. While the City Council repealed the Failure to Appear ordinance in September 2014, many people continue to owe fines and fees stemming from that charge. And the court continues to issue arrest warrants in every case where that charge previously would have been applied. License suspension practices are similarly unchanged. Once issued, arrest warrants can, and frequently do, lead to arrest and time in jail, despite the fact that the underlying offense did not result in a penalty of imprisonment.[49]

Thus, while the municipal court does not generally deem the code violations that come before it as jail-worthy, it routinely views the failure to appear in court to remit payment to the City as jail-worthy, and commonly issues warrants to arrest individuals who have failed to make timely payment. Similarly, while the municipal court does not have any authority to impose a *fine* of over $1,000 for any offense, it is not uncommon for individuals to pay more than this amount to the City of Ferguson — in forfeited bond payments, additional Failure to Appear charges, and added court fees — for what may have begun as a simple code violation. In this way, the penalties that the court imposes are driven not by public safety needs, but by financial interests. And despite the harm imposed by these needless penalties, until recently, the City and court did little to respond to the increasing frequency of Failure to Appear charges, and in many respects made court practices more opaque and difficult to navigate.

1. Court Practices Impose Substantial and Unnecessary Barriers to the Challenge or Resolution of Municipal Code Violations

It is a hallmark of due process that individuals are entitled to adequate notice of the allegations made against them and to a meaningful opportunity to be heard. *See Cole v. Arkansas*, 333 U.S. 196, 201 (1948); *see also Ward v. Vill. of Monroeville*, 409 U.S. 57, 58-62 (1972) (applying due process requirements to case adjudicated by municipal traffic court). As documented below, however, Ferguson municipal court rules and procedures often fail to provide these basic protections, imposing unnecessary barriers to resolving a citation or summons and thus increasing the likelihood of incurring the severe penalties that result if a code violation is not quickly resolved.

We have concerns not only about the obstacles to resolving a charge even when an individual chooses not to contest it, but also about the trial processes that apply in the rare occasion that a person does attempt to challenge a charge. While it is "axiomatic that a fair trial in a fair tribunal is a basic requirement of due process," *Caperton v. A.T. Massey Coal Co., Inc.*, 556 U.S. 868, 876 (2009), the adjudicative tribunal provided by the Ferguson municipal court appears deficient in many respects.[50] Attempts to raise legal claims are met with retaliatory conduct. In an August 2012 email exchange, for instance, the Court Clerk asked what the Prosecuting Attorney does when an attorney appears in a red light camera case, and the Prosecuting Attorney responded: "I usually dismiss them if the attorney merely requests a recommendation. If the attorney goes off on all of the constitutional stuff, then I tell the attorney to come…and argue in front [of] the judge — after that, his client can pay the ticket." We have found evidence of similar adverse action taken against litigants attempting to fulsomely argue a case at trial. The man discussed above who was cited after allowing his child to urinate in a bush attempted to challenge his charges. The man retained counsel who, during trial, was repeatedly interrupted by the court during his cross-examination of the officer. When the attorney objected to the interruptions, the judge told him that, if he continued on this path, "I will hold you in contempt and I will incarcerate you," which, as discussed below, the court has done in the past to others appearing before it. The attorney told us that, believing no line of questioning would alter the outcome, he tempered his defense so as not to be jailed. Notably, at that trial, even though the testifying officer had previously been found untruthful during an official FPD investigation, the prosecuting attorney presented his testimony without informing defendant of that fact, and the court credited that testimony.[51] The evidence thus suggests substantial deficiencies in the manner in which the court conducts trials.

Even where defendants opt not to challenge their charges, a number of court processes make resolving a case exceedingly difficult. City officials and FPD officers we spoke with nearly uniformly asserted that individuals' experiences when they become embroiled in Ferguson's municipal code enforcement are due not to any failings in Ferguson's law enforcement practices, but rather to those individuals' lack of "personal responsibility." But these statements ignore the barriers to resolving a case that court practices impose, including: 1) a lack of transparency regarding rights and responsibilities; 2) requiring in-person appearance to resolve most municipal charges; 3) policies that exacerbate the harms of Missouri's law requiring license suspension where a person fails to appear on a moving violation charge; 4) basic access deficiencies that frustrate a person's ability to resolve even those charges that do not require in-court appearance; and 5) legally inadequate fine assessment methods that do not appropriately consider a person's ability to pay and do not provide alternatives to fines for those living in or near poverty. Together, these barriers impose considerable hardship. We have heard repeated reports, and found evidence in court records, of people appearing in court many times — in some instances on more than ten occasions — to try to resolve a case but being unable to do so, and subsequently having additional fines, fees, and arrest warrants issued against them.

a. Court Practices and Procedural Deficiencies Create a Lack of Transparency Regarding Rights and Responsibilities

It is often difficult for an individual who receives a municipal citation or summons in Ferguson to know how much is owed, where and how to pay the ticket, what the options for payment are, what rights the individual has, and what the consequences are for various actions or oversights. The initial information provided to people who are cited for violating Ferguson's municipal code is often incomplete or inconsistent. Communication with municipal court defendants is haphazard and known by the court to be unreliable. And the court's procedures and operations are ambiguous, are not written down, and are not transparent or even available to the public on the court's website or elsewhere.

The rules and procedures of the court are difficult for the public to discern. Aside from a small number of exceptions, the Municipal Judge issues rules of practice and procedure verbally and on an ad hoc basis. Until recently, on the rare occasion that the Judge issued a written order that altered court practices, those orders were not distributed broadly to court and other FPD officials whose actions they affect and were not readily accessible to the public. Further, Ferguson, unlike other courts in the region, does not include *any* information about its operations on its website other than inaccurate instructions about how to make payment.[52] Court staff acknowledged during our investigation that the public would benefit from increased information about how to resolve cases and about court practices and procedures. Yet neither the court nor other City officials have undertaken efforts to make court operations more transparent in order to ensure that litigants understand their rights or court procedures, or to enable the public to assess whether the court is operating in a fair manner.

Current court practices fail to provide adequate information even to those who are charged with a municipal violation. The lack of clarity about a person's rights and responsibilities often begins from the moment a person is issued a citation. For some offenses, FPD uses state of Missouri uniform citations, and typically indicates on the ticket the assigned court date for the offense. Many times, however, FPD officers omit critical information from the citation, which makes it impossible for a person to determine the specific nature of the offense charged, the amount of the fine owed, or whether a court appearance is required or some alternative method of payment is available. In some cases, citations fail to indicate the offense charged altogether; in November 2013, for instance, court staff wrote FPD patrol to "see what [a] ticket was for" because it "does not have a charge on it." In other cases, a ticket will indicate a charge but omit other crucial information. For example, speeding tickets often fail to indicate the alleged speed observed, even though both the fine owed and whether a court appearance is mandatory depends upon the specific speed alleged. Evidence shows that in some of these cases, a person has appeared in court but been unable to resolve the citation because of the missing information. In June 2014, for instance, a court clerk wrote to an FPD officer: "The above ticket…does not have a speed in it. The guy came in and we had to send him away. Can you email me the speed when you get time." Separate and apart from the difficulties these omissions create for people, the fact that the court staff routinely add the speed to tickets weeks after they are issued raises concerns about the accuracy and reliability of officers' assertions in official records.

We have also found evidence that in issuing citations, FPD officers frequently provide people with incorrect information about the date and time of their assigned court session. In November 2012, court staff emailed the two patrol lieutenants asking: "Would you please be so kind to tell your squads to check their ct. dates and times. We are getting quite a few wrong dates and times[on tickets]." In December 2012, a court clerk emailed an FPD officer to inform him that while he had been putting 6:00 p.m. on his citations that month, the scheduled court session was actually a morning session. More recently, in March 2014, an officer wrote a court clerk because the officer had issued a citation that listed the court date as ten days later than the actual court date assigned. Some of these emails indicate that court staff planned to send a letter to the person who was cited. As noted below, however, such letters often are returned to the court as undeliverable. It is thus unsurprising that, on one occasion, a City employee who works in the building where court was held wrote the Court Clerk to tell her that "[a] few people stopped by tonight looking for court and I referred them to you." The email notes that one person insisted on providing her information so the employee could "vouch for her appearance for Night Court." The email does not identify any other individual who showed up for court that night, nor does it state that any steps were taken to ensure that those assigned the incorrect court date did not have Failure to Appear charges and fines imposed, arrest warrants issued against them, or their licenses suspended.

Even if the citation a person receives has been properly filled out, it is often unclear whether a court appearance is required or if some other method of resolving a case is available. Ferguson has a schedule that establishes fixed fines for a limited number of violations that do not require court appearance. Nonetheless, this list — called the "TVB" or "Traffic Violations Bureau" list — is incomplete and does not provide sufficient clarity regarding whether a court appearance is mandatory. Court staff members have themselves informed us that there are certain offenses for which they will sometimes require a court appearance and other times not, depending on their own assessment of whether an appearance should be required in a given case. That information, however, is not reliably communicated to the person who has been given the citation.

Although the City of Ferguson frequently bears responsibility for giving people misinformation about when they must appear in court, Ferguson does little to ensure that persons who have missed a court date are properly notified of the consequences that result from an additional missed appearance, such as arrest or losing theirdriver's licenses, or that those consequences have already been levied. If a person misses a required appearance, it is the purported practice of court staff to send a letter that sets a new court date and informs the defendant that missing the next appearance will result in an arrest warrant being issued. But court staff do not even claim to send these letters before issuing warrants if an individual is on a payment plan and misses a payment, or if a person already has an outstanding warrant on a different offense; in those cases, the court issues a warrant after a single missed payment or appearance. Further, even for the cases in which the court says it does send such letters prior to issuing a warrant, court records suggest that those letters are often not actually sent. Even where a letter is sent, some are returned to court, and court staff told us that in those cases, they make no additional effort to notify the individual of the new court date or the consequences of non-appearance. Court staff and staff from other municipal courts have informed us that defendants in poverty are more likely not to receive such a letter from court because they frequently change residence.

If an individual misses a second court date, an arrest warrant is issued, without any confirmation that the individual received notice of that second court date. In the past, when the court issued a warrant it would also send notice to the individual that a warrant was issued against them and telling them to appear at the police department to resolve the matter. This notice did not provide the basis of the arrest warrant or describe how it might be resolved. In any case, Ferguson stopped providing even this incomplete notice in 2012. In explaining the decision to stop sending this warrant notice, the Court Clerk wrote in a June 2011 email to Chief Jacksonthat "this will save the cost of warrant cards and postage" and "it is not necessary to send out these cards." Some court employees, however, told us that the notice letter had been useful — at least for those who received it — and that they believe it should still be sent. That the court discontinued what little notice it was providing to people in advance of issuing a warrant is particularly troubling given that, during our investigation, we spoke with several individuals who were arrested without ever knowing that a warrant was outstanding.[53]

Once a warrant is issued, a person can clear the warrant by appearing at the court window in the police department and paying a pre-determined bond. However, that process is itself not communicated to the public and, in any case, is only useful if an individual knows there is a warrant for her or his arrest. Court clerks told us that in some cases they deem sympathetic in their own discretion, they will cancel the warrant without a bond. Further, it appears that if a person is aware of an outstanding warrant but believes that the warrant was issued in error, that person can petition the Municipal Judge to cancel the warrant only after the bond is paid in full. If a person cannot afford to pay the bond, there is no opportunity to seek recourse from the court.

If a person is arrested on an outstanding warrant — or as the result of an encounter with FPD — it is often difficult to secure release with a bond payment, not only because of the inordinately high bond amounts discussed below, but also because of procedural obstacles. In practice, bond procedures depart from those articulated in official policy, and are arbitrary and confusing. FPD staff have told us that correctional officers have at times tried to find a warrant in the court's files to determine the bond amount owed, but have been unable to do so. This is unsurprising given the existence of what has been described to us as "drawers and drawers of warrants." In some cases, people have attempted to pay a bond to secure the release of a family member in FPD custody, but were not even seen by FPD staff. On one occasion, an FPD staff member reported to an FPD captain that a person "came to the station last night and waited to post bond for [a detainee], from 1:00 until 3:30. No one ever came up to get her money and no one informed her that she was going to have to wait that long."

b. Needlessly Requiring In-Court Appearances for Most Code Violations Imposes Unnecessary Obstacles to Resolving Cases

Ferguson requires far more defendants to appear in court than is required under state law. Under Missouri Supreme Court rules, there is a short list of violations that require the violator's appearance in court: any violation resulting in personal injury or property damage; driving while intoxicated; driving without a proper license; and attempting to elude a police officer. *See* Mo. Sup. Ct. R. 37.49. The municipal judge of each court has the discretion to expand this list of "must appears," and Ferguson's municipal court has expanded it exponentially: of 376 actively charged municipal offenses, court staff informed us that approximately 229 typically require an appearance in court before the fine can be paid, including Dog Creating Nuisance, Equipment Violations, No Passing Zone, Housing– Overgrown Vegetation, and Failure to Remove Leaf Debris. Ferguson requires these court appearances regardless of whether the individual is contesting the charges.

Requiring an individual to appear at a specific place and time to pay a citation makes it far more likely that the individual will fail to appear or pay the citation on time, quickly resulting, in Ferguson, in an arrest warrant and a suspended license. Even setting aside the fact that people often receive inaccurate information about when they must appear in court, the inperson appearance requirement imposes particular difficulties on low-wage workers, single parents, and those with limited access to reliable transportation. Requiring an individual to appear in court also imposes particular burdens on those with jobs that have set hours that may conflict with an assigned court session. Court sessions are sometimes set during the workday and sometimes in the early evening. Additionally, while court dates can be set for several months after the citation was issued, in some cases they can also be issued as early as a week after a citation is received. For example, court staff have instructed FPD officers that derelict auto violations must be set for the "very next court date even if it is just a week…or so away." This can add an additional obstacle for those with firmly established employment schedules.

There are also historical reasons, of which the City is well-aware, that many Ferguson residents may not appear in court. Some individuals fear that if they cannot immediately pay the fines they owe, they will be arrested and sent to jail. Ferguson court staff members told us that they believe the high number of missed court appearances in their court is attributable, in part, to this popular belief. These fears are well founded. While Judge Brockmeyer has told us that he has never sentenced someone to jail time for being unable to pay a fine, we have found evidence that the Judge has held people appearing in court for contempt on account of their unwillingness to answer questions and sentenced those individuals to jail time. In December 2013, the FPD officer assigned to provide security at a court session directly emailed the City Manager to provide notice that "Judge Brockmeyer ordered [a defendant] arrested tonight after [he] refused to answer any questions and told the Judge that he had no jurisdiction. This happened on two separate occasions and with the second occasion when [the defendant] continued with his refusal to answer the Judge, he was order[ed] to be arrested and held for 10 days."[54] We also spoke with a woman who told us that, after asking questions in court, FPD officers arrested her for Contempt of Court at the instructions of the Court Clerk. Moreover, we have also received a report of an FPD officer arresting an individual at court for an outstanding warrant. In that instance, which occurred in April 2014, the individual — who was in court to make a fine payment — was approached by an FPD officer, asked to step outside of the court session, and was immediately arrested. In addition, as Ferguson's Municipal Judge confirmed, it is not uncommon for him to add charges and assess additional fines when a defendant challenges the citation that brought the defendant into court. Appearing in court in Ferguson also requires waits that can stretch into hours, sometimes outdoors in inclement weather. Many individuals report being treated dismissively, or worse, by court staff and the Municipal Judge.

Further, as Ferguson officials have told us, many people have experience with the numerous other municipal courts in St. Louis County that informs individuals' expectations about the Ferguson municipal court. Our investigation shows that other municipalities in the area have engaged in a number of practices that have the effect of discouraging people from attending court sessions. For instance, court clerks from other municipalities have told us that they have seen judges order people arrested if they appear in court with an outstanding warrant but are unable to pay the fine owed or post the bond amount listed on the warrant. Indeed, one municipal judge from a neighboring municipality told us that this practice has resulted in what he believes to be a widespread belief that those who attend court but cannot pay will be immediately arrested — a view that municipal judge says is "entirely the municipal courts' fault" for perpetuating because they have not taken steps to correct it. Recent reports have documented other problematic practices. For example, a June 2014 letter from Presiding Circuit Court Judge Maura McShane to municipal court judges in the region discussed troubling and possibly unlawful practices of municipal courts in St. Louis County that served to prevent the public from attending court sessions. These practices included not allowing children in court. Indeed, as late as October 2014, the municipal court website in the neighboring municipality of Bel Ridge — where Judge Brockmeyer serves as prosecutor — stated that children are not allowed in court. While it appears that Ferguson's court has always allowed children, we talked with people who assumed it did not because of their experiences in other courts. One man told us he was aggressively questioned by FPD officers after he left his child outside court with a friend because of this assumption. Thus, even though Ferguson might not engage in some of these practices, and while it may even be the case that other municipalities have themselves implemented reforms, the long history of these practices continues to shape community members' views of what might happen to them if they attend court.

Court officials have told us that Ferguson's expansive list of "must appear" offenses is not driven by any public safety need. That is underscored by the fact that, in some cases, attorneys are allowed to resolve such offenses over the phone without making any appearance in court. Nonetheless, despite the acknowledged obstacles to appearing in person in court and the lack of any articulated need to appear in court in all but a few instances, Ferguson has taken few, if any, steps to reduce the number of cases that require a court appearance.

c. Driver's License Suspensions Mandated by State Law and Unnecessarily Prolonged by Ferguson Make It Difficult to Resolve a Case and Impose Substantial Hardship

For many who have already had a warrant issued against them for failing to either appear or make a required payment, appearing in court is made especially difficult by the fact that their warrants likely resulted in the suspension of their driver's licenses. Pursuant to Missouri state law, anyone who fails to pay a traffic citation for a moving violation on time, or who fails to appear in court regarding a moving traffic violation, has his or her driver's license suspended. Mo. Rev. Stat. § 302.341.1. Thus, by virtue of having their licenses suspended, those who have already missed a required court appearance are more likely to fail to meet subsequent court obligations if they require physically appearing in court — fostering a cycle of missed appearances that is difficult to end. That is particularly so given what some City officials from Ferguson and surrounding communities have called substandard public transportation options. We spoke with one woman who had her license suspended because she received a Failure to Appear charge in Ferguson and so had to rely on a friend to drive her to court. When her friend canceled, she had no other means of getting to court on time, missed court, and had another Failure to Appear charge and arrest warrant issued against her — adding to the charges that required resolution before her license could be reinstated.[55]

To be clear, responsibility for the hardship imposed by automatically suspending a person's license for failing to appear in a traffic case rests largely with this state law. Notably, however, Ferguson's own discretionary practices amplify and prolong that law's impact. A temporary suspension can be lifted with a compliance letter from the municipal court, but the Ferguson municipal court does not issue compliance letters unless a person has satisfied the *entire fine* pending on the charge that caused the suspension. This rule is not mandated by state law, which instead provides a municipality with the authority to decide when to issue a compliance letter. *See* Mo. Rev. Stat. § 302.341.1("Such suspension shall remain in effect until the court with the subject pending charge requests setting aside the noncompliance suspension pending final disposition."). Indeed, Ferguson court staff told us that they will issue compliance letters before full payment has been made for cases that they determine, in their unguided discretion, to be sympathetic.

This rule and the Ferguson practices that magnify its impact underscore how missed court appearancescan have broad ramifications for individuals' ability to maintain a job and care for their families. We spoke with one woman who received three citations during a single incident in 2013 in which she pulled to the side of the road to allow a police car to pass, was confronted by the officer for doing so, and was cited for obstructing traffic, failing to signal, and not wearing a seatbelt. The woman appeared in court to challenge those citations, was told a new trial date would be mailed to her, and instead received notice from the Missouri Department of Revenue several months later that her license was suspended. Upon informing the Court Clerk that she never received notice of her court date, the Clerk told her the trial date had passed two weeks earlier and that there was now a warrant for her arrest pending.[56] Given that the woman's license was suspended only two weeks after her trial date, it appears the court did not send a warning letter before entering a warrant and suspending the license, contrary to purported policy. Court records likewise do not indicate a letter being sent. The woman asked to see the Municipal Judge to explain the situation, but court staff informed her that she could only see the Judge if she was issued a new court date and that she would only be issued a new court date if she paid her $200 bond. With no opportunity to further petition the court, she wrote to Mayor Knowles about her situation, stating:

> Although I feel I have been harassed, wronged and unjustly done by Ferguson...
> [w]hat I am upset and concerned about is my driver's license being suspended. I
> was told that I may not be able to [be] reinstate[d] until the tickets are taken care
> of. I am a hard working mother of two children and I cannot by any means take
> care of my family or work with my license being suspended and being unable to
> drive. I have to have [a] valid license to keep my job because I transport clients that
> I work with not to mention I drive my children back and forth to school, practices
> and rehearsals on a daily basis. I am writing this letter because no one has been
> able to help me and I am really hoping that I can get some help getting this issue
> resolved expediently.

It appears that, at the Mayor's request, the court entered "Not Guilty" dispositions on her cases, several months after they first resulted in the license suspension.

150

d. Court Operations Impose Obstacles to Resolving Even Those Offenses that Do Not Require In-Person Court Appearance

The limited number of code violations that do not require an in-person court appearance can likewise be difficult to resolve, even if a person can afford to do so. The court has accepted mailed payments for some time and has recently begun to accept online payments, but the court's website suggests that in-person payment is required and provides no information that payment online or by mail is an option. As a result, many people try to remit payment to the court window within the police department. But community members have informed us that the court window often closes earlier than the posted hours indicate. Indeed, during our investigation, we observed the court window close at 4:30 p.m. on days where an evening court session was not being held, despite the fact that both the Ferguson City website and the Missouri Courts website state that the window closes at 5:00 p.m.[57] On one such occasion, we observed two different sets of people arrive after 4:30 p.m. but before 5:00 p.m. One man told us his ticket payment was due that day. Another woman arrived in the rain with her small child, unsuccessfully attempted to call someone to the window, and left. Even when the court window is technically open, we have seen people standing at the window waiting for a response to their knocks for long periods of time, sometimes in inclement weather — even as court staff sat inside the police department tending to their normal duties.

As noted above, documents we reviewed showed that even where individuals are successful in talking with court staff about a citation, FPD-issued citations are sometimes so deficient that court staff are unable to determine what the fine, or even charge, is supposed to be. Evidence also shows that court staff have at times been unable to even find a person's case file, often because the FPD officer who issued the ticket failed to properly file a copy. In these cases, a person is left unable to resolve her or his citation.

e. High Fines, Coupled with Legally Inadequate Ability-to-Pay Determinations and Insufficient Alternatives to Immediate Payment, Impose a Significant Burden on People Living In or Near Poverty

It is common for a single traffic stop or other encounter with FPD to give rise to fines in amounts that a person living in poverty is unable to immediately pay. This fact is attributable in part to FPD's practice of issuing multiple citations — frequently three or more — on a single stop. This fact is also attributable to the fine assessment practices of the Ferguson municipal court, including not only the high fine amounts imposed, but also the inadequate process available for those who cannot afford to pay a fine. Even setting aside cases where additional fines and fees were imposed for Failure to Appear violations, our investigation found instances in which the court charged $302 for a single Manner of Walking violation; $427 for a single Peace Disturbance violation; $531 for High Grass and Weeds; $777 for Resisting Arrest; and $792 for Failure to Obey, and $527 for Failure to Comply, which officers appear to use interchangeably.

For many, the hardship of the fine amounts imposed is exacerbated by the fact that they owe similar fines in other, neighboring municipalities. We spoke with one woman who, in addition to owing several hundred dollars in fines to Ferguson, also owed fines to the municipal courts in Jennings and Edmundson. In total, she owed over $2,500 in fines and fees, even after already making over $1,000 in payments and clearing cases in several other municipalities. This woman's case is not unique. We have heard reports from many individuals and even City officials that, in light of the large number of municipalities in the area immediately surrounding Ferguson, most of which have their own police departments and municipal courts, it is common for people to face significant fines from many municipalities.

City officials have extolled that the Ferguson preset fine schedule establishes fines that are "at or near the top of the list" compared with other municipalities across a large number of offenses. A more recent comparison of the preset fines of roughly 70 municipal courts in the region confirms that Ferguson's fine amounts are above regional averages for many offenses, particularly discretionary offenses such as non-speeding-related traffic offenses. That comparison also shows that Ferguson imposes the highest fine of any of those roughly 70 municipalities for the offense of Failing to Provide Proof of Insurance; Ferguson charges $375, whereas the average fine imposed is $186 and the median fine imposed is $175. In 2013 alone, the Ferguson court collected over $286,000 in fines for that offense — more than any other offense except Failure to Appear.

The fines that the court imposes for offenses without preset fines are more difficult to evaluate precisely because they are imposed on a case-by-case basis. Typically, however, in imposing fines for non-TVB offenses during court sessions, the Municipal Judge adopts the fine recommendations of the Prosecuting Attorney — who also serves as the Ferguson City Attorney. As discussed above, court staff have communicated with the Municipal Judge regarding the need to ensure that the prosecutor's recommended fines are sufficiently high because "[w]e need to keep up our revenue." We were also told of at least one incident in which an attorney received a fine recommendation from the prosecutor for his client, but when the client went to court to pay the fine, a clerk refused payment, informing her that there was an additional $100 owed beyond the fine recommended by the prosecutor.

The court imposes these fines without providing any process by which a person can seek a fine reduction on account of financial incapacity. The court does not provide any opportunity for a person unable to pay a preset TVB fine to seek a modification of the fine amount. Nor does the court consider a person's financial ability to pay in determining how much of a fine to impose in cases without preset fines. The Ferguson court's failureto assess a defendant's ability to pay stands in direct tension with Missouri law, which instructs that in determining the amount and the method of payment of a fine, a court "shall, insofar as practicable, proportion the fine to the burden that payment will impose in view of the financial resources of an individual." Mo. Rev. Stat. § 560.026.

In lieu of proportioning a fine to a particular individual's ability to pay or allowing a process by which a person could petition the court for a reduction, the court offers payment plans to those who cannot afford to immediately pay in full. But such payment plans do not serve as a substitute for an ability-to-pay determination, which, properly employed, can enable a person in some cases to pay in full and resolve the case. Moreover, the court's rules regarding payment plans are themselves severe. Unlike some other municipalities that require a $50 monthly payment, Ferguson's standard payment plan requires payments of $100 per month, which remains a difficult amount for many to pay, especially those who are also making payments to other municipalities. Further, the court treats a single missed, partial, or untimely payment as a missed appearance. In such a case, the court immediately issues an arrest warrant without any notice or opportunity to explain why a payment was missed — for example, because the person was sick, or the court closed its doors early that day. The court reportedly has softened this rule during the course of our investigation by allowing a person who has missed a payment to go to court to seek leave for not paying the full amount owed. However, even this softened rule provides minimal relief, as making this request requires a person to appear in court the first Wednesday of the month at 11:00 a.m. If a person misses that session, the court immediately issues an arrest warrant.

Before the court provided this Wednesday morning court session for those on payment plans, court staff frequently rejected requests from payment plan participants to reduce or continue monthly payments — leaving individuals unable to make the required payment with no recourse besides incurring a Failure to Appear charge, receiving additional fines, and having an arrest warrant issued. In July 2014, an assistant court clerk wrote in an email that she rejected a defendant's request for a reduced monthly payment on account of inability to pay and told the defendant,"everyone says [they] can't pay." This is consistent with earlier noted statements by the acting Ferguson prosecutor that he stopped granting "needless requests for continuances from the payment docket." Another defendant who owed $1,002 in fines and fees stemming from a Driving with a Revoked License charge wrote to a City official that he would be unable to make his required monthly payment but hoped to avoid having a warrant issued. He explained that he was unemployed, that the court had put him on a payment plan only a week before his first payment was due, and that he did not have enough time to gather enough money. He implored the City to provide"some kind of community service to work off the fines/fees," stating that "I want to pay you guys what I owe" and "I have been trying to scrape up what I can," but that "with warrants it's hard to get a job." The City official forwarded the request to a court clerk, who noted that the underlying charge dated back to 2007, that five Failure to Appear charges had been levied, and that no payments had yet been made. The clerk responded:"In this certain case [the defendant] will go to warrant." Records show that, only a week earlier, this same clerk asked a court clerk from another municipality to clear a ticket for former Ferguson Police Chief Moonier as a "courtesy." And, only a month later, that same clerk also helped the Ferguson Collector of Revenue clear two citations issued by neighboring municipalities.

Ferguson does not typically offer community service as an alternative to fines. City officials have emphasized to us that Ferguson is one of only a few municipalities in the region to provide *any* form of a community service program, and that the program that is available is well run. But the program, which began in February 2014, is only available on a limited basis, mostly to certain defendants who are 19 years old or younger. We have heard directly from individuals who could not afford to pay their fines — and thus accumulated additional charges and fines and had warrants issued against them — that they requested a community service alternative to monetary payment but were told no such alternative existed. One man who still owes $1,100 stemming from a speeding and seatbelt violation from 2000 told us that he has been arrested repeatedly in connection with the fines he cannot afford to pay, and that "no one is willing to work with him to find an alternative solution." City officials have recognized the need to provide a meaningful community service option. In August 2013, one City Councilmember wrote to the City Manager and the Mayor that, "[f]or a few years now we have talked about offering community service to those who can't afford to pay their fines, but we haven't actually made it happen." The Councilmember noted the benefits of such a program, including that it would "keep those people that simply don't have the money to pay their fines from constantly being arrested and going to jail, only to be released and do it all over again."

2. The Court Imposes Unduly Harsh Penalties for Missed Payments or Appearances

The procedural deficiencies identified above work together to make it exceedingly difficult to resolve a case and exceedingly easy to run afoul of the court's stringent and confusing rules, particularly for those living in or near poverty. That the court is at least in part responsible for causing cases to protract and result in technical violations has not prevented it from imposing significant penalties when those violations occur. AlthoughFerguson's court — unlike many other municipal courts in the region — has ceased imposing the Failure to Appear charge, the court continues to routinely issue arrest warrants for missed appearances and missed payments. The evidence we have found shows that these arrest warrants are used almost exclusively for the purpose of compelling payment through the threat of incarceration. The evidence also shows that the harms of the court's warrant practices are exacerbated by the court's bond procedures, which impose unnecessary obstacles to clearing a warrant or securing release after being arrested on a warrant and often function to furtherprolong a case and a person's involvement in the municipal justice system. These practices — together with the consequences to individuals and communities that result — raise significant due process and equal protection concerns.[58]

a. The Ferguson Municipal Court Uses Arrest Warrants Primarily as a Means of Securing Payment

Ferguson uses its police department in large part as a collection agency for its municipal court. Ferguson's municipal court issues arrest warrants at a rate that police officials have called, in internal emails, "staggering." According to the court's own figures, as of December 2014, over 16,000 people had outstanding arrest warrants that had been issued by the court. In fiscal year 2013 alone, the court issued warrants to approximately 9,007 people. Many of those individuals had warrants issued on multiple charges, as the 9,007 warrants applied to 32,975 different offenses.

In the wake of several news accounts indicating that the Ferguson municipal court issued over 32,000 warrants in fiscal year 2013, court staff determined that it had mistakenly reported to the state of Missouri the number of charged offenses that had warrants (32,975), not the number of people who had warrants outstanding (9,007). Our investigation indicates that is the case. In any event, it is probative of FPD's enforcement practices that those roughly 9,000 warrants were issued for over 32,000 offenses. Moreover, for those against whom a warrant is issued, the number of offenses included within the warrant has tremendous practical importance. As discussed below, the bond amount a person must pay to clear a warrant before an arrest occurs, or to secure release once a warrant has been executed, is often dependent on the number of offenses to which the warrant applies. And, that the court issued warrants for the arrest of roughly 9,000 people is itself not insignificant; even under that calculation, Ferguson has one of the highest warrant totals in the region.

The large number of warrants issued by the court, by any count, is due exclusively to the fact that the court uses arrest warrants and the threat of arrest as its primary tool for collecting outstanding fines for municipal code violations. With extremely limited exceptions, every warrant issued by the Ferguson municipal court was issued because: 1) a person missed consecutive court appearances, or 2) a person missed a single required fine payment as part of a payment plan. Under current court policy, the court issues a warrant in every case where either of those circumstances arises — regardless of the severity of the code violation that the case involves. Indeed, the court rarely issues a warrant for any other purpose. FPD does not request arrest or any other kind of warrants from the Ferguson municipal court; in fact, FPD officers told us that they have been instructed not to file warrant applications with the municipal court because the court does not have the capacity to consider them.

While issuing municipal warrants against people who have not appeared or paid their municipal code violation fines is sometimes framed as addressing the failure to abide by court rules, in practice, it is clear that warrants are primarily issued to coerce payment.[59] One municipal judge from a neighboring municipality told us that the use of the Failure to Appear charge "provides cushion for judges against the attack that the court is operating as a debtor's prison." And the Municipal Judge in Ferguson has acknowledged repeatedly that the warrants the court issues are not put in place for public safety purposes. Indeed, once a warrant issues, there is no urgency within FPD to actually execute it. Court staff reported that they typically take weeks, if not months, to enter warrants into the system that enables patrol officers to determine if a person they encounter has an outstanding warrant. As of December 2014, for example, some warrants issued in September 2014 were not yet detectable to officers in the field. Court staff also informed us that no one from FPD has ever commented on that lag or prioritized closing it. Nor does there seem to be any public safety obstacle to eliminating failure to appear warrants altogether. The court has, in fact, adopted a temporary "warrant recall program" that allows individuals who show up to court to immediately have their warrants recalled and a new court date assigned. And, under longstanding practice, once an attorney makes an appearance in a case, the court automatically discharges any pending warrants.

That the primary role of warrants is not to protect public safety but rather to facilitate fine collection is further evidenced by the fact that the warrants issued by the court are overwhelmingly issued in non-criminal traffic cases that would not themselves result in a penalty of imprisonment. From 2010 to December 2014, the offenses (besides Failure to Appear ordinance violations) that most often led to a municipal warrant were: Driving While License Is Suspended, Expired License Plates, Failure to Register a Vehicle, No Proof of Insurance, and Speed Limit violations. These offenses comprised the majority of offenses that led to a warrant not because they are more severe than other offenses, but rather because every missed appearance or payment on any charge results in a warrant, and these were some of the most common charges brought by FPD during that period.

Even though these underlying code violations would not on their own result in a penalty of imprisonment, arrest and detention are not uncommon once a warrant enters on a case. We have found that FPD officers frequently check individuals for warrants, even when the person is not reasonably suspected of engaging in any criminal activity, and, if a municipal warrant exists, will often make an arrest. City officials have told us that the decision to arrest a person for an outstanding warrant is "highly discretionary" and that officers will frequently not arrest unless the person is "ignorant." Records show, however, that officers do arrest individuals for outstanding municipal warrants with considerable frequency. Jail records are poorly managed, and data on jail bookings is only available as of April 2014. But during the roughly six-month period from April to September 2014, 256 people were booked into the Ferguson City Jail after being arrested at least in part for an outstanding warrant — 96% of whom were African American. Of these individuals, 28 were held for longer than two days, and 27 of these 28 people were black.

Similarly, data collected during vehicle stops shows that, during a larger period of time between October 2012 and October 2014, FPD arrested roughly 460 individuals following a vehicle stop *solely* because they had outstanding warrants. This figure is likely a significant underrepresentation of the total number of people arrested for outstanding warrants during that period, as it does not include those people arrested on outstanding warrants not during traffic stops; nor does it include those people arrested during traffic stops for multiple reasons, but who might not have been stopped, much less arrested, without the officer performing a warrant check on the car and finding an outstanding warrant. Even among this limited pool, the data shows the disparate impact these arrests have on African Americans. Of the 460 individuals arrested during traffic stops solely for outstanding warrants, 443 individuals — or 96% — were African American.

That data also does not include those people arrested by *other* municipal police departments on the basis of an outstanding warrant issued by Ferguson. As has been widely reported in recent months, many municipal police departments in the region identify people with warrants pending in other towns and then arrest and hold those individuals on behalf of those towns. FPD's records show that it routinely arrests individuals on warrants issued by other jurisdictions. And, although we did not review the records of other departments, we have heard reports of many individuals who were arrested for a Ferguson-issued warrant by police officers outside of Ferguson. On some occasions, Ferguson will decline to pick up a person arrested in a different municipality for a Ferguson warrant and, after however long it takes for that decision to be made, the person will be released, sometimes after being required to pay bond. On other occasions, Ferguson will send an officer to retrieve the person for incarceration in the Ferguson City Jail; FPD supervisors have in fact instructed officers to do so "regardless of the charge or the bond amount, or the number of prisoners we have in custody." We found evidence of FPD officers traveling more than 200 miles to retrieve a person detained by another agency on a Ferguson municipal warrant.

Because of the large number of municipalities in the region, many of which have warrant practices similar to Ferguson, it is not unusual for a person to be arrested by one department, have outstanding warrants pending in other police departments, and be handed off from one department to another until all warrants are cleared. We have heard of individuals who have run out of money during this process — referred to by many as the "muni shuffle" — and as a result were detained for a week or longer.

The large number of municipal court warrants being issued, many of which lead to arrest, raises significant due process and equal protection concerns. In particular, Ferguson's practice of automatically treating a missed payment as a failure to appear — thus triggering an arrest warrant and possible incarceration — is directly at odds with well-established law that prohibits "punishing a person for his poverty." *Bearden v. Georgia*, 461 U.S. 660, 671 (1983); *see also Tate v. Short*, 401 U.S. 395, 398 (1971). In *Bearden,* the Supreme Court found unconstitutional a state's decision to revoke probation and sentence a defendant to prison because the defendant was unable to pay a required fine. *Bearden*, 461 U.S. at 672-73. The Court held that before imposing imprisonment, a court must first inquire as to whether the missed payment was attributable to an inability to pay and, if so, "consider alternate measures of punishment other than imprisonment." *Id.* at 672; *see also Martin v. Solem*, 801 F.2d 324, 332 (8th Cir. 1986) (noting that the state court had failed to adequately determine, as required by *Bearden,* whether the defendant had "made sufficient bona fide efforts legally to acquire the resources to pay," but nonetheless denying habeas relief because the defendant's failure to pay was due not to indigency but his "willful refusal to pay").

The Ferguson court, however, has in the past routinely issued arrest warrants when a person is unable to make a required fine payment without any ability-to-pay determination. While the court does not *sentence* a defendant to jail in such a case, the result is often equivalent to what *Bearden* proscribes: the incarceration of a defendant solely because of an inability to pay a fine. In response to concerns about issuing warrants in such cases, Ferguson officials have told us that without issuing warrants and threatening incarceration, they have no ability to secure payment. But the Supreme Court rejected that argument, finding that states are "not powerless to enforce judgments against those financially unable to pay a fine," and noting that — especially in cases like those at issue here in which the court has already made a determination that penological interests do *not* demand incarceration — a court can "establish a reduced fine or alternate public service in lieu of a fine that adequately serves the state's goals of punishment and deterrence, given the defendant's diminished financial resources."[60] *Id.* As discussed above, however, Ferguson has not established any such alternative.[61]

Finally, in light of the significant portion of municipal charges that lead to an arrest warrant, as well as the substantial number of arrest warrants that lead to arrest and detention, we have considerable concerns regarding whether individuals facing charges in Ferguson municipal court are entitled to, and being unlawfully denied, the right to counsel.

b. Ferguson's Bond Practices Impose Undue Hardship on Those Seeking to Secure Release from the Ferguson City Jail

Our investigation found substantial deficiencies in the way Ferguson police and court officials set, accept, refund, and forfeit bond payments. Recently, in response to concerns raised during our investigation, the City implemented several changes to its bond practices, most of which apply to those detained after a warrantless arrest.[62] These changes represent positive developments, but many deficiencies remain.[63] Given the high number of arrest warrants issued by the municipal court — and given that in many cases a person can only clear a pending warrant or secure release from detention by posting bond — the deficiencies identified below impose significant harm to individuals in Ferguson.

Current bond practices are unclear and inconsistent. Information provided by the City reveals a haphazard bond system that results in people being erroneously arrested, and some people paying bond but not getting credit for having done so. Documents describe officers finding hundred dollar bills in their pockets that were given to them for bond payment and not remembering which jail detainee provided them; bond paperwork being found on the floor; and individuals being arrested after their bonds had been accepted because the corresponding warrants were never cancelled. At one point in 2012, Ferguson's Court Clerk called such issues a "daily problem." The City's practices for receiving and tracking bond payments have not changed appreciably since then.

The practices for setting bond are similarly erratic. The Municipal Judge advised us that he sets all bonds upon issuing an arrest warrant. We found, however, that bond amounts are mostly set by court staff, and are rarely even reviewed by the Judge. While court staff told us that the current bond schedule requires a bond of $200 for up to four traffic offenses, $100 for every traffic offense thereafter, $100 for every Failure to Appear charge, and $300 for every criminal offense, FPD's own policy includes a bond schedule that departs from these figures. In practice, bond amounts vary widely. *See* FPD General Order 421.02. Our review of a random sample of warrants indicates that bond is set in a manner that often departs from both the schedule referenced by court staff and the schedule found in FPD policy. In a number of these cases, the bond amount far exceeded the amount of the underlying fine.

The court's bond practices, including the fact that the court often imposes bonds that exceed the amount owed to the court, do not appear to be grounded in any public safety need. In a July 2014 email to Chief Jackson and other police officials, the Court Clerk reported that "[s]tarting today we are going to reduce anyone's bond that calls and is in warrant[] to half the amount," explaining that "[t]his may bring in some extra monies this way." The email identifies no public safety obstacle or other reason not to implement the bond reduction. Notably, the email alsostates that "[w]e will only do this between the hours of 8:30 to 4" and that no half-bond will be accepted after those hours unless the Court Clerk approves it.[64] Thus, as a result of this policy, an individual able to appear at the court window during business hours would pay half as much to clear a warrant as an individual who is actually arrested on a warrant after hours. ThatFerguson's bond practices do not appear grounded in public safety is underscored by the fact that the court will typically cancel outstanding warrants without requiring the posting of *any* bond for people who have an attorney enter an appearance on their behalf. Records show that this practice is also applied haphazardly, and there do not appear to be any rules that govern the apparent discretion court staff have to waive or require bond following an attorney's appearance.

It is not uncommon for an individual charged with only a minor violation to be arrested on a warrant, be unable to afford bond, and have no recourse but to await release. Longstanding court rules provide for a person arrested pursuant to an arrest warrant to be held up to 72 hours before being released without bond, and the court's recent orders do not appear to change this. Records show that individuals are routinely held for 72 hours. FPD's records management system only began capturing meaningful jail data in April 2014; but from April to September 2014 alone, 77 people were detained in the jail for longer than two days, and many of those detentions neared, reached, or exceeded the 72-hour mark. Of those 77 people, 73, or 95%, were black. Many people, including the woman described earlier who was charged with two parking code violations, have reported being held up until the 72-hour limit — despite having no ability to pay.

Indeed, many others report being held for far longer, and documentary evidence is consistent with these reports. In April 2010, for example, the Chief of Police wrote an email to the Captain of the Patrol Division stating that the "intent is that when the watch commander / street supervisor gets the census from the jail he asks who will come up on 72 hrs.," and, if there is any such person, "he can have them given the next available court date and released, or authorize they remain in jail, since he will be the designate." The email continues: "If someone has already been there more than 72 hours, it may be assumed their continued hold was previously authorized." Further, as noted above, while comprehensive jail records do not exist for detentions prior to April 2014, records do show several recent instances in which FPD detained a person for longer than the purported 72-hour limit.

Despite the fact that those arrested by FPD for outstanding municipal warrants can be held for several days if unable to post bond, the Ferguson municipal court does not give credit for time served. As a result, there have been many cases in which a person has been arrested on a warrant, detained for 72 hours or more, and released owing the same amount as before the arrest was made. Court records do not even track the total amount of time a person has spent in jail as part of a case. When asked why this is not tracked, a member of court staff told us: "It's only three days anyway."

These prolonged detentions for those who cannot afford bond are alarming, and raise considerable due process and equal protection concerns. The prolonged detentions are especially concerning given that there is no public safety need for those who receive municipal warrants to be jailed at all. The Ferguson Municipal Judge has acknowledged that for most code violations, it is "probably a good idea to do away with jail time."

Further, there are many circumstances in which court practices preclude a person from making payment against the underlying fine owed — and thus resolving the case, or at least moving the case toward resolution — and instead force the person to pay a bond. If, for example, an individual is jailed on a "must appear" charge and has not yet appeared in court to have the fine assessed, the individual will not be allowed to make payment on the underlying charge. Rather, the person must post bond, receive a new court date, appear in court, and start the process anew. Even when the underlying fine has been assessed, a person in jail may still be forced to make a bond payment instead of a fine payment to secure release if court staff are unavailable to determine the amount the person owes. And when a person attempts to resolve a warrant before they end up arrested, a bond payment will typically be required unless the person can afford to pay the underlying fine in full, as, by purported policy, the court does not accept partial payment of fines outside of a court-sanctioned payment plan.

Bond forfeiture procedures also raise significant due process concerns. Under current practice, the first missed appearance or missed payment following a bond payment results in a warning letter being sent; after the second missed appearance or payment, the court initiates a forfeiture action (and issues another arrest warrant). As with "warrant warning letters" described above, our investigation has been unable to verify that the court *consistently* sends bond forfeiture warning letters. And, as with warrant warning letters, bond forfeiture warning letters are sometimes returned to the court, but court staff members do not appear to make any further attempt to contact the intended recipient.

Upon a bond being forfeited, the court directs the bond money into the City's account and does not apply the amount to the individual's underlying fine. For example, if a person owes a $200 fine payment, is arrested on a warrant, and posts a bond of $200, the forfeiture of the bond will result in the fine remaining $200 and an arrest warrant being issued. If, instead, Ferguson were to allow this $200 to go toward the underlying fine, this would resolve the matter entirely, obviating the need for any warrant or subsequent court appearance. Not applying a forfeited bond to the underlying fine is especially troubling considering that this policy does not appear to be clearly communicated to those paying bonds. Particularly in cases where the bond is set at an amount near the underlying fine owed — which we have found to be common — it is entirely plausible that a person paying bond would mistakenly believe that payment resolves the case.

When asked why the forfeited bond is not applied to the underlying fine, court staff[65] asserted that applicable law prohibits them from doing sowithout the bond payer's consent. That explanation is grounded in an incorrect view of the law. In *Perry v. Aversman*, 168 S.W.3d 541 (Mo. Ct. App. 2005), the Missouri Court of Appeals explicitly upheld a rule requiring that forfeited bonds be applied to pending fines of the person who paid bond and found that such practices are acceptable so long as the court provides sufficient notice. *Id.* at 543-46. In light of the fact that applicable law permits forfeited bonds to be applied to pending fines, Ferguson's longstanding practice of directing forfeited bond money to the City's general fund is troubling. In fiscal year 2013 alone, the City collected forfeited bond amounts of $177,168, which could instead have been applied to the fines of those making the payments.

Ferguson's rules and procedures for *refunding* bond payments upon satisfaction of the underlying fine raise similar concerns. Ferguson requires that when a person pays the underlying fine to avoid bond forfeiture, he or she must pay in person and provide photo identification. Yet, where the underlying fine is less than the bond amount — a common occurrence — the City does not immediately refund the difference to the individual. Rather, pursuant to a directive issued by the current City Finance Director approximately four years ago, bond refunds *cannot* be made in person, and instead must be sent via mail. According to Ferguson's Court Clerk, it is not entirely uncommon for these refund checks to bereturned as undeliverable and become "unclaimed property."

C. Ferguson Law Enforcement Practices Disproportionately Harm Ferguson's African-American Residents and Are Driven in Part by Racial Bias

Ferguson's police and municipal court practices disproportionately harm African Americans. Further, our investigation found substantial evidence that this harm stems in part from intentional discrimination in violation of the Constitution.

African Americans experience disparate impact in nearly every aspect of Ferguson's law enforcement system. Despite making up 67% of the population, African Americans accounted for 85% of FPD's traffic stops, 90% of FPD's citations, and 93% of FPD's arrests from 2012 to 2014. Other statistical disparities, set forth in detail below, show that in Ferguson:

- African Americans are 2.07 times more likely to be searched during a vehicular stop but are 26% less likely to have contraband found on them during a search. They are 2.00 times more likely to receive a citation and 2.37 times more likely to be arrested following a vehicular stop.
- African Americans have force used against them at disproportionately high rates, accounting for 88% of all cases from 2010 to August 2014 in which an FPD officer reported using force. In all 14 uses of force involving a canine bite for which we have information about the race of the person bitten, the person was African American.
- African Americans are more likely to receive multiple citations during a single incident, receiving four or more citations on 73 occasions between October 2012 and July 2014, whereas non-African Americans received four or more citations only twice during that period.
- African Americans account for 95% of Manner of Walking charges; 94% of all Fail to Comply charges; 92% of all Resisting Arrest charges; 92% of all Peace Disturbance charges; and 89% of all Failure to Obey charges.[66]
- African Americans are 68% less likely than others to have their cases dismissed by the Municipal Judge, and in 2013 African Americans accounted for 92% of cases in which an arrest warrant was issued.
- African Americans account for 96% of known arrests made exclusively because of an outstanding municipal warrant.

These disparities are not the necessary or unavoidable results of legitimate public safety efforts. In fact, the practices that lead to these disparities in many ways undermine law enforcement effectiveness. *See, e.g.*, Jack Glaser, *Suspect Race: Causes and Consequence of Racial Profiling Suspect Race: Causes and Consequence of Racial Profiling* 126 (2015) (because profiling can increase crime while harming communities, it has a "high risk" of contravening the core police objectives of controlling crime and promoting public safety). The disparate impact of these practices thus violates federal law, including Title VI and the Safe Streets Act.

The racially disparate impact of Ferguson's practices is driven, at least in part, by intentional discrimination in violation of the Equal Protection Clause of the Fourteenth Amendment. Racial bias and stereotyping is evident from the facts, taken together. This evidence includes: the consistency and magnitude of the racial disparities throughout Ferguson's police and court enforcement actions; the selection and execution of police and court practices that disproportionately harm African Americans and do little to promote public safety; the persistent exercise of discretion to the detriment of African Americans; the apparent consideration of race in assessing threat; and the historical opposition to having African Americans live in Ferguson, which lingers among some today. We have also found explicit racial bias in the communications of police and court supervisors and that some officials apply racial stereotypes, rather than facts, to explain the harm African Americans experience due to Ferguson's approach to law enforcement. "Determining whether invidious discriminatory purpose was a motivating factor demands a sensitive inquiry into such circumstantial and direct evidence of intent as may be available." *Vill. of Arlington Heights v. Metro. Hous. Dev. Corp.*, 429 U.S. 252, 266 (1977).Based on this evidence as a whole, we have found that Ferguson's law enforcement activities stem in part from a discriminatory purpose and thus deny African Americans equal protection of the laws in violation of the Constitution.

1. Ferguson's Law Enforcement Actions Impose a Disparate Impact on African Americans that Violates Federal Law

African Americans are disproportionately represented at nearly every stage of Ferguson law enforcement, from initial police contact to final disposition of a case in municipal court. While FPD's data collection and retention practices are deficient in many respects, the data that is collected by FPD is sufficient to allow for meaningful and reliable analysis of racial disparities. This data — collected directly by police and court officials — reveals racial disparities that are substantial and consistent across a wide range of police and court enforcement actions.

African Americans experience the harms of the disparities identified below as part of a comprehensive municipal justice system that, at each juncture, enforces the law more harshly against black people than others. The disparate impact of Ferguson's enforcement actions is compounding: at each point in the enforcement process there is a higher likelihood that an African American will be subjected to harsher treatment; accordingly, as the adverse consequences imposed by Ferguson grow more and more severe, those consequences are imposed more and more disproportionately against African Americans. Thus, while 85% of FPD's vehicle stops are of African Americans, 90% of FPD's citations are issued to African Americans, and 92% of all warrants are issued in cases against African Americans. Strikingly, available data shows that of those subjected to one of the most severe actions this system routinely imposes — actual arrest for an outstanding municipal warrant — 96% are African American.

a. Disparate Impact of FPD Practices

i. Disparate Impact of FPD Enforcement Actions Arising from Vehicular Stops

Pursuant to Missouri state law on racial profiling, Mo. Rev. Stat. § 590.650, FPD officers are required to collect race and other data during every traffic stop. While some law enforcement agencies collect more comprehensive data to identify and stem racial profiling, this information is sufficient to show that FPD practices exert a racially disparate impact along several dimensions.

FPD reported 11,610 vehicle stops between October 2012 and October 2014. African Americans accounted for 85%, or 9,875, of those stops, despite making up only 67% of the population. White individuals made up 15%, or 1,735, of stops during that period, despite representing 29% of the population. These differences indicate that FPD traffic stop practices may disparately impact black drivers.[67] Even setting aside the question of whether there are racial disparities in FPD's traffic *stop* practices, however, the data collected during those stops reliably shows statistically significant racial disparities in the *outcomes* people receive *after* being stopped. Unlike with vehicle stops, assessing the disparate impact of post-stop outcomes — such as the rate at which stops result in citations, searches, or arrests — is not dependent on population data or on assumptions about differential offending rates by race; instead, the enforcement actions imposed against stopped black drivers are compared directly to the enforcement actions imposed against stopped white drivers.

In Ferguson, traffic stops of black drivers are more likely to lead to searches, citations, and arrests than are stops of white drivers. Black people are significantly more likely to be searched during a traffic stop than white people. From October 2012 to October 2014, 11% of stopped black drivers were searched, whereas only 5% of stopped white drivers were searched.

Despite being searched at higher rates, African Americans are 26% *less* likely to have contraband found on them than whites: 24% of searches of African Americans resulted in a contraband finding, whereas 30% of searches of whites resulted in a contraband finding. This disparity exists even after controlling for the type of search conducted, whether a search incident to arrest, a consent search, or a search predicated on reasonable suspicion. The lower rate at which officers find contraband when searching African Americans indicates either that officers' suspicion of criminal wrongdoing is less likely to be accurate when interacting with African Americans or that officers are more likely to search African Americans without any suspicion of criminal wrongdoing. Either explanation suggests bias, whether explicit or implicit.[68] This lower hit rate for African Americans also underscores that this disparate enforcement practice is ineffective.

Other, more subtle indicators likewise show meaningful disparities in FPD's search practices: of the 31 *Terry* stop searches FPD conducted during this period between October 2012 to October 2014, 30 were of black individuals; of the 103 times FPD asked both the driver and passenger to exit a vehicle during a search, the searched individuals were black in 95 cases; and, while only one search of a white person lasted more than half an hour (1% of all searches of white drivers), 59 searches of African Americans lasted that long (5% of all searches of black drivers).

Of all stopped black drivers, 91%, or 8,987, received citations, while 87%, or 1,501, of all stopped white drivers received a citation.[69] 891 stopped black drivers — 10% of all stopped black drivers — were arrested as a result of the stop, whereas only 63 stopped white drivers — 4% of all stopped white drivers — were arrested. This disparity is explainable in large part by the high number of black individuals arrested for outstanding municipal warrants issued for missed court payments and appearances. As we discuss below, African Americans are more likely to have warrants issued against them than whites and are more likely to be arrested for an outstanding warrant than their white counterparts. Notably, on 14 occasions FPD listed the only reason for an arrest following a traffic stop as "resisting arrest." In all 14 of those cases, the person arrested was black.

These disparities in the outcomes that result from traffic stops remain even after regression analysis is used to control for non-race-based variables, including driver age; gender; the assignment of the officer making the stop; disparities in officer behavior; and the stated reason the stop was initiated. Upon accounting for differences in those variables, African Americans remained 2.07 times more likely to be searched; 2.00 times more likely to receive a citation; and 2.37 times more likely to be arrested than other stopped individuals. Each of these disparities is statistically significant and would occur by chance less than one time in 1,000.[70] The odds of these disparities occurring by chance together are significantly lower still.

ii. DisparateImpact of FPD's Multiple Citation Practices

The substantial racial disparities that exist within the data collected from traffic stops are consistent with the disparities found throughout FPD's practices. As discussed above, our investigation found that FPD officers frequently make discretionary choices to issue multiple citations during a single incident. Setting aside the fact that, in some cases, citations are redundant and impose duplicative penalties for the same offense, the issuance of multiples citations also disproportionately impacts African Americans. In 2013, for instance, more than 50% of all African Americans cited received multiple citations during a single encounter with FPD, whereas only 26% of non-African Americans did. Specifically, 26% of African Americans receiving a citation received two citations at once, whereas only 17% of white individuals received two citations at once. Those disparities are even greater for incidents that resulted in more than two citations: 15% of African Americans cited received three citations at the same time, whereas 6% of cited whites received three citations; and while 10% of cited African Americans received four or more citations at once, only 3% of cited whites received that many during a single incident. Each of these disparities is statistically significant, and would occur by chance less than one time in 1,000. Indeed, related data from an overlapping time period shows that, between October 2012 to July 2014, 38 black individuals received four citations during a single incident, compared with only two white individuals; and while 35 black individuals received five or more citations at once, not a single white person did.[71]

iii. Disparate Impact of Other FPD Charging Practices

From October 2012 to July 2014, African Americans accounted for 85%, or 30,525, of the 35,871 *total* charges brought by FPD — including traffic citations, summonses, and arrests.[72] Non-African Americans accounted for 15%, or 5,346, of all charges brought during that period. These rates vary somewhat across different offenses. For example, African Americans represent a relatively low proportion of those charged with Driving While Intoxicated and Speeding on State Roads or Highways. With respect to speeding offenses for all roads, African Americans account for 72% of citations based on radar or laser, but 80% of citations based on other or unspecified methods. Thus, as evaluated by radar, African Americans violate the law at lower rates than as evaluated by FPD officers. Indeed, controlling for other factors, the disparity in speeding tickets between African Americans and non-African Americans is 48% larger when citations are issued not on the basis of radar or laser, but by some other method, such as the officer's own visual assessment. This difference is statistically significant.

Data on charges issued by FPD from 2011-2013 shows that, for numerous municipal offenses for which FPD officers have a high degree of discretion in charging, African Americans are disproportionately represented relative to theirrepresentation in Ferguson's population. While African Americans make up 67% of Ferguson's population, they make up 95% of Manner of Walking in Roadway charges; 94% of Failure to Comply charges; 92% of Resisting Arrest charges; 92% of Peace Disturbance charges; and 89% of Failure to Obey charges. Because these non-traffic offenses are more likely to be brought against persons who actually live in Ferguson than are vehicle stops, census data here does provide a useful benchmark for whether a pattern of racially disparate policing appears to exist. These disparities mean that African Americans in Ferguson bear the overwhelming burden of FPD's pattern of unlawful stops, searches, and arrests with respect to these highly discretionary ordinances.

iv. Disparate Impact of FPD Arrests for Outstanding Warrants

FPD records show that once a warrant issues, racial disparities in FPD's warrant execution practices make it exceedingly more likely for a black individual with an outstanding warrant to be arrested than a white individual with an outstanding warrant. Arrest data captured by FPD often fails to identify when a person is arrested *solely* on account of an outstanding warrant. Nonetheless, the data FPD collects during traffic stops pursuant to Missouri state requirements does capture information regarding when arrests are made for no other reason than that an arrest warrant was pending. Based upon that data, from October 2012 to October 2014, FPD arrested 460 individuals exclusively because the person had an outstanding arrest warrant. Of those 460 people arrested, 443, or 96%, were black. That African Americans are disproportionately impacted by FPD's warrant execution practices is also reflected in the fact that, during the roughly six-month period from April to September 2014, African Americans accounted for 96% of those booked into the Ferguson City Jail at least *in part* because they were arrested for an outstanding municipal warrant.

v. Concerns Regarding Pedestrian Stops

Although available data enables an assessment of the disparate impact of many FPD practices, many other practices cannot be assessed statistically because of FPD's inadequate data collection. FPD does not reliably collect or track data regarding pedestrian stops, or FPD officers' conduct during those stops. Given this lack of data, we are unable to determine whether African Americans are disproportionately the subjects of pedestrian stops, or the rate of searches, arrests, or other post-pedestrian stop outcomes. We note, however, that during our investigation we have spoken with not only black community members who have been stopped by FPD officers, but also non-black community members and employees of local businesses who have observed FPD conduct pedestrian stops of others, all of whom universally report that pedestrian stops in Ferguson almost always involve African-American youth. Even though FPD does not specifically track pedestrian stops, other FPD records are consistent with those accounts. Arrest and other incident reports sometimes describe encounters that begin with pedestrian stops, almost all of which involve African Americans.

b. Disparate Impact of Court Practices

Our investigation has also found that the rules and practices of the Ferguson municipal court also exert a disparate impact on African Americans. As discussed above, once a charge is filed in Ferguson municipal court, a number of procedural barriers imposed by the court combine to make it unnecessarily difficult to resolve the charge. Data created and maintained by the court show that black defendants are significantly more likely to be adversely impacted by those barriers. An assessment of every charge filed in Ferguson municipal court in 2011 shows that, over time, black defendants are more likely to have their cases persist for longer durations, more likely to face a higher number of mandatory court appearances and other requirements, and more likely to have a warrant issued against them for failing to meet those requirements.[73]

In light of the opaque court procedures previously discussed, the likelihood of running afoul of a court requirement increases when a case lasts for a longer period of time and results in more court encounters. Court cases involving black individuals typically last longer than those involving white individuals. Of the 2,369 charges filed against white defendants in 2011, over 63% were closed after six months. By contrast, only 34% of the 10,984 charges against black defendants were closed within that time period. 10% of black defendants, however, resolved their case between six months and a year from when it was filed, while 9% of white defendants required that much time to secure resolution. And, while 17% of black defendants resolved their charge over a year after it was brought against them, only 9% of white defendants required that much time. Each of these cases was ultimately resolved, in most instances by satisfying debts owed to the court; but this data shows substantial disparities between blacks and whites regarding how long it took to do so.

On average, African Americans are also more likely to have a high number of "events" occur before a case is resolved. The court's records track all activities that occur in a case — from payments and court appearances to continuances and Failure to Appear charges. 11% of cases involving African Americans had three "events," whereas 10% of cases involving white defendants had three events. 14% of cases involving black defendants had four to five events, compared with 9% of cases involving white defendants. Those disparities increase as the recorded number of events per case increases. Data show that there are ten or more events in 17% of cases involving black defendants but only 5% of cases involving white defendants. Given that an "event" can represent a variety of different kinds of occurrences, these particular disparities are perhaps less probative; nonetheless, they strongly suggest that black defendants have, on average, more encounters with the court during a single case than their white peers.

Given the figures above, it is perhaps unsurprising that the municipal court's practice of issuing warrants to compel fine payments following a missed court appearance or missed payment has a disparate impact on black defendants. 92% of all warrants issued in 2013 were issued in cases involving an African-American defendant. This figure is disproportionate to the representation of African Americans in the court's docket. Although the proportion of court cases involving black defendants has increased in recent years — 81% of all cases filed in 2009, compared with 85% of all cases filed in 2013 — that proportion remains substantially below the proportion of warrants issued to African Americans.

These disparities are consistent with the evidence discussed above that African Americans are often unable to resolve municipal charges despite taking appropriate steps to do so, and the evidence discussed below suggesting that court officials exercise discretion in a manner that disadvantages the African Americans that appear before the court.

Notably, the evidence suggests that African Americans are not only disparately impacted by court procedures, but also by the court's discretionary rulings in individual cases. Although court data did not enable a comprehensive assessment of disparities in fines that the court imposes, we did review fine data regarding ten different offenses and offense categories, including the five highly discretionary offenses disproportionately brought against African Americans noted above.[74] That analysis suggests that there may be racial disparities in the court's fine assessment practices. In analyzing the initial fines assessed for those ten offenses for each year from 2011-2013 — 30 data points in total — the average fine assessment was higher for African Americans than others in 26 of the 30 data points. For example, among the 53 Failure to Obey charges brought in 2013 that did not lead to added Failure to Appear fines — 44 of which involved an African-American defendant — African Americans were assessed an average fine of $206, whereas the average fine for others was $147. The magnitude of racial disparities in fine amounts varied across the 30 yearly offense averages analyzed, but those disparities consistently disfavored African Americans.

Further, an evaluation of dismissal rates throughout the life of a case shows that, on average, an African-American defendant is 68% less likely than other defendants to have a case dismissed. In addition to cases that are "Dismissed," court records also show cases that are "Voided" altogether. There are only roughly 400 cases listed as Voided from 2011-2013, but the data that is available for that relatively small number of Voided cases shows that African Americans are three times less likely to receive the Voided outcome than others.

c. Ferguson's Racially Disparate Practices Violate Federal Law

This data shows that police and court practices impose a disparate impact on black individuals that itself violates the law. Title VI and the Safe Streets Act prohibit law enforcement agencies that receive federal financial assistance, such as FPD, from engaging in law enforcement activities that have an unnecessary disparate impact based on race, color, or national origin. 42 U.S.C. § 2000d. Title VI's implementing regulations prohibit law enforcement agencies from using "criteria or methods of administration" that have a n unnecessary disparate impact based on race, color, or national origin. 28 C.F.R. § 42.104(b)(2); *see also Alexander v. Sandoval*, 532 U.S. 275, 281-82 (2001). Similarly, the Safe Streets Act applies not only to intentional discrimination, but also to any law enforcement practices that unnecessarily disparately impact an identified group based on the enumerated factors. 28 C.F.R. § 42.203. *Cf. Charleston Housing Authority v. USDA*, 419 F.3d 729, 741-42 (8th Cir. 2005) (finding in the related Fair Housing Act context that where official action imposes a racially disparate impact, the action can only be justified through a showing that it is necessary to nondiscriminatory objectives).

Thus, under these statutes, the discriminatory impact of Ferguson's law enforcement practices — which is both unnecessary and avoidable — is unlawful regardless of whether it is intentional or not. As set forth below, these practices also violate the prohibitions against intentional discrimination contained within Title VI, the Safe Streets Act, and the Fourteenth Amendment.

2. Ferguson's Law Enforcement Practices Are Motivated in Part by Discriminatory Intent in Violation of the Fourteenth Amendment and Other Federal Laws

The racebased disparities created by Ferguson's law enforcement practices cannot be explained by chance or by any difference in the rates at which people of different races adhere to the law. These disparities occur, at least in part, because Ferguson law enforcement practices are directly shaped and perpetuated by racial bias. Those practices thus operate in violation of the Fourteenth Amendment's Equal Protection Clause, which prohibits discriminatory policing on the basis of race. *Whren*, 517 U.S. at 813; *Johnson v. Crooks,* 326 F.3d 995, 999 (8th Cir. 2003).[75]

An Equal Protection Clause violation can occur where, as here, the official administration of facially neutral laws or policies results in a discriminatory effect that is motivated, at least in part, by a discriminatory purpose. *See Washington v. Davis*, 426 U.S. 229, 239-40 (1976). In assessing whether a given practice stems from a discriminatory purpose, courts conduct a "sensitive inquiry into such circumstantial and direct evidence of intent as may be available," including historical background, contemporaneous statements by decision makers, and substantive departures from normal procedure. *Vill. of Arlington Heights*, 429 U.S. at 266; *United States v. Bell*, 86 F.3d 820, 823 (8th Cir. 1996). To violate the Equal Protection Clause, official action need not rest *solely* on racially discriminatory purposes; rather, official action violates the Equal Protection Clause if it is motivated, at least in part, by discriminatory purpose. *Personnel Adm'r of Mass. v. Feeney*, 442 U.S. 256, 279 (1979).

We have uncovered significant evidence showing that racial bias has impermissibly played a role in shaping the actions of police and court officials in Ferguson. That evidence, detailed below, includes: 1) the consistency and magnitude of the racial disparities found throughout police and court enforcement actions; 2) direct communications by police supervisors and court officials that exhibit racial bias, particularly against African Americans; 3) a number of other communications by police and court officials that reflect harmful racial stereotypes; 4) the background and historic context surrounding FPD's racially disparate enforcement practices; 5) the fact that City, police, and court officials failed to take any meaningful steps to evaluate or address the race-based impact of its law enforcement practices despite longstanding and widely reported racial disparities, and instead consistently reapplied police and court practices known to disparately impact African Americans.

a. Consistency and Magnitude of Identified Racial Disparities

In assessing whether an official action was motivated in part by discriminatory intent, the actual impact of the action and whether it "bears more heavily on one race or another" may "provide an important starting point." *Vill. of Arlington Heights*, 429 U.S. at 266 (internal citations and quotation marks omitted). Indeed, in rare cases, statistical evidence of discriminatory impact may be sufficiently probative to itself establish discriminatory intent. *Hazelwood School Dist. v. United States*, 433 U.S. 299, 307-08 (1977) (noting in the Title VII context that where "gross statistical disparities can be shown, they alone may in a proper case constitute prima facie proof of a pattern or practice of discrimination").

The race-based disparities we have found are not isolated or aberrational; rather, they exist in nearly every aspect of Ferguson police and court operations. As discussed above, statistical analysis shows that African Americans are more likely to be searched but less likely to have contraband found on them; more likely to receive a citation following a stop and more likely to receive multiple citations at once; more likely to be arrested; more likely to have force used against them; more likely to have their case last longer and require more encounters with the municipal court; more likely to have an arrest warrant issued against them by the municipal court; and more likely to be arrested solely on the basis of an outstanding warrant. As noted above, many of these disparities would occur by chance less than one time in 1000.

These disparities provide significant evidence of discriminatory intent, as the "impact of an official action is often probative of why the action was taken in the first place since people usually intend the natural consequences of their actions." *Reno v. Bossier Parish Sch. Bd.*, 520 U.S. 471, 487 (1997); *see also Davis*, 426 U.S. at 242("An invidious discriminatory purpose may often be inferred from the totality of the relevant facts, including the fact, if it is true, that the [practice] bears more heavily on one race than another."). These disparities are unexplainable on grounds other than race and evidence that racial bias, whether implicit or explicit, has shaped law enforcement conduct.[76]

b. Direct Evidence of Racial Bias

Our investigation uncovered direct evidence of racial bias in the communications of influential Ferguson decision makers. In email messages and during interviews, several court and law enforcement personnel expressed discriminatory views and intolerance with regard to race, religion, and national origin. The content of these communications is unequivocally derogatory, dehumanizing, and demonstrative of impermissible bias.

We have discovered evidence of racial bias in emails sent by Ferguson officials, all of whom are current employees, almost without exception through their official City of Ferguson email accounts, and apparently sent during work hours. These email exchanges involved several police and court supervisors, including FPD supervisors and commanders. The following emails are illustrative:

- A November 2008 email stated that President Barack Obama would not be President for very longbecause "what black man holds a steady job for four years."
- A March 2010 email mocked African Americans through speech and familial stereotypes, using a story involving child support. One line from the email read: "I be so glad that dis be my last child support payment! Month after month, year after year, all dose payments!"
- An April 2011 email depicted President Barack Obama as a chimpanzee.
- A May 2011 email stated: "An African-American woman in New Orleans was admitted into the hospital for a pregnancy termination. Two weeks later she received a check for $5,000. She phoned the hospital to ask who it was from. The hospital said, 'Crimestoppers.'"
- A June 2011 email described a man seeking to obtain "welfare" for his dogs because they are "mixed in color, unemployed, lazy, can't speak English and have no frigging clue who their Daddies are."
- An October 2011 email included a photo of a bare-chested group of dancing women, apparently in Africa, with the caption,"Michelle Obama's High School Reunion."
- A December 2011 email included jokes that are based on offensive stereotypes about Muslims.

Our review of documents revealed many additional email communications that exhibited racial or ethnic bias, as well as other forms of bias. Our investigation has not revealed any indication that any officer or court clerk engaged in these communications was ever disciplined. Nor did we see a single instance in which a police or court recipient of such an email asked that the sender refrain from sending such emails, or any indication that these emails were reported as inappropriate. Instead, the emails were usually forwarded along to others.[77]

Critically, each of these email exchanges involved supervisors of FPD's patrol and court operations.[78] FPD patrol supervisors are responsible for holding officers accountable to governing laws, including the Constitution, and helping to ensure that officers treat all people equally under the law, regardless of race or any other protected characteristic. The racial animus and stereotypes expressed by these supervisors suggest that they are unlikely to hold an officer accountable for discriminatory conduct or to take any steps to discourage the development or perpetuation of racial stereotypes among officers.

Similarly, court supervisors have significant influence and discretion in managing the court's operations and in processing individual cases. As discussed in Parts I and III.B of this report, our investigation has found that a number of court rules and procedures are interpreted and applied entirely at the discretion of the court clerks. These include: whether to require a court appearance for certain offenses; whether to grant continuances or other procedural requests; whether to accept partial payment of an owed fine; whether to cancel a warrant without a bond payment; and whether to provide individuals with documentation enabling them to have a suspended driver's license reinstated before the full fine owed has been paid off. Court clerks are also largely responsible for setting bond amounts. The evidence we found thus shows not only racial bias, but racial bias by those with considerable influence over the outcome of any given court case.

This documentary evidence of explicit racial bias is consistent with reports from community members indicating that some FPD officers use racial epithets in dealing with members of the public. We spoke with one African-American man who, in August 2014, had an argument in his apartment to which FPD officers responded, and was immediately pulled out of the apartment by force. After telling the officer,"you don't have a reason to lock me up," he claims the officer responded:"N*****, I can find something to lock you up on." When the man responded, "good luck with that," the officer slammed his face into the wall, and after the man fell to the floor, the officer said,"don't pass out motherf****r because I'm not carrying you to my car." Another young man described walking with friends in July 2014 past a group of FPD officers who shouted racial epithets at them as they passed.

Courts have widely acknowledged that direct statements exhibiting racial bias are exceedingly rare, and that such statements are not necessary for establishing the existence of discriminatory purpose. *See, e.g., Hayden v. Paterson,* 594 F.3d 150, 163 (2d Cir. 2010) (noting that "discriminatory intent is rarely susceptible to direct proof"); *see also Thomas v. Eastman Kodak Co.,* 183 F.3d 38, 64 (1st Cir. 1999) (noting in Title VII case that "[t]here is no requirement that a plaintiff...must present direct, 'smoking gun' evidence of racially biased decision making in order to prevail"); *Robinson v. Runyon,* 149 F.3d 507, 513 (6th Cir. 1998) (noting in Title VII case that "[r]arely will there be direct evidence from the lips of the defendant proclaiming his or her racial animus"). Where such evidence does exist, however, it is highly probative of discriminatory intent. That is particularly true where, as here, the communications exhibiting bias are made by those with considerable decision-making authority. *See Doe v. Mamaroneck,* 462 F. Supp. 2d 520, 550 (S.D.N.Y. 2006); *Eberhart v. Gettys,* 215 F. Supp. 2d 666, 678 (M.D.N.C. 2002).

c. Evidence of Racial Stereotyping

Several Ferguson officials told us during our investigation that it is a lack of "personal responsibility" among African-American members of the Ferguson community that causes African Americans to experience disproportionate harm under Ferguson's approach to law enforcement. Our investigation suggests that this explanation is at odd with the facts. While there are people of all races who may lack personal responsibility, the harm of Ferguson's approach to law enforcement is largely due to the myriad systemic deficiencies discussed above. Our investigation revealed African Americans making extraordinary efforts to pay off expensive tickets for minor, often unfairly charged, violations, despite systemic obstacles to resolving those tickets. While our investigation did not indicate that African Americans are disproportionately irresponsible, it did reveal that, as the above emails reflect, some Ferguson decision makers hold negative stereotypes about African Americans, and lack of personal responsibility is one of them. Application of this stereotype furthers the disproportionate impact of Ferguson's police and court practices. It causes court and police decision makers to discredit African Americans' explanations for not being able to pay tickets and allows officials to disown the harms of Ferguson's law enforcement practices.

The common practice among Ferguson officials of writing off tickets further evidences a double standard grounded in racial stereotyping. Even as Ferguson City officials maintain the harmful stereotype that black individuals lack personal responsibility — and continue to cite this lack of personal responsibility as the cause of the disparate impact of Ferguson's practices — white City officials condone a striking lack of personal responsibility among themselves and their friends. Court records and emails show City officials, including the Municipal Judge, the Court Clerk, and FPD supervisors assisting friends, colleagues, acquaintances, and themselves in eliminating citations, fines, and fees. For example:

- In August 2014, the Court Clerk emailed Municipal Judge Brockmeyer a copy of a Failure to Appear notice for a speeding violation issued by the City of Breckenridge, and asked: "[FPD patrol supervisor] came to me this morning, could you please take [care] of this for him in Breckenridge?" The Judge replied: "Sure." Judge Brockmeyer also serves as Municipal Judge in Breckenridge.
- In October 2013, Judge Brockmeyer sent Ferguson's Prosecuting Attorney an email with the subject line "City of Hazelwood vs. Ronald Brockmeyer." The Judge wrote: "Pursuant to our conversation, attached please find the red light camera ticket received by the undersigned. I would appreciate it if you would please see to it that this ticket is dismissed." The Prosecuting Attorney, who also serves as prosecuting attorney in Hazelwood,responded: "I worked on red light matters today and dismissed the ticket that you sent over. Since I entered that into the system today, you may or may not get a second notice– you can just ignore that."
- In August 2013, an FPD patrol supervisor wrote an email entitled "Oops" to the Prosecuting Attorney regarding a ticket his relative received in another municipality for traveling 59 miles per hour in a 40 miles-per-hour zone, noting "[h]aving it dismissed would be a blessing." The Prosecuting Attorney responded that the prosecutor of that other municipality promised to nolle pros the ticket. The supervisor responded with appreciation, noting that the dismissal "[c]ouldn't have come at a better time."
- Also in August 2013, Ferguson's Mayor emailed the Prosecuting Attorney about a parking ticket received by an employee of a non-profit day camp for which the Mayor sometimes volunteers. The Mayor wrote that the person "shouldn't have left his car unattended there, but it was an honest mistake" and stated, "I would hate for him to have to pay for this, can you help?" The Prosecuting Attorney forwarded the email to the Court Clerk, instructing her to "NP [nolle prosequi, or not prosecute] this parking ticket."
- In November 2011, a court clerk received a request from a friend to "fix a parking ticket" received by the friend's coworker's wife. After the ticket was faxed to the clerk, she replied:"It's gone baby!"
- In March 2014, a friend of the Court Clerk's relative emailed the Court Clerk with a scanned copy of a ticket asking if there was anything she could do to help. She responded:"Your ticket of $200 has magically disappeared!" Later, in June 2014, the same person emailed the Court Clerk regarding two tickets and asked: "Can you work your magic again? It would be deeply appreciated." The Clerk later informed him one ticket had been dismissed and she was waiting to hear back about the second ticket.

These are just a few illustrative examples. It is clear that writing off tickets between the Ferguson court staff and the clerks of other municipal courts in the region is routine. Email exchanges show that Ferguson officials secured or received ticket write-offs from staff in a number of neighboring municipalities. There is evidence that the Court Clerk and a City of Hazelwood clerk "fixed" at least 12tickets at each other's request, and that the Court Clerk successfully sought help with a ticket from a clerk in St. Ann. And in April 2011, a court administrator in the City of Pine Lawn emailed the Ferguson Court Clerk to have a warrant recalled for a person applying for a job with the Pine Lawn Police Department. The court administrator explained that "[a]fter he gets the job, he will have money to pay off his fines with Ferguson."

The Court Clerk recalled the warrant and issued a new court date for more than two months after the request was made.

City official s' application of the stereotype that African Americans lack "personal responsibility" to explain why Ferguson's practices harm African Americans, even as these same City officials exhibit a lack of personal — and professional — responsibility in handling their own and their friends' code violations, is further evidence of discriminatory bias on the part of decision makers central to the direction of law enforcement in Ferguson.

d. Historical Background

Until the 1960s, Ferguson was a "sundown town" where Af rican Americans were banned from the City after dark. The City would block off the main road from Kinloch, which was a poor, all-black suburb, "with a chain and construction materials but kept a second road open during the day so housekeepers and nannies could get from Kinloch to jobs in Ferguson."[79] During our investigative interviews, several older African-American residents recalled this era in Ferguson and recounted that African Americans knew that, for them, the City was "off-limits."

The Ferguson of half a century ago is not the same Ferguson that exists today. We heard from many residents — black and white — who expressed pride in their community, especially with regard to the fact that Ferguson is one of the most demographically diverse communities in the area. Pride in this aspect of Ferguson is well founded; Ferguson is more diverse than most of the United States, and than many of its surrounding cities. It is clear that many Ferguson residents of different races genuinely embrace that diversity.

But we also found evidence during our investigation that some within Ferguson still have difficultycoming to terms with Ferguson's changing demographics and seeing Ferguson's African American and white residents as equals in civic life. While total population rates have remained relatively constant over the last three decades, the portion of Ferguson residents who are African American has increased steadily but dramatically, from 25% in 1990 to 67% in 2010. Some individuals, including individuals charged with discretionary enforcement decisions in either the police department or the court, have expressed concerns about the increasing number of African Americans that have moved to Ferguson in recent years. Similarly, some City officials and residents we spoke with explicitly distinguished Ferguson's African-American residents from Ferguson's "normal" residents or "regular" people. One white third-generation Ferguson resident told us that inmany ways Ferguson is "progressive and quite vibrant," while in another it is "typical — trying to hang on to its 'whiteness.'"

On its own, Ferguson's historical backdrop as a racially segregated community that did not treat African Americans equally under the law does not demonstrate that law enforcement practices today are motivated by impermissible discriminatory intent. It is one factor to consider, however, especially given the evidence that, among some in Ferguson, these attitudes persist today. As courts have instructed, the historical background of an official practice that leads to discriminatory effects is, together with other evidence, probative as to whether that practice is grounded in part in discriminatory purposes. *See Vill. of Arlington Heights*, 429 U.S. at 267; *see also Rogers v. Lodge*, 458 U.S. 613, *passim* (1982).

e. Failure to Evaluate or Correct Practices that Have Long Resulted in a Racially Disparate Impact

That the discriminatory effect of Ferguson's law enforcement practices is the result of intentional discrimination is further evidenced by the fact that City, police, and court officials have consistently failed to evaluate or reform — and in fact appear to have redoubled their commitment to — the very practices that have plainly and consistently exerted a disparate impact on African Americans.

The disparities we have identified appear to be longstanding. The statistical analysis performed as part of our investigation relied upon police and court data from recent years, but FPD has collected data related to vehicle stops pursuant to state requirements since 2000. Each year, that information is gathered by FPD, sent to the office of the Missouri Attorney General, and published on the Missouri Attorney General's webpage.[80] The data show disparate impact on

African Americans in Ferguson for as long as that data has been reported. Based on that racial profiling data,Missouri publishes a "Disparity Index" for each reporting municipality, calculated as the percent of stops of a certain racial group compared with that group's local population rate. In each of the last 14 years, thedata show that African Americans are "over represented" in FPD's vehicular stops.[81] That data also shows that in most years, FPD officers searched African Americans at higher rates than others, but found contraband on African Americans at lower rates.

In 2001, for example, African Americans comprised about the same proportion of the population as whites, but while stops of white drivers accounted for 1,495 stops, African Americans accounted for 3,426, more than twice as many. While a white person stopped that year was searched in 6% of cases, a black person stopped was searched in 14% of cases. That same year, searches of whites resulted in a contraband finding in 21% of cases, but searches of African Americans only resulted in a contraband finding in 16% of cases. Similar disparities were identified in most other years, with varying degrees of magnitude. In any event, the data reveals a pattern of racial disparities in Ferguson's police activities. That pattern appears to have been ignored by Ferguson officials.

That the extant racial disparities are intentional is also evident in the fact that Ferguson has consistently returned to the unlawful practices described in Parts III.A. and B. of this Report knowing that they impose a persistent disparate impact on African Americans. City officials have continued to encourage FPD to stop and cite aggressively as part of its revenue generation efforts, even though that encouragement and increased officer discretion has yielded disproportionate African-American representation in FPD stops and citations. Until we recommended it during our investigation, FPD officials had not restricted officer discretion to issue multiple citations at once, even though the application of that discretion has led officers to issue far more citations to African Americans at once than others, on average, and even though only black individuals (35 in total) ever received five or more citations at once over a three-year period. FPD has not provided further guidance to constrain officer discretion in conducting searches, even though FPD officers have, for years, searched African Americans at higher rates than others but found contraband during those searches less often than in searches of individuals of other races.

Similarly, City officials have not taken any meaningful steps to contain the discretion of court clerks to grant continuances, clear warrants, or enable driver's license suspensions to be lifted, even though those practices have resulted in warrants being issued and executed at highly disproportionate rates against African Americans. Indeed, until the City of Ferguson repealed the Failure to Appear statute in September 2014 — after this investigation began — the City had not taken meaningful steps to evaluate or reform any of the court practices described in this Report, even though the implementation of those practices has plainly exerted a disparate impact on African Americans.

FPD also has not significantly altered its use-of-force tactics, even though FPD records make clear that current force decisions disparately impact black suspects, and that officers appear to assess threat differently depending upon the race of the suspect. FPD, for example, has not reviewed or revised its canine program, even though available records show that canine officers have exclusively set their dogs against black individuals, often in cases where doing so was not justified by the danger presented. In many incidents in which officers used significant levels of force, the facts as described by the officers themselves did not appear to support the force used, especially in light of the fact that less severe tactics likely would have been equally effective. In some of these incidents, law enforcement experts with whom we consulted could find no explanation other than race to explain the severe tactics used.

During our investigation, FPD officials told us that their police tactics are responsive to the scenario at hand. But records suggest that, where a suspect or group of suspects is white, FPD applies a different calculus, typically resulting in a more measured law enforcement response. In one 2012 incident, for example, officers reported responding to a fight in progress at a local bar that involved white suspects. Officers reported encountering "40-50 people actively fighting, throwing bottles and glasses, as well as chairs." Thereport noted that "one subject had his ear bitten off." While the responding officers reported using force, they only used "minimal baton and flashlight strikes as well as fists, muscling techniques and knee strikes." While the report states that "due to the amount of subjects fighting, no physical arrests were possible," it notes also that four subjects were brought to the station for "safekeeping." While we have found other evidence that FPD later issued a wanted for two individuals as a result of the incident, FPD's response stands in stark contrast to the actions officers describe taking in many incidents involving black suspects, some of which we earlier described.

Based on this evidence, it is apparent that FPD requires better training, limits on officer discretion, increased supervision, and more robust accountability systems, not only to ensure that officers act in accordance with the Fourth Amendment, but with the Fourteenth Amendment as well. FPD has failed to take any such corrective action, and instead has actively endorsed and encouraged the perpetuation of the practices that have led to such stark disparities. This, together with the totality of the facts that we have found, evidences that those practices exist, at least in part, on account of an unconstitutional discriminatory purpose. *See Feeney*, 442 U.S. at 279 n.24 (noting that the discriminatory intent inquiry is "practical," because what "any official entity is 'up to' may be plain from the results its actions achieve, or the results they avoid").

D. Ferguson Law Enforcement Practices Erode Community Trust, Especially Among Ferguson's African-American Residents, and Make Policing Less Effective, More Difficult, and Less Safe

The unlawful police misconduct and court practices described above have generated great distrust of Ferguson law enforcement, especially among African Americans.[82] As described below, other FPD practices further contribute to distrust, including FPD's failure to hold officers accountable for misconduct, failure to implement community policing principles, and the lack of diversity within FPD. Together, these practices severely damaged the relationship between African Americans and the Ferguson Police Department long before Michael Brown's shooting death in August 2014. This divide has made policing in Ferguson less effective, more difficult, and more likely to discriminate.

1. Ferguson's Unlawful Police and Court Practices Have Led to Distrust and Resentment Among Many in Ferguson

The lack of trust between a significant portion of Ferguson's residents, especially its African-American residents, and the Ferguson Police Department has become, since August 2014, undeniable. The causes of this distrust and division, however, have been the subject of debate. City and police officials, and some other Ferguson residents, have asserted that this lack of meaningful connection with much of Ferguson's African-American community is due to the fact that they are "transient" renters; that they do not appreciate how much the City of Ferguson does for them; that "pop-culture" portrays alienating themes; or because of "rumors" that the police and municipal court are unyielding because they are driven by raising revenue.

Our investigation showed that the disconnect and distrust between much of Ferguson's African-American community and FPD is caused largely by years of the unlawful and unfair law enforcement practices by Ferguson's police department and municipal court described above. In the documents we reviewed, the meetings we observed and participated in, and in the hundreds of conversations Civil Rights Division staff had with residents of Ferguson and the surrounding area, many residents, primarily African-American residents, described being belittled, disbelieved, and treated with little regard for their legal rights by the Ferguson Police Department. One white individual who has lived in Ferguson for 48 years told us that it feels like Ferguson's police and court system is "designed to bring a black man down... [there are] no second chances." We heard from African-American residents who told us of Ferguson's "long history of targeting blacks for harassment and degrading treatment," and who described the steps they take to avoid this — from taking routes to work that skirt Ferguson to moving out of state. An African-American minister of a church in a nearby community told us thathe doesn't allow his two sons to drive through Ferguson out of "fear that they will be targeted for arrest."

African Americans' views of FPD are shaped not just by *what* FPD officers do, but by *how* they do it. During our investigation, dozens of African Americans in Ferguson told us of verbal abuse by FPD officers during routine interactions, and these accounts are consistent with complaints people have made about FPD for years. In December 2011, for example, an African-American man alleged that as he was standing outside of Wal-Mart, an officer called him a "stupid motherf****r" and a "bastard." According to the man, a lieutenant was on the scene and did nothing to reproach the officer, instead threatening to arrest the man. In April 2012, officers allegedly called an African-American woman a "bitch" and a "mental case" at the jail following an arrest. In June 2011, a 60-year-old man complained that an officer verbally harassed him while he stood in line to see the judge in municipal court. According to the man, the officer repeatedly ordered him to move forward as the line advanced and, because he did not advance far enough, turned to the other court-goers and joked, "he is hooked on phonics."

Another concern we heard from many African-American residents, and saw in the files we reviewed, was of casual intimidation by FPD officers, including threats to draw or fire their weapons, often for seemingly little or no cause. In September 2012, a 28-year resident of Ferguson complained to FPD about a traffic stop during which a lieutenant approached with a loud and confrontational manner with his hand on his holstered gun. The resident, who had a military police background, noted that the lieutenant's behavior, especially having his hand on his gun, ratcheted up the tension level, and he questioned why the lieutenant had been so aggressive. In another incident captured on video and discussed below in more detail, an officer placed his gun on a wall or post and pointed it back and forth to each of two store employees as he talked to them while they took the trash out late one night. In another case discussed above, a person reported that an FPD officer removed his ECW during a traffic stop and continuously tapped the ECW on the roof of the person's car. These written complaints reported to FPD are consistent with complaints we heard from community members during our investigation about officers casually threatening to hurt or even shoot them.

It appears that many police and City officials were unaware of this distrust and fear of Ferguson police among African Americans prior to August 2014. Ferguson's Chief, for example, told us that prior to the Michael Brown shooting he thought community-police relations were good. During our investigation, however, City and police leadership, and many officers of all ranks, acknowledged a deep divide between police and some Ferguson residents, particularly black residents. Mayor Knowles acknowledged that there is "clearly mistrust" of FPD by many community members, including a "systemic problem" with youth not wanting to work with police. One FPD officer estimated that about a quarter of the Ferguson community distrusts the police department.

A growing body of research, alongside decades of police experience, is consistent with what our investigation found in Ferguson: that when police and courts treat people unfairly, unlawfully, or disrespectfully, law enforcement loses legitimacy in the eyes of those who have experienced, or even observed, the unjust conduct. *See, e.g.,* Tom R. Tyler & Yuen J. Huo, *Trust in the Law: Encouraging Public Cooperation with the Police and Courts* (2002). Further, this loss of legitimacy makes individuals more likely to resist enforcement efforts and less likely to cooperate with law enforcement efforts to prevent and investigate crime. *See, e.g.,* Jason Sunshine & Tom R. Tyler, *The Role of Procedural Justice and Legitimacy in Shaping Public Support for Policing,* 37 Law & Soc'y Rev. 513, 534-36 (2003); *Promoting Cooperative Strategies to Reduce Racial Profiling* 20-21(U.S. Dep't of Justice, Office of Community Oriented Policing Services, 2008) ("Being viewed as fair and just is critical to successful policing in a democracy. When the police are perceived as unfair in their enforcement, it will undermine their effectiveness."); Ron Davis et al., *Exploring the Role of the Police in Prisoner Reentry*Reentry14 (Nat'l Inst. of Justice, New Perspectives in Policing, July 2012)("Increasingly, research is supporting the notion that legitimacy is an important factor in the effectiveness of law, and the establishment and maintenance of legitimacy are particularly important in the context of policing.") (citations omitted). To improve community trust and police effectiveness, Ferguson must ensure not only that its officers act in accord with the Constitution, but that they treat people fairly and respectfully.

2. FPD's Exercise of Discretion, Even When Lawful, Often Undermines Community Trust and Public Safety

Even where lawful, many discretionary FPD enforcement actions increase distrust and significantly decrease the likelihood that individuals will seek police assistance even when they are victims of crime, or that they will cooperate with the police to solve or prevent other crimes. Chief Jackson toldus "we don't get cooperating witnesses" from the apartment complexes. Consistent with this statement, our review of documents and our conversations with Ferguson residents revealed many instances in which they are reluctant to report being victims of crime or to cooperate with police, and many instances in which FPD imposed unnecessary negative consequences for doing so.

In one instance, for example, a woman called FPD to report a domestic disturbance. By the time the police arrived, the woman's boyfriend had left. The police looked through the house and saw indications that the boyfriend lived there. When the woman told police that only she and her brother were listed on the home's occupancy permit, the officer placed the woman under arrest for the permit violation and she was jailed. In another instance, after a woman called police to report a domestic disturbance and was given a summons for an occupancy permit violation, she said, according to the officer's report, that she "hated the Ferguson Police Department and will never call again, even if she is being killed."

In another incident, a young African-American man was shot while walking on the road with three friends. The police department located and interviewed two of the friends about the shooting. After the interview, they arrested and jailed one of these cooperating witnesses, who was 19 years old, on an outstanding municipal warrant.

We also reviewed many instances in which FPD officers arrested individuals who sought to care for loved ones who had been hurt. In one instance from May 2014, for example, a man rushed to the scene of a car accident involving his girlfriend, who was badly injured and bleeding profusely when he arrived. He approached and tried to calm her. When officers arrived they treated him rudely, according to the man, telling him to move away from his girlfriend, which he did not want to do. They then immediately proceeded to handcuff and arrest him, which, officers assert, he resisted. EMS and other officers were not on the scene during this arrest, so the accident victim remained unattended, bleeding from her injuries, while officers were arresting the boyfriend. Officers charged the man with five municipal code violations (Resisting Arrest, Disorderly Conduct, Assault on an Officer, Obstructing Government Operations, and Failure to Comply) and had his vehicle towed and impounded. In an incident from 2013, a woman sought to reach her fiancé, who was in a car accident. After she refused to stay on the sidewalk as the officer ordered, she was arrested and jailed. While it is sometimes both essential and difficult to keep distraught family from being in close proximity to their loved ones on the scene of an accident, there is rarely a need to arrest and jail them rather than, at most, detain them on the scene.

Rather than view these instances as opportunities to convey their compassion for individuals at times of crisis even as they maintain order, FPD appears instead to view these and similar incidents we reviewed as opportunities to issue multiple citations and make arrests. For very little public safety benefit, FPD loses opportunities to build community trust and respect, and instead further alienates potential allies in crime prevention.

3. FPD's Failure to Respond to Complaints of Officer Misconduct Further Erodes Community Trust

Public trust has been further eroded by FPD's lack of any meaningful system for holding officers accountable when they violate law or policy. Through its system for taking, investigating, and responding to misconduct complaints, a police department has the opportunity to demonstrate that officer misconduct is unacceptable and unrepresentative of how the law enforcement agency values and treats its constituents. In this way, a police department's internal affairs process provides an opportunity for the department to restore trust and affirm its legitimacy. Similarly, misconduct investigations allow law enforcement the opportunity to provide community members who have been mistreated a constructive, effective way to voice their complaints. And, of course, effective internal affairs processes can be a critical part of correcting officer behavior, and improving police training and policies.

Ferguson's internal affairs system fails t o respond meaningfully to complaints of officer misconduct. It does not serve as a mechanism to restore community members' trust in law enforcement, or correct officer behavior. Instead, it serves to contrast FPD's tolerance for officer misconduct against the Department's aggressive enforcement of even minor municipal infractions, lending credence to a sentiment that we heard often from Ferguson residents: that a "different set of rules" applies to Ferguson's police than to its African-American residents, and that making a complaint about officer misconduct is futile.

Despite the statement in FPD's employee misconduct investigation policy that "[t]he integrity of the police department depends on the personal integrity and discipline of each employee," FPD has done little to investigate external allegations that officers have not followed FPD policy or the law, or, with a few notable exceptions, to hold officers accountable when they have not. Ferguson Police Department makes it difficult to make complaints about officer conduct, and frequently assumes that the officer is telling the truth and the complainant is not, even where objective evidence indicates that the reverse is true.

It is difficult for individuals to make a misconduct complaint against an officer in Ferguson, in part because Ferguson both discourages individuals from making complaints and discourages City and police staff from accepting them. In a March 2014 email, for example, a lieutenant criticized a sergeant for taking a complaint from a man on behalf of his mother, who stayed in her vehicle outside the police station. Despite the fact that Ferguson policy requires that complaints be taken "from any source, identified or anonymous," the lieutenant stated "I would have had him bringher in, or leave." In another instance, a City employee took a complaint of misconduct from a Ferguson resident and relayed it to FPD. An FPD captain sent an email in response that the City employee viewed as being "lectured" for taking the complaint. The City Manager agreed, calling the captain's behavior "not only disrespectful and unacceptable, but it is dangerous in [that] it is inciteful [sic]and divisive." Nonetheless, there appeared to be no follow-up action regarding the captain, and the complaint was never logged as such or investigated.

While official FPD policy states clearly that officers must "never attempt to dissuade any citizen from lodging a complaint," FPD General Order 301.3, a contrary leadership message speaks louder than policy. This message is reflected in statements by officers that indicate a need to justify their actions when they do accept a civilian complaint. In one case, a sergeant explained: "Nothing I could say helped, he demanded the complaint forms which were provided." In another: "I spoke to [two people seeking to make a complaint] …but after the conversation, neither had changed their mind and desired still to write out a complaint." We saw many instances in which people complained of being prevented from making a complaint, with no indication that FPD investigated those allegations. In one instance, for example, a man alleging significant excessive force reported the incident to a commander after being released from jail, stating that he was unable to make his complaint earlier because several different officers refused to let him speak to a sergeant to make a complaint about the incident and threatened to keep him in jail longer if he did not stop asking to make a complaint.

Some individuals also fear that they will suffer retaliation from officers if they report misconduct or even merely speak out as witnesses when approached by someone from FPD investigating a misconduct complaint. For instance, in one case FPD acknowledged that a witness to the misconduct was initially reluctant to complete a written statement supporting the complainant because he wanted no "repercussions" from the subject officer or other officers. In another case involving alleged misconduct at a retail store that we have already described, the store's district manager told the commander he did not want an investigation — despite how concerned he was by video footage showing an officer training his gun on two store employees as they took out the trash — because he wanted to "stay on the good side" of the police.

Even when individuals do report misconduct, there is a significant likelihood it will not be treated as a complaint and investigated. In one case, FPD failed to open an investigation of an allegation made by a caller who said an officer had kicked him in the side of the head and stepped on his head and back while he was face down with his hands cuffed behind his back, all the while talking about having blood on him from somebody else and "being tired of the B.S." The officer did not stop until the other officer on the scene said words to the effect of, "[h]ey, he's not fighting he's cuffed." The man alleged that the officer then ordered him to "get the f*** up" and lifted him by the handcuffs, yanking his arms backward. The commander taking the call reported that the man stated that he supported the police and knew they had a tough job but was reporting the incident because it appeared the officer was under a lot of stress and needed counseling, and because he was hoping to prevent others from having the experience he did. The commander's email regarding the incident expressed no skepticism about the veracity of the caller's report and was able to identify the incident (and thus the involved officers). Yet FPD did not conduct an internal affairs investigation of this incident, based on our review of all of FPD's internal investigation files. There is not even an indication that a use-of-force report was completed.

In another case, an FPD commander wrote to a sergeant that despite a complainant being "pretty adamant that she was profiled and that the officer was rude," the commander "didn't even bother to send it to the chief for a control number" before hearing the sergeant's account of the officer's side of the story. Upon getting the officer's account second hand from the sergeant, the commander forwarded the information to the PoliceChief so that it could be "filed in the non- complaint file." FPD officers and commanders also often seek to frame complaints as being entirely related to complainants' guilt or innocence, and therefore not subject to a misconduct investigation, even though the complaint clearly alleges officer misconduct. In one instance, for example, commanders told the complainant to go to court to fight her arrest, ignoring the complainant's statement that the officer arrested her for Disorderly Conduct and Failure to Obey only after she asked for the officer's name. In another instance, a commander stated that the complainant made no allegations unrelated to the merits of the arrest, even though the complainant alleged rudeness and being "intimidated" during arrest, among a number of other non-guilt related allegations.

FPD appears to intentionally *not* treat allegations of misconduct as complaints even where it believes that the officer in fact committed the misconduct. In one incident, for example, a supervisor wrote an email directly to an officer about a complaint the Police Chief had received about an officer speeding through the park in a neighboring town. The supervisor informed the officer that the Chief tracked the car number given by the complainant back to the officer, but assured the officer that the supervisor's email was "[j]ust for your information. No need to reply and there is no record of this other than this email." In another instance referenced above, the district manager of a retail store called a commander to tell him that he had a video recording that showed an FPD officer pull up to the store at about midnight while two employees were taking out the trash, take out his weapon, and put it on top of a concrete wall, pointed at the two employees. When the employees said they were just taking out the trash and asked the officer if he needed them to take off their coats so that he could see their uniforms, the officer told the employees that he knew they were employees and that if he had not known "I would have put you on the ground." The commander related in an email to the sergeant and lieutenant that "there is no reason to doubt the Gen. Manager because he said he watched the video and he clearly saw a weapon — maybe the sidearm or the taser." Nonetheless, despite noting that "we don't need cowboy" and the "major concern" of the officer taking his weapon out of his holster and placing it on a wall, the commander concluded, "[n]othing for you to do with this other than make a mental note and for you to be on the lookout for that kind of behavior."[83]

In another case, an officer investigating a report of a theft at a dollar store interrogated a minister pumping gas into his church van about the theft. The man alleged that he provided his identification to the officer and offered to return to the store to prove he was not the thief. The officer instead handcuffed the man and drove him to the store. The store clerk reported that the detained man was not the thief, but the officer continued to keep the man cuffed, allegedly calling him "f*****g stupid" for asking to be released from the cuffs. The man went directly to FPD to file a complaint upon being released by the officer. FPD conducted an investigation but, because the complainant did not respond to a cell phone message left by the investigator within 13 days, reclassified the complaint as "withdrawn," even as the investigator noted that the complaint of improper detention would otherwise have been sustained, and noted that the "[e]mployee has been counseled and retraining is forthcoming." In still another case, a lieutenant of a neighboring agency called FPD to report that a pizza parlor owner had complained to him that an off-duty FPD officer had become angry upon being told that police discounts were only given to officers in uniform and said to the restaurant owner as he was leaving, "I hope you get robbed!" The allegation was not considered a complaint and instead, despite its seriousness, was handled through counseling at the squad level.[84]

Even where a complaint is actually investigated, unless the complaint is made by an FPD commander, and sometimes not even then, FPD consistently takes the word of the officer over the word of the complainant, frequently even where the officer's version of events is clearly at odds with the objective evidence. On the rare occasion that FPD does sustain an external complaint of officer misconduct, the discipline it imposes is generally too low to be an effective deterrent.[85]

Our investigation raised concerns in particular about how FPD responds to untruthfulness by officers. In many departments, a finding of untruthfulness pursuant to internal investigation results in an officer's termination because the officer's credibility on police reports and in providing testimony is subsequently subject to challenge. In FPD, untruthfulness appears not even to always result in a formal investigation, and even where sustained, has little effect. In one case we reviewed, FPD sustained a charge of untruthfulness against an officer after he was found to have lied to the investigator about whether he had engaged in an argument with a civilian over the loudspeaker of his police vehicle. FPD imposed only a 12-hour suspension on the officer. In addition, FPD appears not to have taken the officer's untruthfulness into sufficient account in several subsequent complaints, including in at least one case in which the complainant alleged conduct very similar to that alleged in the case in which FPD found the officer untruthful. Nor, as discussed above, has FPD or the City disclosed this information to defendants challenging charges brought by the officer. In another case a supervisor was sustained for false testimony during an internal affairs investigation and was given a written reprimand. In another case in which an officer was clearly untruthful, FPD did not sustain the charge.[86] In that case, an officer in another jurisdiction was assigned to monitor an intersection in that city because an FPDmarked vehicle allegedly had repeatedly been running the stop sign at that intersection. While at that intersection, and while receiving a complaint from a person about the FPD vehicle, the officer saw that very vehicle "dr[iving] through the stop sign without tapping a brake," according to a sergeant with the other jurisdiction. When asked to respond to these allegations, the officer wrote, unequivocally, "I assure you I don't run stop signs." It is clear from the investigative file that FPD found that he did, in fact, run stop signs, as the officer was given counseling. Nonetheless, the officer received a counseling memo that made no mention of the officer's written denial of the misconduct observed by another law enforcement officer. This officer continues to write reports regarding significant uses of force, several of which our investigation found questionable.[87]

By failing to hold officers accountable, FPD leadership sends a message that FPD officers can behave as they like, regardless of law or policy, and even if caught, that punishment will be light. This message serves to condone officer misconduct and fuel community distrust.

4. FPD's Lack of Community Engagement Increases the Likelihood of Discriminatory Policing and Damages Public Trust

Alongside its divisive law enforcement practices and lack of meaningful response to community concerns about police conduct, FPD has made little effort in recent years to employ community policing or other community engagement strategies. This lack of community engagement has precluded the possibility of bridging the divide caused by Ferguson's law enforcement practices, and has increased the likelihood of discriminatory policing.

Community policing and related community engagement strategies provide the opportunity for officers and communities to work together to identify the causes of crime and disorder particular to their community, and to prioritize law enforcement efforts. *See Community Policing Defined* 1-16 (U.S. Dep't of Justice, Office of Community Oriented Policing Services, 2014). The focus of these strategies — in stark contrast to Ferguson's current law enforcement approach — is on crime prevention rather than on making arrests. *See Effective Policing and Crime Prevention: A Problem Oriented Guide for Mayors, City Managers, and County Executives* 1-62 (U.S. Dep't of Justice, Office of Community Oriented Policing Services, 2009). When implemented fully, community policing creates opportunities for officers and community members to have frequent, positive interactions with each other, and requires officers to partner with communities to solve particular public safety problems that, together, they have decided to address. Research and experience show that community policing can be more effective at crime prevention and at making people feel safer. *See* Gary Cordner, *Reducing Fear of Crime: Strategies for Police* 47 (U.S. Dep't of Justice, Office of Community Oriented Policing Services, Jan. 2010) ("Most studies of community policing have found that residents like community policing and feel safer when it is implemented where they live and work.") (citations omitted).

Further, research and law enforcement experience show that community policing and engagement can overcome many of the divisive dynamics that disconnected Ferguson residents and City leadership alike describe, from a dearth of positive interactions to racial stereotyping and racial violence. *See, e.g.*, Glaser, *supra*, at 207-11 (discussing research showing that community policing and similar approaches can help reduce racial bias and stereotypes and improve community relations); L. Song Richardson & Phillip Atiba Goff, *Interrogating Racial Violence*, 12 Ohio St. J. of Crim. L. 115, 143-47 (2014) (describing how fully implemented and inclusive community policing can help avoid racial stereotyping and violence); *Strengthening the Relationship Between Law Enforcement and Communities of Color: Developing an Agenda for Action* 1-20 (U.S. Dep't of Justice, Office of Community Oriented Policing Services, 2014).

Ferguson's community policing efforts appear always to have been somewhat modest, but have dwindled to almost nothing in recent years. FPD has no community policing or community engagement plan. FPD currently designates a single officer the "Community Resource Officer." This officer attends community meetings, serves as FPD's public relations liaison, and is charged with collecting crime data. No other officers play any substantive role in community policing efforts. Officers we spoke with were fairly consistent in their acknowledgment of this, and of the fact that this move away from community policing has been due, at least in part, to an increased focus on code enforcement and revenue generation in recent years. As discussed above, our investigation found that FPD redeployed officers to 12-hour shifts, in part for revenue reasons. There is some evidence that community policing is more difficult to carry out when patrol officers are on 12-hour shifts, and this appears to be the case in difficult to carry out when patrol officers are on 12-hour shifts, and this appears to be the case in hour shift has undermined community policing. One officer said that "FPD used to have a strong community policing ethic — — hour day." Another officer told us that the 12- hour schedule, combined with a lack of any attempt to have officers remain within their assigned area, has resulted in a lack of any geographical familiarity by FPD officers. This same officer told us that it is viewed as more positive to write tickets than to "talk with your businesses." Another officer told us that FPD officers should put less energy into writing tickets and instead "get out of their cars" and get to know community members.

One officer told us that officers could spend more time engaging with community members and undertaking problem-solving projects if FPD officers were not so focused on activities that generate revenue. This officer told us, "everything's about the courts…the court's enforcement priorities are money." Another officer told us that officers cannot "get out of the car and play basketball with the kids," because "we've removed all the basketball hoops — there's an ordinance against it." While one officer told us that there was a police substation in Canfield Green when FPD was more committed to community policing, another told us that now there is "nobody in there that anybody knows."

City and police officials note that there are several active neighborhood groups in Ferguson. We reached out to each of these during our investigation and met with each one that responded. Some areas of Ferguson are well-represented by these groups. But City and police officials acknowledge that, since August 2014, they have realized that there are entire segments of the Ferguson community that they have never made an effort to know, especially African Americans who live in Ferguson's large apartment complexes, including Canfield Green. While some City officials appear well-intentioned, they have also been too quick to presume that outreach to more disconnected segments of the Ferguson community will be futile. One City employee told us, "they think they do outreach, but they don't," and that some Ferguson residents do not even realize their homes are in Ferguson. Our investigation indicated that, while the City and police department may have to use different strategies for engagement in some parts of Ferguson than in others, true community policing efforts can have positive results. As an officer who has patrolled the area told us, "most of the people in Canfield are good people. They just don't have a lot of time to get involved."

5. Ferguson's Lack of a Diverse Police Force Further Undermines Community Trust

While approximately two-thirds of Ferguson's residents are African American, only four of Ferguson's 54 commissioned police officers are African American. Since August 2014, there has been widespread discussion about the impact this comparative lack of racial diversity within FPD has on community trust and police behavior. During this investigation we also heard repeated complaints about FPD's lack of racial diversity from members of the Ferguson community. Our investigation indicates that greater diversity within Ferguson Police Department has the potential to increase community confidence in the police department, but may only be successful as part of a broader police reform effort.

While it does appear that a lack of racial diversity among officers decreases African Americans' trust in a police department, this observation must be qualified. Increasing a police department's racial diversity does not necessarily increase community trust or improve officer conduct. There appear to be many reasons for this. One important reason is that African-American officers can abuse and violate the rights of African-American civilians, just as white officers can. And African-American officers who behave abusively can undermine community trust just as white officers can. Our investigation indicates that in Ferguson, individual officer behavior is largely driven by a police culture that focuses on revenue generation and is infected by race bias. While increased vertical and horizontal diversity, racial and otherwise, likely is necessary to change this culture, it probably cannot do so on its own.

Consistent with our findings in Ferguson and other departments, research more broadly shows that a racially diverse police force does not guarantee community trust or lawful policing. *See Diversity in Law Enforcement: A Literature Review* 4 n.v. (U.S. Dep't of Justice, Civil Rights Division, Office of Justice Programs, & U.S. Equal Employment Opportunity Commission, Submission to President's Task Force on 21st Century Policing, Jan. 2015). The picture is far more complex. Some studies show that Africa-American officers are less prejudiced than white officers as a whole, are more familiar with African-American communities, are more likely to arrest white suspects and less likely to arrest black suspects, and receive more cooperation from African Americans with whom they interact on the job. *See* David A. Sklansky, *Not Your Father's Police Department: Making Sense of the New Demographics of Law Enforcement*, 96 J. Crim. L. & Criminology 1209, 1224-25 (2006). But studies also show that African Americans are equally likely to fire their weapons, arrest people, and have complaints made about their behavior, and sometimes harbor prejudice against African-American civilians themselves. *Id.*

While a diverse police department does not guarantee a constitutional one, it is nonetheless critically important for law enforcement agencies, and the Ferguson Police Department in particular, to strive for broad diversity among officers and civilian staff. In general, notwithstanding the above caveats, a more racially diverse police department has the potential to increase confidence in police among African Americans in particular. *See* Joshua C. Cochran & Patricia Y. Warren, *Racial, Ethnic, and Gender Differences in, Perceptions of the Police: The Salience of Officer Race Within the Context of Racial Profiling*, 28(2) J. Contemp. Crim. Just. 206, 206-27 (2012). In addition, diversity of all types — including race, ethnicity, sex, national origin, religion, sexual orientation and gender identity — can be beneficial both to police-community relationships and the culture of the law enforcement agency. Increasing gender and sexual orientation diversity in policing in particular may be critical in re-making internal police culture and creating new assumptions about what makes policing effective. *See, e.g.*, Sklansky, *supra*, at 1233-34; Richardson & Goff, *supra*, at 143-47; Susan L. Miller, Kay B. Forest, & Nancy C. Jurik, *Diversity in Blue, Lesbian and Gay Police Officers in a Masculine Occupation*, 5 Men and Masculinities 355, 355-85 (Apr. 2003).[88] Moreover, aside from the beneficial impact a diverse police force may have on the culture of the department and police-community relations, police departments are obligated under law to provide equal opportunity for employment. *See* Title VII of the Civil Rights Act of 1964, 42 U.S.C. § 2000e *et seq.*

Our investigation indicates that Ferguson can and should do more to attract and hire a more diverse group of qualified police officers.[89] However, for these efforts to be successful at increasing the diversity of its workforce, as well as effective at increasing community trust and improving officer behavior, they must be part of a broader reform effort within FPD. This reform effort must focus recruitment efforts on attracting qualified candidates of *all* demographics with the skills and temperament to police respectfully and effectively, and must ensure that *all* officers — regardless of race — are required to police lawfully and with integrity.

V. CHANGES NECESSARY TO REMEDY FERGUSON'S UNLAWFUL LAW ENFORCEMENT PRACTICES AND REPAIR COMMUNITY TRUST

The problems identified within this letter reflect deeply entrenched practices and priorities that are incompatible with lawful and effective policing and that damage community trust. Addressing those problems and repairing the City's relationship with the community will require a fundamental redirection of Ferguson's approach to law enforcement, including the police and court practices that reflect and perpetuate this approach.

Below we set out broad recommendations for changes that Ferguson should make to its police and court practices to correct the constitutional violations our investigation identified. Ensuring meaningful, sustainable, and verifiable reform will require that these and other measures be part of a court-enforceable remedial process that includes involvement from community stakeholders as well as independent oversight. In the coming weeks, we will seek to work with the City of Ferguson toward developing and reaching agreement on an appropriate framework for reform.

A. Ferguson Police Practices

1. Implement a Robust System of True Community Policing

Many of the recommendations included below would require a shift from policing to raise revenue to policing in partnership with the entire Ferguson community. Developing these relationships will take time and considerable effort. FPD should:

    a. Develop and put into action a policy and detailed plan for comprehensive implementation of community policing and problem-solving principles. Conduct outreach and involve the entire community in developing and implementing this plan;

    b. Increase opportunities for officers to have frequent, positive interactions with people outside of an enforcement context, especially groups that have expressed high levels of distrust of police. Such opportunities may include police athletic leagues and similar informal activities;

    c. Develop community partnerships to identify crime prevention priorities, with a focus on disconnected areas, such as Ferguson's apartment complexes, and disconnected groups, such as much of Ferguson's African-American youth;

    d. Modify officer deployment patterns and scheduling (such as moving away from the current 12-hour shift and assigning officers to patrol the same geographic areas consistently) to facilitate participating in crime prevention projects and familiarity with areas and people;

    e. Train officers on crime-prevention, officer safety, and anti-discrimination advantages of community policing. Train officers on mechanics of community policing and their role in implementing it;

    f. Measure and evaluate individual, supervisory, and agency police performance on community engagement, problem-oriented-policing projects, and crime prevention, rather than on arrest and citation productivity.

2. Focus Stop, Search, Ticketing and Arrest Practices on Community Protection

FPD must fundamentally change the way it conducts stops and searches, issues citations and summonses, and makes arrests. FPD officers must be trained and required to abide by the law. In addition, FPD enforcement efforts should be reoriented so that officers are required to take enforcement action because it promotes public safety, not simply because they have legal authority to act. To do this, FPD should:

    a. Prohibit the use of ticketing and arrest quotas, whether formal or informal;

b. Require that officers report in writing all stops, searches and arrests, including pedestrian stops, and that their reports articulate the legal authority for the law enforcement action and sufficient description of facts to support that authority;

c. Require documented supervisory approval prior to:

1) Issuing any citation/summons that includes more than two charges;

2) Making an arrest on any of the following charges:

i. Failure to Comply/Obey;

ii. Resisting Arrest;

iii. Disorderly Conduct/Disturbing the Peace;

iv. Obstruction of Government Operations;

3) Arresting or ticketing an individual who sought police aid, or who is cooperating with police in an investigation;

4) Arresting on a municipal warrant or wanted;

d. Revise Failure to Comply municipal code provision to bring within constitutional limits, and provide sufficient guidance so that all stops, citations, and arrests based on the provision comply with the Constitution;

e. Train officers on proper use of Failure to Comply charge, including elements of the offense and appropriateness of the charge for interference with police activity that threatens public safety;

f. Require that applicable legal standards are met before officers conduct pat-downs or vehicle searches. Prohibit searches based on consent for the foreseeable future;

g. Develop system of correctable violation, or "fix-it" tickets, and require officers to issue fix-it tickets wherever possible and absent contrary supervisory instruction;

h. Develop and implement policy and training regarding appropriate police response to activities protected by the First Amendment, including the right to observe, record, and protest police action;

i. Provide initial and regularly recurring training on Fourth Amendment constraints on police action, as well as responsibility within FPD to constrain action beyond what Fourth Amendment requires in interest of public safety and community trust;

j. Discontinue use of "wanteds" or "stop orders" and prohibit officers from conducting stops, searches, or arrests on the basis of "wanteds" or "stop orders" issued by other agencies.

3. Increase Tracking, Review, and Analysis of FPD Stop, Search, Ticketing and Arrest Practices

At the first level of supervision and as an agency, FPD must review more stringently officers' stop, search, ticketing, and arrest practices to ensure that officers are complying with the Constitution and department policy, and to evaluate the impact of officer activity on police legitimacy and community trust. FPD should:

a. Develop and implement a plan for broader collection of stop, search, ticketing, and arrest data that includes pedestrian stops, enhances vehicle stop data collection, and requires collection of data on all stop and post-stop activity, as well as location and demographic information;

b. Require supervisors to review all officer activity and review all officer reports before the supervisor leaves shift;

c. Develop and implement system for regular review of stop, search, ticketing, and arrest data at supervisory and agency level to detect problematic trends and ensure consistency with public safety and community policing goals;

d. Analyze race and other disparities shown in stop, search, ticketing, and arrest practices to determine whether disparities can be reduced consistent with public safety goals.

4. Change Force Use, Reporting, Review, and Response to Encourage De-Escalation and the Use of the Minimal Force Necessary in a Situation

FPD should reorient officers' approach to using force by ensuring that they are trained and skilled in using tools and tactics to de-escalate situations, and incentivized to avoid using force wherever possible. FPD also should implement a system of force review that ensures that improper force is detected and responded to effectively, and that policy, training, tactics, and officer safety concerns are identified. FPD should:

a. Train and require officers to use de-escalation techniques wherever possible both to avoid a situation escalating to where force becomes necessary, and to avoid unnecessary force even where it would be legally justified. Training should include tactics for slowing down a situation to increase available options;

b. Require onsite supervisory approval before deploying any canine, absent documented exigent circumstances; require and train canine officers to take into account the nature and severity of the alleged crime when deciding whether to deploy a canine to bite; require and train canine officers to avoid sending a canine to apprehend by biting a concealed suspect when the objective facts do not suggest the suspect is armed and a lower level of force reasonably can be expected to secure the suspect;

c. Place more stringent limits on use of ECWs, including limitations on multiple ECW cycles and detailed justification for using more than one cycle;

d. Retrain officers in use of ECWs to ensure they view and use ECWs as a tool of necessity, not convenience. Training should be consistent with principles set out in the *2011 ECW Guidelines*;

e. Develop and implement use-of-force reporting that requires the officer using force to complete a narrative, separate from the offense report, describing the force used with particularity, and describing with specificity the circumstances that required the level of force used, including the reason for the initial stop or other enforcement action. Some levels of force should require all officers observing the use of force to complete a separate force narrative;

f. Develop and implement supervisory review of force that requires the supervisor to conduct a complete review of each use of force, including gathering and considering evidence necessary to understand the circumstances of the force incident and determine its consistency with law and policy, including statements from individuals against whom force is used and civilian witnesses;

g. Prohibit supervisors from reviewing or investigating a use of force in which they participated or directed;

h. Ensure that complete use-of-force reporting and review/investigation files — including all offense reports, witness statements, and medical, audio/video, and other evidence — are kept together in a centralized location;

i. Develop and implement a system for higher-level, inter-disciplinary review of some types of force, such as lethal force, canine deployment, ECWs, and force resulting in any injury;

j. Improve collection, review, and response to use-of-force data, including information regarding ECW and canine use;

k. Implement system of zero tolerance for use of force as punishment or retaliation rather than as necessary, proportionate response to counter a threat;

l. Discipline officers who fail to report force and supervisors who fail to conduct adequate force investigations;

m. Identify race and other disparities in officer use of force and develop strategies to eliminate avoidable disparities;

n. Staff jail with at least two correctional officers at all times to ensure safety and minimize need for use of force in dealing with intoxicated or combative prisoners. Train correctional officers in de-escalation techniques with specific instruction and training on minimizing force when dealing with intoxicated and combative prisoners, as well as with passive resistance and noncompliance.

5. Implement Policies and Training to Improve Interactions with Vulnerable People

Providing officers with the tools and training to better respond to persons in physical or mental health crisis, and to those with intellectual disabilities, will help avoid unnecessary injuries, increase community trust, and make officers safer. FPD should:

a. Develop and implement policy and training for identifying and responding to individuals with known or suspected mental health conditions, including those observably in mental health crisis, and those with intellectual or other disabilities;

b. Provide enhanced crisis intervention training to a subset of officers to allow for ready availability of trained officers on the scenes of critical incidents involving individuals with mentally illness;

c. Require that, wherever possible, at least one officer with enhanced crisis intervention training respond to any situation concerning individuals in mental health crisis or with intellectual disability, when force might be used;

d. Provide training to officers regarding how to identify and respond to more commonly occurring medical emergencies that may at first appear to reflect a failure to comply with lawful orders. Such medical emergencies may include, for example, seizures and diabetic emergencies.

6. Change Response to Students to Avoid Criminalizing Youth While Maintaining a Learning Environment

FPD has the opportunity to profoundly impact students through its SRO program. This program can be used as a way to build positive relationships with youth from a young age and to support strategies to keep students in school and learning. FPD should:

a. Work with school administrators, teachers, parents, and students to develop and implement policy and training consistent with law and best practices to more effectively address disciplinary issues in schools. This approach should be focused on SROs developing positive relationships with youth in support of maintaining a learning environment without unnecessarily treating disciplinary issues as criminal matters or resulting in the routine imposition of lengthy suspensions;

b. Provide initial and regularly recurring training to SROs, including training in mental health, counseling, and the development of the teenage brain;

c. Evaluate SRO performance on student engagement and prevention of disturbances, rather than on student arrests or removals;

d. Regularly review and evaluate incidents in which SROs are involved to ensure they meet the particular goals of the SRO program; to identify any disparate impact or treatment by race or other protected basis; and to identify any policy, training, or equipment concerns.

7. Implement Measures to Reduce Bias and Its Impact on Police Behavior

Many of the recommendations listed elsewhere have the potential to reduce the level and impact of bias on police behavior (e.g., increasing positive interactions between police and the community; increasing the collection and analysis of stop data; and increasing oversight of the exercise of police discretion). Below are additional measures that can assist in this effort. FPD should:

a. Provide initial and recurring training to all officers that sends a clear, consistent and emphatic message that bias-based profiling and other forms of discriminatory policing are prohibited. Training should include:

1) Relevant legal and ethical standards;

2) Information on how stereotypes and implicit bias can infect police work;

3) The importance of procedural justice and police legitimacy on community trust, police effectiveness, and officer safety;

4) The negative impacts of profiling on public safety and crime prevention;

b. Provide training to supervisors and commanders on detecting and responding to biasbased profiling and other forms of discriminatory policing;

c. Include community members from groups that have expressed high levels of distrust of police in officer training;

d. Take steps to eliminate all forms of workplace bias from FPD and the City.

8. Improve and Increase Training Generally

FPD officers receive far too little training as recruits and after becoming officers. Officers need a better knowledge of what law, policy, and integrity require, and concrete training on how to carry out their police responsibilities. In addition to the training specified elsewhere in these recommendations, FPD should:

a. Significantly increase the quality and amount of all types of officer training, including recruit, field training (including for officers hired from other agencies), and in-service training;

b. Require that training cover, in depth, constitutional and other legal restrictions on officer action, as well as additional factors officers should consider before taking enforcement action (such as police legitimacy and procedural justice considerations);

c. Employ scenario-based and adult-learning methods.

9. Increase Civilian Involvement in Police Decision Making

In addition to engaging with all segments of Ferguson as part of implementing community policing, FPD should develop and implement a system that incorporates civilian input into all aspects of policing, including policy development, training, use-of-force review, and investigation of misconduct complaints.

10. Improve Officer Supervision

The recommendations set out here cannot be implemented without dedicated, skilled, and welltrained supervisors who police lawfully and without bias. FPD should:

a. Provide all supervisors with specific supervisory training prior to assigning them to supervisory positions;

b. Develop and require supervisors to use an "early intervention system" to objectively detect problematic patterns of officer misconduct, assist officers who need additional attention, and identify training and equipment needs;

c. Support supervisors who encourage and guide respectful policing and implement community policing principles, and evaluate them on this basis. Remove supervisors who do not adequately review officer activity and reports or fail to support, through words or actions, unbiased policing;

d. Ensure that an adequate number of qualified first-line supervisors are deployed in the field to allow supervisors to provide close and effective supervision to each officer under the supervisor's direct command, provide officers with the direction and guidance necessary to improve and develop as officers, and to identify, correct, and prevent misconduct.

11. Recruiting, Hiring, and Promotion

There are widespread concerns about the lack of diversity, especially race and gender diversity, among FPD officers. FPD should modify its systems for recruiting hiring and promotion to:

a. Ensure that the department's officer hiring and selection processes include an objective process for selection that employs reliable and valid selection devices that comport with best practices and federal anti-discrimination laws;

b. In the case of lateral hires, scrutinize prior training and qualification records as well as complaint and disciplinary history;

c. Implement validated pre-employment screening mechanisms to ensure temperamental and skill-set suitability for policing.

12. Develop Mechanisms to More Effectively Respond to Allegations of Officer Misconduct

Responding to allegations of officer misconduct is critical not only to correct officer behavior and identify policy, training, or tactical concerns, but also to build community confidence and police legitimacy. FPD should:

a. Modify procedures and practices for accepting complaints to make it easier and less intimidating for individuals to register formal complaints about police conduct, including providing complaint forms online and in various locations throughout the City and allowing for complaints to be submitted online and by third parties or anonymously;

b. Require that all complaints be logged and investigated;

c. Develop and implement a consistent, reliable, and fair process for investigating and responding to complaints of officer misconduct. As part of this process, FPD should:

1) Investigate all misconduct complaints, even where the complainant indicates he or she does not want the complaint investigated, or wishes to remain anonymous;

2) Not withdraw complaints without reaching a disposition;

d. Develop and implement a fair and consistent system for disciplining officers found to have committed misconduct;

e. Terminate officers found to have been materially untruthful in performance of their duties, including in completing reports or during internal affairs investigations;

f. Timely provide in writing to the Ferguson Prosecuting Attorney all impeachment information on officers who may testify or provide sworn reports, including findings of untruthfulness in internal affairs investigations, for disclosure to the defendant under *Brady v. Maryland*, 373 U.S. 83 (1963);

g. Document in a central location all misconduct complaints and investigations, including the nature of the complaint, the name of the officer, and the disposition of the investigation;

h. Maintain complete misconduct complaint investigative files in a central location;

i. Develop and implement a community-centered mediation program to resolve, as appropriate, allegations of officer misconduct.

13. Publically Share Information about the Nature and Impact of Police Activities

Transparency is a key component of good governance and community trust. Providing broad information to the public also facilitates constructive community engagement. FPD should:

a. Provide regular and specific public reports on police stop, search, arrest, ticketing, force, and community engagement activities, including particular problems and achievements, and describing the steps taken to address concerns;

b. Provide regular public reports on allegations of misconduct, including the nature of the complaint and its resolution;

c. Make available online and regularly update a complete set of police policies.

B. Ferguson Court Practices

1. Make Municipal Court Processes More Transparent

Restoring the legitimacy of the municipal justice system requires increased transparency regarding court operations to allow the public to assess whether the court is operating in a fair manner. The municipal court should:

a. Make public — through a variety of means, including prominent display on the City, police, and municipal court web pages — all court-related fines, fees, and bond amounts, and a description of the municipal court payment process, including court dates, payment options, and potential consequences for non-payment or missed court dates;

b. Create, adopt, and make public written procedures for all court operations;

c. Collect all orders currently in effect and make those orders accessible to the public, including by posting any such materials on the City, police, and municipal court web pages. Make public all new court orders and directives as they are issued;

d. Initiate a public education campaign to ensure individuals can have an accurate and complete understanding of how Ferguson's municipal court operates, including that appearance in court without ability to pay an owed fine will not result in arrest;

e. Provide broadly available information to individuals regarding low-cost or cost-free legal assistance;

f. Enhance public reporting by ensuring data provided to the Missouri Courts Administrator is accurate, and by making that and additional data available on City and court websites, including monthly reports indicating:

1) The number of warrants issued and currently outstanding;

2) The number of cases heard during the previous month;

3) The amount of fines imposed and collected, broken down by offense, including by race;

4) Data regarding the number of Missouri Department of Revenue license suspensions initiated by the court and the number of compliance letters enabling license reinstatement issued by the court.

g. Revise the municipal court website to enable these recommendations to be fully
implemented.

2. Provide Complete and Accurate Information to a Person Charged with a Municipal Violation

In addition to making its processes more transparent to the public, the court should ensure that those with cases pending before the court are provided with adequate and reliable information about their case. The municipal court, in collaboration with the Patrol Division, should:

a. Ensure all FPD citations, summonses, and arrests are accompanied by sufficient, detailed information about the recipient's rights and responsibilities, including:

1) The specific municipal violation charged;

2) A person's options for addressing the charge, including whether in-person appearance is required or if alternative methods, including online payment, are available, and information regarding all pending deadlines;

3) A person's right to challenge the charge in court;

4) The exact date and time of the court session at which the person receiving the charge must or may appear;

5) Information about how to seek a continuance for a court date;

6) The specific fine imposed, if the offense has a preset fine;

7) The processes available to seek a fine reduction for financial incapacity, consistent with recommendation four set forth below;

8) The penalties for failing to meet court requirements.

b. Develop and implement a secure online system for individuals to be able to access specific details about their case, including fines owed, payments made, and pending requirements and deadlines.

3. Change Court Procedures for Tracking and Resolving Municipal Charges to Simplify Court Processes and Expand Available Payment Options

The municipal court should:

a. Strictly limit those offenses requiring in-person court appearance for resolution to those for which state law requires the defendant to make an initial appearance in court;

b. Establish a process by which a person may seek a continuance of a court date, whether or not represented by counsel;

c. Continue to implement its online payment system, and expand it to allow late payments, payment plan installments, bond payments, and other court payments to be made online;

d. Continue to develop and transition to an electronic records management system for court records to ensure all case information and events are tracked and accessible to court officials and FPD staff, as appropriate. Ensure electronic records management system has appropriate controls to limit user access and ability to alter case records;

e. Ensure that the municipal court office is consistently staffed during posted business hours to allow those appearing at the court window of the police department seeking to resolve municipal charges to do so;

f. Accept partial payments from individuals, and provide clear information to individuals about payment plan options.

4. Review Preset Fine Amounts and Implement System for Fine Reduction

The municipal court should:

a. Immediately undertake a review of current fine amounts and ensure that they are consistent not only with regional but also statewide fine averages, are not overly punitive, and take into account the income of Ferguson residents;

b. Develop and implement a process by which individuals can appear in court to seek proportioning of preset fines to their financial ability to pay.

5. Develop Effective Ability-to-Pay Assessment System and Improve Data Collection Regarding Imposed Fines

The municipal court should:

a. Develop and implement consistent written criteria for conducting an assessment of an individual's ability to pay prior to the assessment of any fine, and upon any increase in the fine or related court costs and fees. The ability-to-pay assessment should include not only a consideration of the financial resources of an individual, but also a consideration of any documented fines owed to other municipal courts;

b. Improve current procedures for collecting and tracking data regarding fine amounts imposed. Track initial fines imposed as an independent figure separate from any additional charges imposed during a case;

c. Regularly conduct internal reviews of data regarding fine assessments. This review should include an analysis of fines imposed for the same offenses, including by race of the defendant, to ensure fine assessments for like offenses are set appropriately.

6. Revise Payment Plan Procedures and Provide Alternatives to Fine Payments for Resolving Municipal Charges

The municipal court should:

a. Develop and implement a specific process by which a person can enroll in a payment plan that requires reasonable periodic payments. That process should include an assessment of a person's ability to pay to determine an appropriate periodic payment amount, although a required payment shall not exceed $100. That process should also include a means for a person to seek a reduction in their monthly payment obligation in the event of a change in their financial circumstances;

b. Provide more opportunities for a person to seek leave to pay a lower amount in a given month beyond the court's current practice of requiring appearance the first Wednesday of the month at 11:00 a.m. Adopt procedures allowing individuals to seek their first request for a one-time reduction outside of court, and to have such requests be automatically granted. Such procedures should provide that subsequent requests shall be granted liberally by the Municipal Judge, and denials of requests for extensions or reduced monthly payments shall be accompanied by a written explanation of why the request was denied;

c. Cease practice of automatically issuing a warrant when a person on a payment plan misses a payment, and adopt procedures that provide for appropriate warnings following a missed payment, consistent with recommendation eight set forth below;

d. Work with community organizations and other regional groups to develop alternative penalty options besides fines, including expanding community service options. Make all individuals eligible for community service.

7. Reform Trial Procedures to Ensure Full Compliance with Due Process Requirements

The municipal court should take all necessary steps to ensure that the court's trial procedures fully comport with due process such that defendants are provided with a fair and impartial forum to challenge the charges brought against them. As part of this effort, the court shall ensure that defendants taking their case to trial are provided with all evidence relevant to guilt determinations consistent with the requirements of *Brady v. Maryland*, 373 U.S. 83 (1963), and other applicable law.

8. Stop Using Arrest Warrants as a Means of Collecting Owed Fines and Fees

As Ferguson's own Municipal Judge has recognized, municipal code violations should result in jail in only the rarest of circumstances. To begin to address these problems, Ferguson should only jail individuals for a failure to appear on or pay a municipal code violation penalty, if at all, if the following steps have been attempted in a particular case and have failed:

a. Enforcement of fines through alternative means, including:

1) Assessment of reasonable late fees;

2) Expanding options for payment through community service;

3) Modified payment plans with reasonable amounts due and payment procedures;

4) A show cause hearing on why a warrant should not issue, including an assessment of ability to pay, where requested. At this hearing the individual has a right to counsel and, if the individual is indigent, the court will assign counsel to represent the individual. *See* Mo. Sup. Ct. R. 37.65; Mo. Mun. Benchbook, Cir. Ct., Mun. Divs. § 13.8;

b. Personal service on the individual of the Order to Show Cause Motion that provides notice of the above information regarding right to counsel and the consequences of non-appearance; and

c. If the above mechanisms are unsuccessful at securing payment or otherwise resolving the case, the court should ensure that any arrest warrant issued has the instruction that it be executed only on days that the court is in session so that the individual can be brought immediately before the court to enable the above procedures to be implemented. *See* Mo. Mun. Benchbook, Cir. Ct., Mun. Divs. §

13.8("If a defendant fails to appear in court on the return date of the order to show cause or motion for contempt, *a warrant should be issued to get the defendant before the court for the hearing.*") (emphasis added).

9. Allow Warrants to be Recalled Without the Payment of Bond

Ferguson recently extended its warrant recall program, also called an "amnesty" program, which allows individuals to have municipal warrants recalled and to receive a new court date without paying a bond. This program should be made permanent. The municipal court should:

    a. Allow all individuals to seek warrant recall in writing or via telephone, whether represented by an attorney or not;

    b. Provide information to a participating individual at the time of the warrant recall, including the number of charges pending, the fine amount due if a charge has been assessed, the options available to pay assessed fines, the deadlines for doing so, and the requirements, if any, for appearing in court.

10. Modify Bond Amounts and Bond and Detention Procedures

Ferguson has two separate municipal code bond schedules and processes: one for warrantless arrests, and another for arrests pursuant to warrants issued by the municipal court. Ferguson's municipal court recently limited the number of municipal code violations for which officers can jail an individual without a warrant, and reduced the amount of time the jail may hold a defendant who is unable to post bond from 72 to 12 hours. These changes are a positive start, but further reforms are necessary. The City and municipal court should:

    a. Limit the amount of time the jail may hold a defendant unable to post bond on *all* arrests for municipal code violations or municipal arrest warrants to 12 hours;

    b. Establish procedures for setting bond amounts for warrantless and warrant-based detaineesthat are consistent with the Equal Protection Clause's prohibition on incarcerating individuals on the basis of indigency, and that ensure bond shall in no case exceed $100 for a person arrested pursuant to a municipal warrant, regardless of the number of pending charges;

    c. At the time of bond payment, provide individuals with the option of applying a bond fee to underlying fines and costs, including in the event of forfeiture;

    d. Take steps necessary, including the continued development of a computerized court records management system as discussed above, to enable court staff, FPD officers, and FPD correctional officers to access case information so that a person has the option of paying the full underlying fine owed in lieu of bond upon being arrested;

    e. Increase options for making a bond payment, including allowing bond payment by credit card and through the online payment system, whether by a person in jail or outside of the jail;

    f. Institute closer oversight and tracking of bond payment acceptance by FPD officers and FPD correctional officers;

    g. Initiate practice of issuing bond refund checks immediately upon a defendant paying their fine in full and being owed a bond refund;

    h. Ensure that all court staff, FPD officers, and FPD correctional officers understand Ferguson's bond rules and procedures.

11.Consistently Provide "Compliance Letters" Necessary for Driver's License Reinstatement After a Person Makes an Appearance Following a License Suspension

Per official policy, the municipal court provides people who have had their licenses suspended pursuant to Mo. Rev. Stat. § 302.341.1 with compliance letters enabling the suspension to be lifted only once the underlying fine has been paid in full. Court staff told us, however, that in "sympathetic cases," they provide compliance letters that enable people to have their licenses reinstated. The court should adopt and implement a policy of providing individuals with compliance letters immediately upon a person appearing in court following a license suspension pursuant to this statute.

12. Close Cases that Remain on the Court's Docket Solely Because of Failure to Appear Charges or Bond Forfeitures

In September 2014, the City of Ferguson repealed Ferguson Mun. Code § 13-58, which allowed the imposition of an additional "Failure to Appear" charge, fines, and fees in response to missed appearances and payments. Nonetheless, many cases remain pending on the court's docket solely on account of charges, fines, and fees issued pursuant to this statute or because of questionable bond forfeiture practices. The City and municipal court should:

> a. Close all municipal cases in which the individual has paid fines equal or greater to the amount of the fine assessed for the original municipal code violation — through Failure to Appear fines and fees or forfeited bond payments — and clear all associated warrants;
>
> b. Remove all Failure to Appear related charges, fines, and fees from current cases, and close all cases in which only a Failure to Appear charge, fine, or fee remains pending;
>
> c. Immediately provide compliance letters so that license suspensions are lifted for all individuals whose cases are closed pursuant to these reforms.

13. Collaborate with Other Municipalities and the State of Missouri to Implement Reforms

These recommendations should be closely evaluated and, as appropriate, implemented by other municipalities. We also recommend that the City and other municipalities work collaboratively with the state of Missouri on issues requiring statewide action, and further recommend:

> a. Reform of Mo. Rev. Stat. § 302.341.1, which requires the suspension of individuals' driving licenses in certain cases where they do not appear or timely pay traffic charges involving moving violations;
>
> b. Increased oversight of municipal courts in St. Louis County and throughout the state of Missouri to ensure that courts operate in a manner consistent with due process, equal protection, and other requirements of the Constitution and other laws.

VI. CONCLUSION

Our investigation indicates that Ferguson as a City has the capacity to reform its approach to law enforcement. A small municipal department may offer greater potential for officers to form partnerships and have frequent, positive interactions with Ferguson residents, repairing and maintaining police-community relationships. *See, e.g.*, Jim Burack, *Putting the "Local" Back in Local Law Enforcement, in, American Policing in 2022: Essays on the Future of the Profession* 79-83 (Debra R. Cohen McCullough & Deborah L. Spence, eds., 2012). These reform efforts will be well worth the considerable time and dedication they will require, as they have the potential to make Ferguson safer and more united.

Footnotes

1.   The threshold determination that a case meets the standard for indictment rests with the prosecutor, *Wayte v. United States*, 470 U.S. 598, 607 (1985), and is "one of the most considered decisions a federal prosecutor makes." USAM 9-27.200, Annotation.

2.   With the exception of Darren Wilson and Michael Brown, the names of individuals have been redacted as a safeguard against an invasion of their personal privacy.

3.   Witness 147 was jointly interviewed by SLCPD detectives and federal agents and prosecutors on August 19, 2014. He then testified before the county grand jury on September 16, 2014. Witness 147 never documented what Wilson told him during those initial few minutes after the shooting. Witness 147 acknowledged that while talking to Wilson, he was also focused on the shooting scene and crowd safety.

4.   The Ferguson Market store clerk's daughter stated that Brown used a similar statement when her father tried to stop Brown from stealing cigarillos, *i.e.* , "What you gonna do?" While it might seem odd that a person in Brown's position would verbally confront a police officer, the fact that another witness at a separate location described Brown as speaking similarly a few minutes earlier tends to corroborate Wilson.

5.   According to Wilson's sergeant, Witness 147, Wilson told him that Brown made that comment later when Brown was charging at Wilson in the roadway. Witness 147 remembered this part of Wilson's account when he testified before the county grand jury, and not when he was interviewed by state and federal authorities. In every other account, Wilson stated that Brown made that comment as soon as he withdrew his gun.

6.   During his second interview with SLCPD detectives, Wilson stated he was unsure with which hand Brown reached for Wilson's gun. During all other statements, when asked, Wilson said that Brown used his right hand.

7.   According to Witness 147, he spoke to Wilson while Wilson was seated in his SUV.

8.   Federal prosecutors were aware of and reviewed prior complaints against Wilson, as well as media reports, alleging Wilson engaged in misconduct. Such allegations were not substantiated, and do not contain information admissible in federal court in support of a prosecution.

9.   The locations of the shell casings are consistent with Wilson's account and the credible witness accounts. However, shell casings provide limited evidentiary value relative to the precise location of the shooter and bullet trajectory because they tend to bounce and roll unpredictably after being ejected from the firearm and before coming to rest.

10.   Crime scene detectives also noted a hole in the wall of an apartment building located on the south side of Canfield Drive, east of Wilson's SUV. They removed a small section of siding, but were unable to determine whether there was a projectile within the wall without causing significant structural damage to the building. There is no evidence to indicate what caused the hole or when it was made.

11.   As noted below, the blood in the roadway was determined to be Brown's blood.

12.   It was never determined to whom these bracelets belong or when they were left in the street.

13.   Soot typically appears if the muzzle is within less than one foot of the target and stippling typically appears if the muzzle is within two to three feet of the target.

14.   This fact was critical for prosecutors in evaluating the credibility of witness accounts that stated that Brown continued moving toward Wilson after Wilson ceased firing shots.

15.   Although Brown's shirt was blood soaked, the private forensic pathologist noted the following with regard to Brown's shorts and socks, "Examination of the clothing...shows small dried blood drops on his khaki shorts and yellow socks most consistent with drops from the hand wound." This was significant to prosecutors because it is not inconsistent with Brown lowering his hands and/or putting his hand(s) near his waistband.

16.   This evidence was significant to prosecutors when determining the credibility of those witness accounts that stated that Wilson shot Brown in the back.

17.   This evidence was significant to prosecutors when determining the credibility of those witness accounts that stated that Wilson choked or grabbed Brown by the neck at the outset of the struggle at the SUV.

18.   Post mortem abrasions are consistent with Brown's hands hitting the ground after the final shot to the vortex of the head. It is less likely that they were inflicted during removal of Brown's body because Brown's hands were secured in brown paper bags prior to transport.

19.   While it is possible that Wilson inadvertently transferred Brown's blood from his own hand to his gun either after the struggle or while packaging his gun (even though Wilson claimed to have already washed his hands), such a possibility is speculative. The autopsy results and bullet trajectory are consistent with Brown's DNA being present on the gun as a result of the struggle over the gun. Regardless, the absence of Brown's DNA on Wilson's gun would not change the prosecutive decision.

20.   The grips and hammer, the latter of which was where blood was recovered on Wilson's gun, are textured, making it difficult to lift latent prints.

21.   Fingerprint analysis would not have changed the prosecutive decision. Had the gun yielded Brown's fingerprints, such evidence would further corroborate Wilson's account. If the gun did not test positive for Brown's fingerprints, the state of the evidence would remain the same.

22.   Brown's actions on the surveillance video at that moment mimicked the way in which Wilson described Brown again handing the cigarillos to Witness 101 minutes later as Brown assaulted Wilson in the SUV.

23.   As detailed below, the Monte Carlo in question was white.

24.   The person who recorded this video claimed that yet another person, "Chris," made that statement.

25.   There is no indication that Witness 139 ever gave a media interview that was broadcast to the public.

26.   Autopsy results indicate that Brown was shot on his right side.

27.   Witness 120 cited to media reports as to why he knew that Brown was shot in the arm.

28.   The media has widely reported that there is witness testimony that Brown said "don't shoot" as he held his hands above his head. In fact, our investigation did not reveal any eyewitness who stated that Brown said "don't shoot."

29.   *See 2012 Census of Governments*, U.S. Census Bureau (Sept. 2013), *available at* http://factfinder.census.gov/bkmk/table/1.0/en/COG/2012/ORG13.ST05P?slice= GEO-{}0400000US29 (last visited Feb. 26, 2015).

30.   *See 2010 Census*, U.S. Census Bureau (2010), *available at* http://factfinder.census. gov/bkmk/table/1.0/en/DEC/10_SF1/QTP3/1600000US2923986 (last visited Feb. 26, 2015).

31.   *See 1990 Census of Population General Population Characteristics Missouri*, U.S. Census Bureau (Apr. 1992), *available at* ftp://ftp2.census.gov/library/publications/1992/ dec/cp\protect\unhbox\voidb@x\penalty\@M\hskip\z@skip-\discretionary{}{}{}\ penalty\@M\hskip\z@skip{}1\protect\unhbox\voidb@x\penalty\@M\hskip\z@ skip-\discretionary{}{}{}\penalty\@M\hskip\z@skip{}27.pdf (last visited Feb. 26, 2015).

32.   *See Race Alone or in Combination: 2000*, U.S. Census Bureau (2000), *available at* http:// factfinder.census.gov/ bkmk/table/1.0/en/DEC/00_SF1/QTP5/1600000US2923986 (last visited Feb. 26, 2015).

33.   *2010 Census, supra* note 2.

34.   *See Poverty Status in the Past 12 Months 2009-2013 American Community Survey 5-Year Estimates*, U.S. Census Bureau (2014), available at http://factfinder.census.gov/bkmk/ table/1.0/en/ACS/13_5YR/S1701/1600000US2923986 (last visited Feb. 26, 2015).

35.   This is evidenced not only by FPD's own records, but also by Uniform Crime Reports data for Ferguson, which show a downward trend in serious crime over the last ten years. *See Uniform Crime Reports,* Federal Bureau of Investigation, http://www.fbi.gov/about\protect\unhbox\voidb@x\penalty\@M\hskip\z@skip-\ discretionary{}{}{}\penalty\@M\hskip\z@skip{}us/cjis/ucr/crime\protect\unhbox\ voidb@x\penalty\@M\hskip\z@skip-\discretionary{}{}{}\penalty\@M\hskip\z@ skip{}in\protect\unhbox\voidb@x\penalty\@M\hskip\z@skip-\discretionary{}{}{}\ penalty\@M\hskip\z@skip{}the\protect\unhbox\voidb@x\penalty\@M\hskip\z@ skip-\discretionary{}{}{}\penalty\@M\hskip\z@skip{}u.s (last visited Feb. 26, 2015).

36.   Each of these yearly totals excludes certain court fees that are designated for particular purposes, but that nonetheless are paid directly to the City. For example, $2 of the court fee that accompanies every citation for a municipal code violation is set aside to be used for police training. That fee is used only by the City of Ferguson and is deposited in the City's general fund; nonetheless, the City's budget does not include that fee in its totals for "municipal court" revenue. In 2012 and 2013, the police training fee brought in, respectively, another $24,724 and $22,938 in revenue.

37.   FPD's financial focus has also led FPD to elevate municipal enforcement over state-law enforcement. Even where individuals commit violations of state law, if there is an analogous municipal code provision, the police department will nearly always charge the offense under municipal law. A senior member of FPD's command told us that all Ferguson police officers understand that, when a fine is the likely punishment, municipal rather than state charges should be pursued so that Ferguson will reap the financial benefit.

38.   After a recommendation we made during this investigation, Ferguson has recently begun a very limited "correctable violation" or "fix-it" ticket program, under which charges for certain violations can be dismissed if corrected within a certain period of time.

39.   Katherine Smith, *Ferguson to Increase Police Ticketing to Close City's Budget Gap*,
        Bloomberg News (Dec.   12, 2014), http://www.bloomberg.com/news/articles/
        2014\protect\unhbox\voidb@x\penalty\@M\hskip\z@skip-\discretionary{}{}{}\
        penalty\@M\hskip\z@skip{}12\protect\unhbox\voidb@x\penalty\@M\hskip\z@
        skip-\discretionary{}{}{}\penalty\@M\hskip\z@skip{}12/ferguson\protect\unhbox\
        voidb@x\penalty\@M\hskip\z@skip-\discretionary{}{}{}\penalty\@M\hskip\z@
        skip{}to\protect\unhbox\voidb@x\penalty\@M\hskip\z@skip-\discretionary{}{}{}\
        penalty\@M\hskip\z@skip{}increase\protect\unhbox\voidb@x\penalty\@M\
        hskip\z@skip-\discretionary{}{}{}\penalty\@M\hskip\z@skip{}police\protect\
        unhbox\voidb@x\penalty\@M\hskip\z@skip-\discretionary{}{}{}\penalty\@M\
        hskip\z@skip{}ticketing\protect\unhbox\voidb@x\penalty\@M\hskip\z@skip-\
        discretionary{}{}{}\penalty\@M\hskip\z@skip{}to\protect\unhbox\voidb@x\
        penalty\@M\hskip\z@skip-\discretionary{}{}{}\penalty\@M\hskip\z@skip{}close\
        protect\unhbox\voidb@x\penalty\@M\hskip\z@skip-\discretionary{}{}{}\penalty\
        @M\hskip\z@skip{}city\protect\unhbox\voidb@x\penalty\@M\hskip\z@skip-\
        discretionary{}{}{}\penalty\@M\hskip\z@skip{}s\protect\unhbox\voidb@x\penalty\
        @M\hskip\z@skip-\discretionary{}{}{}\penalty\@M\hskip\z@skip{}budget\protect\
        unhbox\voidb@x\penalty\@M\hskip\z@skip-\discretionary{}{}{}\penalty\@M\
        hskip\z@skip{}gap.

40.   Ferguson officials have asserted that in the last fiscal year revenue from the municipal
        court comprised only 12% of City revenue, but they have not made clear how they cal-
        culated this figure. It appears that 12% is the proportion of Ferguson's *total* revenue
        (forecasted to amount to $18.62 million in 2014) derived from fines and fees (fore-
        casted to be $2.09 million in 2014). Guidelines issued by the Missouri State Auditor
        in December 2014 provide, however, that the 30% cap outlined in Mo. Rev. Stat.
        § 302.341.2 imposes a limit on the makeup of fines and fees in *general* use revenue,
        excluding any revenue designated for a particular purpose. Notably, the current 30%
        state cap only applies tofines and fees derived from "traffic violations." It thus appears
        that, for purposes of the state cap, Ferguson must ensure that its traffic-relatedfines
        and fees do not exceed 30% of its "General Fund" revenue. In 2014, Ferguson's Gen-
        eral Fund revenue was forecasted to be $12.33 million.

41.   FPD policy states that "[o]fficers should document" all field contacts and field inter-
        rogation "relevant to criminal activity and identification of criminal suspects on the
        appropriate Department approvedcomputer entry forms." FPD General Order 407.00.
        Policy requires that a "Field Investigation Report" be completed for persons and ve-
        hicles "in all instances when an officer feels" that the subject"may be in the area for
        a questionable or suspicious purpose." FPD General Order 422.01. In practice, how-
        ever, FPD officers do not reliably document field contacts, particularly of pedestrians,
        and the department does not evaluate such field contacts.

42.   FPD officers are not consistent in how they label this charge in their reports. They
        refer to violations of Section 29-16 as both "Failure to Comply" and "Failure to Obey."
        This report refers to all violations of this code provision as "Failure to Comply."

43.   Other broad quality-of-life ordinances in the Ferguson municipal code, such as the
        disorderly conduct provision, may also be vulnerable to attack as unconstitutionally
        vague or overbroad. *See* Ferguson Mun. Code § 29-94 (defining disorderly conduct to
        include the conduct of "[a]ny person, while in a public place, who utters in a loud, abu-
        sive or threatening manner, any obscene words, epithets *or similar abusive language*")
        (emphasis added).

44.   The ordinance on interfering with arrest, detention, or stop, Ferguson Mun. Code §
        29-17, does not actually permit arrest unless the subject uses or threatens violence,

which did not occur here. Another code provision the officer may have relied on, §
29-19, is likely unconstitutionally overbroad because it prohibits obstruction of government operations "in any manner whatsoever." *See Hill*, 482 U.S. at 455, 462, 466
(invalidating ordinance that made it unlawful to "in any manner oppose, molest, abuse,
or interrupt any policeman in the execution of his duty").

45.   This set, however, did not include any substantive information on the August 9, 2014
shooting of Michael Brown by Officer Darren Wilson. That incident is being separately investigated by the Criminal Section of the Civil Rights Division and the U.S.
Attorney's Office for the Eastern District of Missouri.

46.   ECWs have two modes. In dart mode, an officer fires a cartridge thatsends two darts
or prongs into a person's body, penetrating the skin and delivering a jolt of electricity
of a length determined by the officer. In drive-stun mode, sometimes referred to as
"pain compliance" mode, an officer pressesthe weapon directly against a person's body,
pulling the trigger to activate the electricity. Many agencies strictly limit the use of
ECWs in drive-stun mode because of the potential for abuse.

47.   The Ferguson-Florissant School District serves over 11,000 students, about
80% of whom are African American. *See* Ferguson-Florissant District Demographic Data 2014 & 2015,Mo. Dep't of Elementary & Secondary Educ.,
http://mcds.dese.mo.gov/guidedinquiry/Pages/District\protect\unhbox\voidb@x\
penalty\@M\hskip\z@skip-\discretionary{}{}{}\penalty\@M\hskip\z@skip{}and\
protect\unhbox\voidb@x\penalty\@M\hskip\z@skip-\discretionary{}{}{}\penalty\
@M\hskip\z@skip{}School\protect\unhbox\voidb@x\penalty\@M\hskip\z@skip-\
discretionary{}{}{}\penalty\@M\hskip\z@skip{}Information.aspx (last visited Feb.
26, 2015).

48.   The influence of revenue on the court, described both in Part II and in Part III.B.
of this Report, may itself be unlawful. *See Ward v. Vill. of Monroeville*, 409 U.S. 57,
58-62 (1972) (finding a violation of the due process right to a fair and impartial trial
where a town mayor served as judge and was also responsible for the town's finances,
which were substantially dependent on "fines,forfeitures, costs, and fees" collected by
the court).

49.   As with many of the problematic court practices that we identify in this report, other
municipalities in St. Louis County also have imposed a separate Failure to Appear
charge, fine, and fee for missed court appearances and payments. Many continue to
do so.

50.   As discussed in Part II of this report, City officials have acknowledged several of these
procedural deficiencies. In 2012, a City Councilmember, citing specific examples,
urged against reappointing Judge Brockmeyer because he "often times does not listen
to the testimony, does not review the reports or the criminal history of defendants,
and doesn't let all the pertinent witnesses testify before rendering a verdict."

51.   This finding of untruthfulness by a police officer constitutes impeachment evidence
that must be disclosed in any trial in which the officer testifies for the City. Under the Fourteenth Amendment, the failure to disclose evidence that is "favorable to
an accused" violates due process "where the evidence is material either to guilt or to
punishment, irrespective of the good faith or bad faith of the prosecution." *Brady
v. Maryland*, 373 U.S. 83, 87 (1963). This duty applies to impeachment evidence,
United States v. Bagley, 473 U.S. 667, 676 (1985), and it applies even if the defendant
does not request the evidence, *United States v. Agurs*, 427 U.S. 97, 107 (1976). The
duty encompasses, furthermore, information that should be known to the prosecutor,
including information known solely by the police department. *Kyles v. Whitley*, 514

U.S. 419, 437 (1995). This constitutional duty to disclose appears to extend to municipal court cases, which can result in jail terms of up to three months under Section 29-2 of Ferguson's municipal code. *See City of Kansas City v. Oxley*, 579 S.W.2d 113, 114 (Mo. 1979) (en banc) (holding that the due process standard of proof beyond a reasonable doubt applied in a municipal court speeding case because "the violation has criminal overtones"); *see also City of Cape Girardeau v. Jones*, 725 S.W.2d 904, 907-09 (Mo. Ct. App. 1987) (explaining that reasonable doubt standard applied to municipal trespass prosecution because municipal ordinance violations are "quasi-criminal," and reversing two convictions based on privilege against self- incrimination). We are aware of at least two cases, from January 2015, in which the City called this officer as a witness without disclosing the finding of untruthfulness to the defense.

52.   *See City Courts*, City of Ferguson, http://www.fergusoncity.com/60/The\ protect\unhbox\voidb@x\penalty\@M\hskip\z@skip-\discretionary{}{}{}\ penalty\@M\hskip\z@skip{}City\protect\unhbox\voidb@x\penalty\@M\hskip\ z@skip-\discretionary{}{}{}\penalty\@M\hskip\z@skip{}Of\protect\unhbox\ voidb@x\penalty\@M\hskip\z@skip-\discretionary{}{}{}\penalty\@M\hskip\ z@skip{}Ferguson\protect\unhbox\voidb@x\penalty\@M\hskip\z@skip-\ discretionary{}{}{}\penalty\@M\hskip\z@skip{}Municipal\protect\unhbox\ voidb@x\penalty\@M\hskip\z@skip-\discretionary{}{}{}\penalty\@M\hskip\z@ skip{}Courts (last visited Feb. 26, 2015). By contrast, the neighboring municipality of Normandy operates a court website with an entire page containing information regarding fine due dates, methods of payment, and different payment options, including the availability of payment plans for those who cannot afford to pay a fine in full. *See How Do I Pay a Ticket / Fine?*, City of Normandy, http://www.cityofnormandy.gov/index.aspx?NID=570 (last visited Feb. 26, 2015).

53.   Prior to September 2014, a second missed court appearance (or a single missed payment) would result not only in a warrant being issued, but also the imposition of an additional Failure to Appear *charge*. This charge was imposed automatically. It does not appear that there was any attempt by the court to inform individuals that a failure to appear could be excused upon a showing of good cause, or to provide individuals with an opportunity to make such a showing. Additionally, just as the court does not currently send any notice informing a defendant that an arrest warrant has been issued, the court did not send any notice that this additional Failure to Appear charge had been brought.

54.   The email reports that the defendant, a black male, was booked into jail. This email does not provide the full context of the circumstances that led to the 10-day jail sentence and further information is required to assess the appropriateness of that order. Nonetheless, the email suggests that the court jailed a defendant for refusing to answer questions, which raises significant Fifth Amendment concerns. There is also no indication as to whether the defendant was represented or, if not, was allowed or afforded representation to defend against the contempt charge and 10-day sentence.

55.   While Missouri provides a process to secure a temporary waiver of a license suspension, we have heard from many that this process can be difficult and, in any case, is only available in certain circumstances.

56.   By initiating the license suspension procedure after a single missed appearance and without first providing notice or an opportunity to remedy the missed appearance, the court appears to have violated Missouri law. *See* Mo. Rev. Stat. § 302.341.1 (providing that after a missed appearance associated with a moving violation, a court "shall within ten days…inform the defendant by ordinary mail at the last address shown on

the court records that the court will order the director of revenue to suspend the defendant's driving privileges if the charges are not disposed of and fully paid within thirty days from the date of mailing").

57.   *See City Courts,* City of Ferguson, http://www.fergusoncity.com/60/The\protect\unhbox\voidb@x\penalty\@M\hskip\z@skip-\discretionary{}{}{}\penalty\@M\hskip\z@skip{}City\protect\unhbox\voidb@x\penalty\@M\hskip\z@skip-\discretionary{}{}{}\penalty\@M\hskip\z@skip{}Of\protect\unhbox\voidb@x\penalty\@M\hskip\z@skip-\discretionary{}{}{}\penalty\@M\hskip\z@skip{}Ferguson\protect\unhbox\voidb@x\penalty\@M\hskip\z@skip-\discretionary{}{}{}\penalty\@M\hskip\z@skip{}Municipal\protect\unhbox\voidb@x\penalty\@M\hskip\z@skip-\discretionary{}{}{}\penalty\@M\hskip\z@skip{}Courts (last visited Feb. 26, 2015); *Ferguson Municipal Court,* Your Missouri Courts, http://www.courts.mo.gov/page.jsp?id=8862 (last visited Feb. 26, 2015).

58.   Recently, the court has allowed some individuals over age 19 to resolve fines through community service, but that remains a rarity. *See City of Ferguson Continues Court Reform Initiative by Offering Community Service Program,* City of Ferguson (Dec. 15, 2014), http://www.fergusoncity.com/CivicAlerts.aspx?AID=370&ARC=699 (stating community service program was launched in partnership with Ferguson Youth Initiative in February 2014 "to assist teenagers and certain other defendants").

59.   As stated in the Missouri Municipal Court Handbook produced by the Circuit Court: "Defendants who fail or refuse to pay their fines and costs can be extremely difficult to deal with, but if there is a credible threat of incarceration if they do not pay, the job of collection becomes much easier." Mo. Mun. Benchbook, Cir. Ct., Mun. Divs. § 13.6 (2010).

60.   Ferguson officials have also told us that the arrest warrant is issued not because of the missed payment per se, but rather because the person missing the payment failed to abide by the court's rules. But the Supreme Court has rejected that contention, too. In *Bearden,*the Court noted that the sentencing court's stated concern "was that the petitioner had disobeyed a prior court order to pay the fine," but found that the sentence nonetheless "is no more than imprisoning a person solely because he lacks funds" to pay. *Bearden,* 461 U.S. at 674.

61.   Additionally,Ferguson's municipal code provides: "When a sentence for violation of any provision of this Code or other ordinance of the city...includes a fine and such fine is not paid, or if the costs of prosecution adjudged against an offender are not paid, the person under sentence shall be imprisoned one day for every ten dollars ($10.00) of any such unpaid fine or costs...not to exceed a total of four (4) months." Ferguson Mun. Code § 1-16. Our investigation did not uncover any evidence that the court has sentenced anyone to imprisonment pursuant to this statute in the past several years. Nonetheless, it is concerning that this statute, which unconstitutionally sanctions imprisonment for failing to pay a fine, remains in effect. *Cf. Bearden v. Georgia,* 461 U.S. 660, 671 (1983).

62.   In December 2014, the court set forth a bond schedule for warrantless arrests, which provides that, for all but 14 code violations, a person arrested pursuant to a municipal code violation and brought to Ferguson City Jail shall be issued a citation or summons and released on his or her own recognizance without any bond payment required. For those 14 code violations requiring a bond, the court has set "fixed" bond amounts, although these are subject to the court's discretion to raise or lower those amounts at the request of the City or the detained individual. The court's recent order further

provides that, even if an individual does not pay the bond required, he or she shall in any case be released after 12 hours, rather than the previous 72-hour limit.

63. For example, the recent orders fail to specify that, in considering whether to adjust the bond imposed, the court shall make an assessment of an individual's ability to pay, and assign bond proportionately. *Cf. Pugh v. Rainwater*, 572 F.2d 1053, 1057 (5th Cir. 1978) (en banc) (noting that the incarceration of those who cannot afford to meet the requirements of a fixed bond schedule "without meaningful consideration of other possible alternatives" infringes on due process and equal protection requirements).

64. The court's website states that the court window is open from 8:30 a.m. to 5:00 p.m., not 4:00 p.m. *See City Courts,* City of Ferguson, http://www.fergusoncity.com/60/The\protect\unhbox\voidb@x\penalty\@M\hskip\ z@skip-\discretionary{}{}{}\penalty\@M\hskip\z@skip{}City\protect\unhbox\ voidb@x\penalty\@M\hskip\z@skip-\discretionary{}{}{}\penalty\@M\hskip\z@ skip{}Of\protect\unhbox\voidb@x\penalty\@M\hskip\z@skip-\discretionary{}{}{}\ penalty\@M\hskip\z@skip{}Ferguson\protect\unhbox\voidb@x\penalty\@M\hskip\ z@skip-\discretionary{}{}{}\penalty\@M\hskip\z@skip{}Municipal\protect\unhbox\ voidb@x\penalty\@M\hskip\z@skip-\discretionary{}{}{}\penalty\@M\hskip\z@ skip{}Courts (last visited Feb. 26, 2015).

65. Critically, however, when a person attends court after paying a bond and is assessed a fine, court staff members *do* automatically apply the bond already paid to the fine owed, and in fact require application of the bond to the fine regardless of the defendant's wishes. Thus, the court has simultaneously asserted that it *can* apply a bond to a fine without a defendant's consent when the bond would otherwise be returned to the defendant, but that it *cannot* apply a bond to a fine without a defendant's consent when the bond would otherwise be forfeited into the City's own accounts.

66. As noted above, FPD charges violations of Municipal Code Section 29-16 as both Failure to Obey and Failure to Comply. Court data carries forward this inconsistency.

67. While there are limitations to using basic population data as a benchmark when evaluating whether there are racial disparities in vehicle stops, it is sufficiently reliable here. In fact, in Ferguson, black drivers might account for *less* of the driving pool than would be expected from overall population rates because a lower proportion of blacks than whites is at or above the minimum driving age. *See 2009-2013 5-Year American Community Survey*, U.S. Census Bureau (2015) (showing higher proportion of black population in under-15 and under-19 age categories than white population). Ferguson officials have told us that they believe that black drivers account for *more* of the driving pool than their 67% share of the population because the driving pool also includes drivers traveling from neighboring municipalities — many of which have higher black populations than Ferguson. Our investigation casts doubt upon that claim. An analysis of zip-code data from the 53,850 summonses FPD issued from January 1, 2009 to October 14, 2014, shows that the African-American makeup for all zip codes receiving a summons — weighted by population size and the number of summonses received by people from that zip code — is 63%. Thus, there is substantial reason to believe that the share of drivers in Ferguson who are black is in fact *lower* than population data suggests.

68. Assessing contraband or "hit rates" is a generally accepted practice in the field of criminology to "operationaliz[e] the concept of 'intent to discriminate.'" The test shows "bias against a protected group if the success rate of searches on that group is lower than on another group." Nicola Persico & Petra Todd, *The Hit Rates Test for Racial Bias in Motor-Vehicle Searches*, 25 Justice Quarterly 37, 52 (2008). Indeed, as noted

below, in assessing whether racially disparate impact is motivated by discriminatory intent for Equal Protection Clause purposes, disparity can itself provide probative evidence of discriminatory intent.

69. As noted above, African Americans received 90% of all citations issued by FPD from October 2012 to July 2014. This data shows that 86% of people receiving citations following an FPD traffic stop between October 2012 and October 2014 were African American.

70. It is generally accepted practice in the field of statistics to consider any result that would occur by chance less than five times out of 100 to be statistically significant.

71. Similar to the post-stop outcome disparities — which show disparities in FPD practices after an initial stop has been made — these figures show disparities in FPD practices after a decision to issue a citation has been made. Thus, these disparities are not based in any part on population data.

72. Although the state-mandated racial profiling data collected during traffic stops captures ethnicity in addition to race, most other FPD reports capture race only. As a result, these figures for non-African Americans include not only whites, but also non-black Latinos. That FPD's data collection methods do not consistently capture ethnicity does not affect this report's analysis of the disparate impact imposed on African Americans, but it has prevented an analysis of whether FPD practices also disparately impact Latinos. In 2010, Latinos comprised 1% of Ferguson's population. *See 2010 Census*, U.S. Census Bureau (2010), *available at* http://factfinder.census.gov/bkmk/table/1.0/en/DEC/10_SF1/QTP3/1600000US2923986 (last visited Feb. 26, 2015)

73. The universe of cases in this and subsequent analyses consisted of cases filed in 2011 because, given that some cases endure for years, a more recent sample would have excluded a greater amount of data from case events that have not yet occurred.

74. The ten offenses or offense categories analyzed include: 1) Manner of Walking in Roadway; 2) Failure to Comply; 3) Resisting Arrest; 4) Peace Disturbance; 5) Failure to Obey; 6) High Grass and Weeds; 7) One Headlight; 8) Expired License Plate; 9) aggregated data for 14 different parking violation offenses; and 10) aggregated data for four different headlight offenses, including: One Headlight; Defective Headlights; No Headlights; and Failure to Maintain Headlights.

75. Ferguson's discriminatory practices also violate Title VI and the Safe Streets Act, which, in addition to prohibiting some forms of unintentional conduct that has a disparate impact based on race, also prohibit intentionally discriminatory conduct that has a disparate impact. *See* 42 U.S.C. § 2000d; 42 U.S.C. § 3789d.

76. Social psychologists have long recognized the influence of implicit racial bias on decision making, and law enforcement experts have similarly acknowledged the impact of implicit racial bias on law enforcement decisions. *See, e.g.*, R. Richard Banks, Jennifer L. Eberhardt, & Lee Ross, *Discrimination and Implicit Bias in a Racially Unequal Society*, 94 Cal. L. Rev. 1169 (2006); Tracey G. Gove, *Implicit Bias and Law Enforcement*, The Police Chief (October 2011).

77. We did find one instance in 2012 in which the City Manager forwarded an email that played upon stereotypes of Latinos, but within minutes of sending it, sent another email to the recipient in which he stated he had not seen the offensive part of the email and apologized for the "inappropriate and offensive" message. Police and court staff took no such corrective action, and indeed in many instances expressed amusement at the offensive correspondence.

78. We were able to review far more emails from FPD supervisors than patrol officers. City officials informed us that, while many FPD supervisors have their email accounts on hard drives in the police department, most patrol officers use a form of webmail that does not retain messages once they are deleted.

79. Richard Rothstein, *The Making of Ferguson*, Econ. Policy Inst. (Oct. 2014), *available at* http://www.epi.org/publication/making\protect\unhbox\voidb@x\penalty\@M\hskip\z@skip-\discretionary{}{}{}\penalty\@M\hskip\z@skip{}ferguson/.

80. *See Missouri Vehicle Stops Report*, Missouri Attorney General, http://ago.mo.gov/VehicleStops/Reports.php?lea=161 (last visited Feb. 13, 2015).

81. Data for the entire state of Missouri shows an even higher "Disparity Index" for those years than the disparity index present in Ferguson. This raises, by the state's own metric, considerable concerns about policing outside of Ferguson as well.

82. Although beyond the scope of this investigation, it appears clear that individuals' experiences with other law enforcement agencies in St. Louis County, including with the police departments in surrounding municipalities and the County Police, in many instances have contributed to a general distrust of law enforcement that impacts interactions with the Ferguson police and municipal court.

83. This incident raises another concern regarding whether a second-hand informal account of a complaint, often the only record Ferguson retains, conveys the seriousness of the allegation of misconduct. In this illustrative instance, our conversation with a witness to this incident indicates that the officer pointed his weapon at each employee as he spoke to him, and threatened to shoot both, despite knowing that they were simply employees taking out the trash.

84. We found additional examples of FPD officers behaving in public in a manner that reflects poorly on FPD and law enforcement more generally. In November 2010, an officer was arrested for DUI by an Illinois police officer who found his car crashed in a ditch off the highway. Earlier that night he and his squad mates — including his sergeant — were thrown out of a bar for bullying a customer. The officer received a thirty-day suspension for the DUI. Neither the sergeant nor any officers was disciplined for their behavior in the bar. In September 2012, an officer stood by eating a sandwich while a fight broke out at an annual street festival. After finally getting involved to break up the fight, he publically berated and cursed at his squad mates, screamed and cursed at the two female street vendors who were fighting, and pepper-sprayed a handcuffed female arrestee in the back of his patrol car. The officer received a written reprimand.

85. While the Chief's "log" of Internal Affairs ("IA") investigations contains many sustained allegations, most of these were internally generated; that is, the complaint was made by an FPD employee, usually a commander. In addition, we found that a majority of complaints are never investigated as IA cases, or even logged as complaints. The Chief's log, which he told us included all complaint investigations, includes 56 investigations from January 2010 through July 2014. Our review indicates that there were significantly more complaints of misconduct during this time period. Despite repeated requests, FPD provided us no other record of complaints received or investigated.

86. FPD may have initially accepted this as a formal complaint, but then informally withdrew it after completion of the investigation. No rationale is provided for doing so, but the case does not appear on the Chief's IA investigation log, and another case with this same IA number appears instead.

87.   Our review of FPD's handling of misconduct complaints is just one source of our concern about FPD's efforts to ensure that officers are truthful in their reports and testimony, and to take appropriate measures when they are not. As discussed above, our review of FPD offense and force reports also raises this concern.

88.   While the emphasis in Ferguson has been on racial diversity, FPD also, like many police agencies, has strikingly disparate gender diversity: in Ferguson, approximately 55% of residents are female, but FPD has only four female officers. *See* 2010 *Census*, U.S. Census Bureau (2010), *available at* factfinder.census.gov/bkmk/table/1.0/en/DEC /10_DP/DPDP1/1600000US2923986 (last visited Feb. 26, 2015). During our investigation we received many complaints about FPD's lack of gender diversity as well.

89.   While not the focus of our investigation, the information we reviewed indicated that Ferguson's efforts to retain qualified female and black officers may be compromised by the same biases we saw more broadly in the department. In particular, while the focus of our investigation did not permit us to reach a conclusive finding, we found evidence that FPD tolerates sexual harassment by male officers, and has responded poorly to allegations of sexual harassment that have been made by female officers.

Made in the USA
Coppell, TX
03 September 2020

36468667R10120